LEE H. HAMILTON

CONGRESS, PRESIDENTS, AND AMERICAN POLITICS

Fifty Years of Writings and Reflections

INDIANA UNIVERSITY PRESS
Bloomington and Indianapolis

This book is a publication of

Indiana University Press
Office of Scholarly Publishing
Herman B Wells Library 350
1320 East 10th Street
Bloomington, Indiana 47405 USA

iupress.indiana.edu

The paper used in this publication meets the minimum requirements of
the American National Standard for Information Sciences—Permanence
of Paper for Printed Library Materials, ANSI Z39.48–1992.

Manufactured in the United States of America

Library of Congress Cataloging-in-Publication Data

Names: Hamilton, Lee, author.
Title: Congress, presidents, and American politics : fifty years
    of writings and reflections / Lee H. Hamilton.
Description: Bloomington : Indiana University Press, 2016. | Includes index.
Identifiers: LCCN 2015050743| ISBN 9780253020864 (cloth :
    alk. paper) | ISBN 9780253020970 (ebook)
Subjects: LCSH: United States—Politics and government—1945–1989. |
    United States—Politics and government—1989– | Hamilton, Lee.
Classification: LCC E839.5 .H36 2016 | DDC 320.97309/04—dc23
    LC record available at http://lccn.loc.gov/2015050743

1 2 3 4 5   21 20 19 18 17 16

My main debt of gratitude is to my wife Nancy, who is deeply missed by us all, and our children, Tracy, Debbie, and Doug, each of whom has given me pride and support in the years gone by.

CONTENTS

Acknowledgments

This book has benefited from the contributions of many people. The talented staff who assisted me in the writing of the commentaries over the thirty-four years I was in Congress are too numerous to mention individually, but I greatly appreciated their assistance. They contributed a great deal to these pieces—and to my office—over the years. Since I left Congress, Rob Gurwitt has been particularly helpful with the style and readability of my commentaries. I also owe a debt of gratitude to Ken Nelson, with whom I have worked productively for more than thirty years. Ken helped me select the commentaries for the book, and his suggestions on content were invaluable. Rebecca Tolen and Nancy Lightfoot from IU Press provided important guidance throughout the writing and editing process, and meticulous copyediting was provided by Eric Levy.

Of the many sources of information for the book, I would especially note three that were helpful in pulling together the Key Facts sections for the various Congresses: *Landmark Legislation, 1774–2012*, by Stephen W. Stathis (CQ Press, 2014), "Vital Statistics on Congress," by Norman J. Ornstein, Thomas E. Mann, Michael J. Malbin, Andrew Rugg, and Raffaela Wakeman (http://www.brookings.edu), and *CQ Almanac* (CQ Press, various years).

CONGRESS, PRESIDENTS, AND AMERICAN POLITICS

INTRODUCTION

FROM MY EARLIEST DAYS IN CONGRESS I BELIEVED STRONGLY IN the importance of an informed electorate and the regular dialogue between representative and represented. So in March 1965, after being in office for only two months, I wrote my first newsletter for constituents—on the Vietnam War. In December 2014 the commentary that closed out my fiftieth year of writing these was on the need for Congress to focus on long-term economic growth. In between I wrote some two thousand commentaries giving my observations on Congress and American politics, usually on a weekly basis.

I am not aware of a similar effort as extensive by another member of Congress. It took a fair amount of work, both by me and by my staff. And it could be difficult, especially during busy times in Congress, to produce a thousand-word statement each week on key issues of the day, but I felt it was worth the effort. Congress can be a bewildering institution even to those of us who have worked in it for several years; it's even more confusing for the people back home.

The idea for the commentaries arose from what I saw as several needs. When I first went to Congress, my immediate impression was that Washington, DC, needed a lot of explaining to the people back home. I also saw the complexity of the issues early on, and I was not pleased with the coverage of Congress in the media. Plus, from meetings back home I would get a sense about concepts that were not well understood by the public, and I felt that my commentaries could contribute to enhancing the quality of the relationship between elected official and voter. I also found writing the commentaries to be a good way to educate myself—helping me to organize my thoughts and giving me some resources that I could use when I'd go back to the district for public meetings, so I could do my best to explain complicated issues of the day in understandable, fairly simple terms.

The commentaries covered a wide range of topics, as illustrated in the list below, which shows the subjects of my weekly Washington Reports in a typical year, 1980. The following year I also started writing a separate Foreign Affairs Newsletter, on a monthly basis, and a few of these are also included in this volume.

WASHINGTON REPORT TOPICS FOR 1980
1. The Future Face of Farming
2. The 1980 Economic Outlook
3. The 96th Congress, First Session
4. The Challenge of Education
5. The Soviet Invasion of Afghanistan: Questions and Answers
6. The Presidential Messages: The State of the Union
7. The Presidential Messages: The Federal Budget
8. The Abscam Affair
9. Judging Candidates
10. Gasohol: Questions and Answers
11. Improvements in National Defense
12. Controlling Government Spending
13. President Carter's Anti-Inflation Program
14. Helping Small Business
15. The Mood of the Voters
16. How Congressional Staff Help Hoosiers
17. Nominating Presidents: Ideas for Reform
18. The Hostage Crisis Worsens
19. The Second Decade
20. Cutting the Cost of Health Care
21. The Underground Economy
22. Trouble for America's Automakers
23. Hazardous Waste

There is no claim that my commentaries presented a lot of original research and scholarship. Most of the facts and figures came from resources that would typically come across a member of Congress's desk. Reports from the nonpartisan Congressional Research Service at the Library of Congress were particularly valuable, and I would often run commentary drafts by CRS policy experts to have the facts checked for accuracy.

The commentaries were produced with considerable help from a long list of talented staff members over five decades. The pieces always reflected my thoughts and the key points I wanted to get across, but a lot of research was done by staff to help me fill them in. I would initiate the ideas, develop the overall content, and give my views on the politics of the situation. The commentaries would typically go through several drafts and I would review and rework them multiple times (though perhaps not as many times as my staff would say).

Distribution of the commentaries in Indiana was extensive and over the years they developed a good following. They were mailed out weekly to some eight thousand constituents who asked to receive them, and they were published in several newspapers in the state—most of them weeklies, but also some of the larger dailies. I recorded radio versions each week, which were picked up by many small radio stations in my district. Most of my Washington Reports were also printed in the Congressional Record. While the commentaries I wrote while in Congress went primarily to people in southern Indiana, my post-Congress commentaries have been distributed mainly to small regional newspapers around the country, and each commentary has typically run in well over one hundred newspapers.

The area I represented in Congress was the Ninth District, located in southeastern Indiana. It was mainly a small-town, rural district, covering a wide geographical area—usually over twenty-one counties. It was located between three large media markets (Indianapolis, Louisville, and Cincinnati), with no large media itself, so my commentaries on local radio stations or in local papers had a good audience. The political makeup of the residents was moderate to conservative, with a strong dose of pragmatism and a good degree of skepticism about Washington and big government. The people had strong midwestern values: patriotic, churchgoing, hardworking. Solid citizens with a lack of pretense but a lot of pride in their local communities. Not a large proportion of college graduates, but good common sense, good judgment.

I would regularly receive comments about my Washington Reports—often in public meetings, sometimes in writing. Certainly not all of the comments were positive, but even the critical ones gave me feedback from constituents and an opportunity to further explain my views and carry on the discussion. I felt that the commentaries were very much a part of the dialogue that lies at the heart of representative democracy.

My emphasis in the commentaries was educational: I wanted them to be more about the issues and important concepts than about me. So I sometimes heard the criticism that they were too educational and too balanced and that I wasn't taking a clear position. I didn't think that was a valid criticism—most of them had a distinct point of view. But I leave that to the reader to judge.

The nature of the commentaries has varied over the years. Some in the early years were intended to give a sense of what it was like to be a new member of Congress and to discuss some of the major issues during the turbulent times of the 1960s and '70s. Many in the middle years were pro/con discussions of key legislative issues of the day as well as, increasingly, key issues in American foreign policy, which was becoming a major focus of mine. Many of the commentaries after I left Congress in 1999 were what I'd call "Poli-Sci 101" commentaries: they tried to improve public understanding of the basics of how Congress works and why citizen involvement is important. In the most recent years, many of the commentaries dealt with the difficulties Congress was experiencing—they were critical of the current situation but also constructive, suggesting how the functioning of Congress could be improved.

Of the roughly two thousand commentaries, the one hundred included in this book were selected for several different reasons: some for historical interest, because they give a good sense of the issues and challenges of the times; others because they make broader statements about our country and system of government or because they discuss a particularly difficult policy issue that is still relevant today; still others because they indicate specific ways in which Congress can work better. It is my hope that they provide not only an interesting look back but also some important lessons for the future.

The pieces reflect my view that a member of Congress needs to be both a partner in the governing process and also a critic. It's a difficult balance to strike. Too often members fall into the pattern of being a *partner* when the president is of their party and a *critic* when he is not.

Also coming through in these commentaries is my interest in process and reform in Congress. This may have developed from my training as a lawyer, but it also reflects my conviction that good process is the key to the functioning of Congress: if the process by which Congress handles legislation is basically fair, then there are not many complaints from members. But if members are excluded, they get angry, and the institution and its work product suffer.

As the years went on, the pieces reflected the increasing responsibility I felt as a senior member of Congress to try to make the institution work. As often happens with senior members, I became more of an institutionalist—looking not just at the politics of specific issues but also at what impact they would have on the standing and integrity of the institution of the Congress.

Over the fifty years of these commentaries, the workings of Congress changed considerably. At the time of the 89th Congress the institution was functioning well, with both parties working together to address the major issues and challenges of the day. In fact, it was criticized for working too well—passing too many major bills at *too* rapid a pace. In the last Congress covered in the book—the 113th—it was just the opposite: highly polarized, often dysfunctional, unable to do even its most basic work. At some point during the span of those fifty years, Congress went seriously off track. This is reflected in my commentaries. A few of my earlier commentaries would discuss problems with Congress, but that became a primary focus of my later commentaries as I devoted more and more attention to what was wrong with Congress and how it could do its work better.

Yet through it all, I still have maintained a deep respect for the institution. I increasingly express my disappointment about how Congress is working, and I probably propose more remedies than could easily be carried out at any one time. But it is disappointment with the performance of Congress, not with the institution itself. I try to come at it from a constructive point of view, and I still, after all I've seen over these fifty years, retain a fundamental confidence in representative democracy.

I continue to write such commentaries regularly. Now in my fifty-first year of putting them together, the format has changed quite a bit from the early days—now blogs and e-mails rather than mimeographed mailings—and most of the topics have changed. Yet I hope they continue to serve an educational purpose, stimulating some reflection on our remarkable system of government and contributing in some way to advancing the national dialogue for getting Congress back on track—improving its ability to once again function as the Founders intended, at the heart of our system of representative democracy.

ONE

THE JOHNSON YEARS
(1965–68)
A Remarkable Time to Begin in Congress

THE NOVEMBER 1964 ELECTION THAT BROUGHT ME TO CONGRESS was also the Lyndon Johnson landslide over Barry Goldwater. The four years that I would serve in Congress during the Johnson years—in the 89th and 90th Congresses—were a memorable, tumultuous time.

Legislation came at us very quickly. I was sworn into office on January 4, 1965, and by April we had passed the Elementary and Secondary Education Act, the first of sixty major bills we passed that Congress. President Johnson felt he had a clear mandate from the election, and he was poised to strike. Much of the legislation had been developed by President Kennedy, so Johnson had an agenda handed to him. And many of the major bills were fully aired and, to Johnson's mind, fully settled during the campaign. So it was full speed ahead.

The 89th was a Congress in which the president clearly took the lead, and Johnson was relentless in pursuing his agenda and in his follow-up with Congress. He had great energy and focus, and a thorough knowledge of the institution and its members. He enjoyed the legislative process and had been involved in it for much of his life. He was constantly on the phone to members of Congress, making dozens of calls every day. Like other members I was cornered by Johnson on several occasions, his index finger poking against my chest as he told me why a bill needed to be passed. The question on his mind was always, How do I get your vote? Johnson was a dealmaker and he used the full powers of his office—which were considerable—to close the deal, whether it was promising a federal building or bridge for your district, offering you a trip overseas, or appointing someone you knew to an office. Anything he needed to do, he'd do.

He was proud of the accomplishments of the 89th Congress, and at the end of the two years hosted a reception at the White House for what he called "the fabulous 89th," saying its record exceeded that of any previous Congress. Impressive as the accomplishments were, I did have some reservations. At midsession I wrote the president, saying that it might be a "time to pause" in the legislative flurry. We were passing a lot of major legislation—aid to education, Medicare, War on Poverty—all of broad magnitude, and I was concerned about implementation. I took numerous trips back home, almost every weekend, to hold public meetings with constituents to discuss what we were doing, and there was clear skepticism about the rush of legislation. It took the 1966 elections, when the Democrats lost several seats in the House, to slow us down.

I had a good personal relationship with President Johnson. He took a special interest in me as a new member of Congress, for reasons I never fully understood—perhaps he overestimated the significance of my being president of the incoming House class. He was always accessible and open to my requests, and once he even came out to my district for a campaign appearance, which was an unusual thing for a president to do for a member of the House. Later in his term I offered one of the first amendments in the House to reduce funding for the Vietnam War. Our effort wasn't successful, but it received more votes than expected. It so happened that I went to the White House that evening for a reception. President Johnson came directly over as soon as he saw me. I still remember the disappointed look in his eyes when he said, "Lee, how could you do that to me?" But to his great credit, we stayed on good terms. As a master politician he knew that down the road he would need my vote or support on something else.

I actually had a less direct relationship with the House leadership early on. In the 1960s the general advice from the congressional leadership to new members was to keep your mouth shut your first few terms in Congress, and we were told—not altogether in jest—that the senior members didn't even learn your name until your third or fourth term. In my second term in office, in January 1967, I did receive a phone call from Speaker John McCormack—a surprising "Lee, how are you?" call, since I don't think he would have recognized me if I walked unannounced into his room. He said a vote for Speaker was coming up in the caucus and he hoped I'd be with him. I told him I'd be voting for Mo Udall, and then I heard the phone slam down. McCormack was reelected Speaker, but he never held my vote against me. And from then on he did know who I was. He was never vindictive, always nice, and ready to be helpful. Both he and Johnson showed me that to be a successful politician you don't hold grudges, and you think about the battles ahead, not those in the past.

The Democratic and Republican leaders in the House—Speaker McCormack, Majority Leader Carl Albert, and Minority Leader Gerald Ford—were all political professionals who got along well. They had regular meetings, and there was a sense of civility and accommodation. Make no mistake: there was partisanship. The leaders were strong and articulate advocates for their party caucuses. But the overall sense of working together for the good of the nation was quite unlike the way it is in Congress today.

I was impressed not only with the leadership but also with the quality of the members of the House—their integrity, their competence, their many abilities. I remember thinking to myself that these people were good, and that I was both honored and challenged to be among them.

At one point early on, when I was still learning my way around Congress, I was managing a minor bill on the House floor for the Democrats and made a small parliamentary mistake that would have doomed its fate. At the direction of the Republican leadership, Bill Bray, a prominent Republican also from Indiana, came over to me, put his arm on my shoulder, and gently pointed out how I could fix my blunder—and this was on a bill they *opposed*. They didn't want even a new Democratic member of Congress to look foolish. It is simply unimaginable that something like that could happen in Congress today.

The 89th Congress was a remarkable time to start a career in Congress. It was a two-year period of accomplishments unlike anything seen since. It was also a time when the public had a high regard for Congress. I don't think I appreciated it enough initially, thinking that maybe that was the way it always worked in Congress. But as the Congress progressed, I came to recognize the uniqueness of what we had done.

The 89th Congress: Key Facts

· January 4, 1965, through October 22, 1966, during the first two years of the second Johnson administration
· House of Representatives controlled by the Democrats, 295 to 140
· Senate controlled by the Democrats, 68 to 32
· 810 bills enacted
· Major accomplishments included passing the Older Americans Act, Medicare and Medicaid, the Voting Rights Act of 1965, the Elementary and Secondary Education Act, the Higher Education Act, the Water Quality Act, a minimum wage increase, the Freedom of Information Act, the Highway Safety Act, and the Financial Institutions Supervisory Act; and setting up the Department of Housing and Urban Development and the Department of Transportation
· Support for President Johnson's position in the House: Democrats 82 percent, Republicans 46 percent; in the Senate: Democrats 73 percent, Republicans 54 percent

The 90th Congress: Key Facts

· January 10, 1967, through October 14, 1968, during the last two years of the second Johnson administration
· House of Representatives controlled by the Democrats, 246 to 187 (2 other)
· Senate controlled by the Democrats, 64 to 36
· 640 bills enacted
· Major accomplishments included passing the Investment Tax Credit Act, the Public Broadcasting Act, the Air Quality Control Act, the Wholesome Meat Act, the Age Discrimination in Employment Act, an increase in Social Security benefits, the Civil Rights Act of 1968 (housing), the Truth in Lending Act, the Omnibus Crime Control and Safe Streets Act, the Juvenile Delinquency Prevention and Control Act, the Housing and Urban Development Act, the National Trails System Act, and the Gun Control Act; and Senate ratification of the first US-USSR bilateral treaty

· Support for President Johnson's position in the House: Democrats 79 percent, Republicans 55 percent; in the Senate: Democrats 69 percent, Republicans 60 percent

THE FACTS ABOUT THE MEDICARE BILL

In the 1964 campaign, my first campaign for Congress, I had several debates in southern Indiana on Medicare, as well as on federal aid to education—those were the two big domestic issues. So I was reasonably familiar with the main questions and controversies about Medicare when I came to Congress. Often my debates were with doctors rather than with other politicians. The American Medical Association was the main group opposed to Medicare—calling it socialized medicine—and they found doctors to debate me in various forums.

I was only in Congress for six months before Medicare came up for consideration and for a vote, and it was a good learning experience for me. Two lessons stand out:

I was impressed by the way Chairman Wilbur Mills and ranking member John Byrnes handled the bill on the House floor. They had complete command of the details, and the debate consisted basically of Mills answering questions about every aspect of the bill, with Byrnes's help. It was a good lesson about the importance of mastering the details of a bill—if you are bringing a bill to the floor, you need to know more about it than anyone else.

I also learned a lot from Wilbur Mills about consensus building and respect for minority views. The Democrats at that time had an overwhelming majority in the House—more than two to one—and many of us felt that we should just pass the Medicare bill we wanted. But Mills argued persuasively that it would be unwise not to give some significant concessions to the Republicans. He recognized that what matters is not just passing a bill but also its implementation, and that there would be a much better chance of successful implementation if something passed with bipartisan support. The bill received many Republican votes on final passage, making it a significant bipartisan accomplishment.

Mills was constantly talking to members of both parties about legislation he was developing, and if he spotted a potential problem he would go back to his committee to try to find a way to fix it—which meant that the bills he brought to the floor almost always passed by wide margins and with strong bipartisan support. He was the most impressive legislator I saw during my years in Congress, and to my mind the greatest legislator of the twentieth century, responsible for shaping a broad range of our nation's basic legislation, from Social Security and the tax code to trade agreements and welfare.

April 28, 1965: "The Facts about the Medicare Bill"
Report from Washington
Vol. I, No. 7
On April 8, 1965, the House of Representatives by an over-whelming majority of 313 to 115 passed an historic bill providing for medical care for persons sixty-five years or older.
The bill actually provides

1. basic hospital insurance under Social Security;
2. voluntary supplementary health benefits through private insurance in part paid by government; and
3. an expanded medical assistance program for the needy.

In addition, the bill provides for improvements in the Social Security program itself, including a general increase in benefits of 7 percent.
I voted wholeheartedly in favor of this bill because it is of monumental significance to all residents of the Ninth District.
Because the subject of medical care for the aged has been under discussion for so long, I think you are entitled to a thorough review of the issues involved.

The Problem
There was unanimous agreement in the Congress that a real problem exists. Persons over sixty-five years of age are a growing segment of our society. Nearly one out of every ten Americans is in this age group and their numbers are increasing every year.

Medical care is a serious matter of concern to all citizens, but this group faces special problems:

Less Income: Of the eighteen million persons over sixty-five, more than half have incomes of less than $1000 a year. The average for two-person families is just $2530. This level of income will buy very little hospital care today.

Fewer Assets: One-third of the persons over sixty-five, numbering six million Americans, have no assets at all. Half of all persons over sixty-five have assets amounting to less than $1,000. Yet, when a husband or wife is hospitalized, half the aged couples today have total medical bills exceeding $800 a year.

Ill Longer: Persons over sixty-five use three times as much hospital care as younger people. When they go to the hospital they stay twice as long for each illness on the average.

Costs Hurt: Since their productive years ended, bringing sharp cuts in annual income, these persons have experienced great increases in medical costs. Those costs have increased 63 percent since 1950. In that same period, the cost of hospital rooms has gone up 154 percent. Few older persons have savings adequate to meet these mounting costs that, as one grows older, cannot be avoided.

No amount of oratory about self-reliance is going to keep our older citizens from getting sick. Nor will it put money in the savings accounts of retired persons who have exhausted their savings and can't get a job.

Weighing the Proposals

Some constituents wrote that not enough study had been given to this legislation.

I would disagree and point to the fact that rarely in the history of the Congress has any piece of legislation been more carefully studied. In the 85th, 86th, 87th, and 88th and the present 89th Congress, the Ways and Means Committee held public hearings for forty-six days, heard 641 witnesses who presented thirteen volumes and 7601 pages of testimony, accepted hundreds of additional statements, and devoted seventy-seven more days to private discussion of the legislation.

Such a record can hardly be held up as evidence of undue haste on the part of Congress.

The Real Issue

The legislation reported by the Ways and Means Committee for consideration by the full House brought together the best features of all the proposals. The major portions of the legislation were accepted by Republicans and Democrats alike, with no debate.

All the testimony, the research, the probing and weighing of all the various factors that were important to such a hugely important bill have borne fruit.

Congressman Byrnes, the chief Republican spokesman, said, "Let me point out at the very beginning, that we on the Committee, Democrats and Republicans alike, are in general agreement with respect to the provisions in the bill as reported by the Committee relating to the old-age and survivors system, the disability system, and even as far as the Kerr-Mills system is concerned . . . my objection to the Committee bill is not on the basis of cost. My objection is to the means used to finance the benefits; namely, the payroll tax."

We Chose the Conservative Course

Wilbur Mills (D. Ark.), chairman of the Ways and Means Committee, argued persuasively that the payroll tax was the surest, most conservative path to prevent a program whose benefit payments would become a runaway monster draining the federal treasury. He said, "The Social Security . . . system is actuarially sound and has been for over thirty years. How many times have we had a balanced budget of the general fund of the treasury into which the gentleman [Mr. Byrnes] proposes to put this [Medicare] system? I am trying to say this, to emphasize the point I have made repeatedly—a payroll tax will tend to limit the growth of the benefit and will tend to do so to a greater extent than will be the case if that benefit cost is placed in the general fund of the treasury."

THE OTHER WAR IN VIETNAM

I went to Congress supporting the Vietnam War. It was the first war I had to deal with as a member of Congress, and I felt the need to delve into it in great detail. I spent a lot of time trying to understand what was happening there—through various reports, briefings, and discussions with colleagues, as well as through visits to the region. By October 1966 I was beginning to see more clearly the limits of military power in dealing with the complexities of Vietnam.

In 1966, Robert McNamara was secretary of defense and Dean Rusk was secretary of state. Persuasion was a large part of their responsibilities. Both were very knowledgeable, with an extensive command of the facts about what was going on and what our role was. Watching them it was clear what being a good cabinet member was all about: mastering their brief down to every detail and presenting it consistently and thoroughly to all kinds of audiences all over the country.

A lot of it was about measurement: the number of enemy soldiers killed, the number of villages pacified, the number of new roads or new schools built. All elaborately stated, all put on colorful charts and graphs for members of Congress in an effort to sell a war that was becoming increasingly controversial.

McNamara and Rusk testified before Congress persuasively. They and other administration officials looked at the economic, political, and social side, not just the military side, and I was impressed by that. But I was starting to become skeptical about some of the statistics. On one of my visits to Vietnam I went along on a combat patrol. Several hundred yards ahead some of our soldiers encountered Viet Cong soldiers, and we could clearly hear the gunfire. Afterward I saw the captain writing up his report. I asked him about it, and he said he reported ten enemy soldiers killed in action. I asked him how he got that number, and his response was that they shot at the bushes so long they must have killed at least ten. It was just a guess, with no physical evidence, no bodies found, but those are the kinds of numbers that go up the line and would later be presented with great certainty to members of Congress in congressional hearings.

This report reflects my optimism at that time about the war, but it also shows the extent to which I was basically regurgitating information the administration was giving me about progress in Vietnam. Soon I started to have serious concerns about the war and about my dependence on the administration for facts about Vietnam. So I began searching for other sources of information.

October 1, 1966: "The Other War in Vietnam"
Washington Report
Vol. II, No. 53

We read and talk about Vietnam in terms of military operations. And we overlook an important "other war" in that country—the struggle to overcome human misery and want.

The Viet Cong has been attempting to throttle South Vietnam's economy for years. In the last seven months alone, 3,015 school teachers, health workers, village chiefs, and agriculture workers—people who could help lead the country to social stability—have been murdered or kidnapped by the Viet Cong.

The United States is providing technical advice and material help to this other "war." But it remains primarily a Vietnamese effort to preserve the economic stability of the country, to organize new programs of health education and welfare, and to establish a representative government.

The success in the efforts toward a responsible government was demonstrated last September 11 in the election for a constitutional government. Between 70 and 80 percent of the eligible voters went to the polls.

As the military conflict has progressed, more money has been pumped into the Vietnamese economy than could be readily absorbed, creating inflation. To check this threat to the country's economy, the US and Vietnamese governments have agreed upon a devaluation of the Vietnamese currency, an overhauling of the fiscal systems, and the establishment of budget and wage restraints.

US sources report that in the countryside, the battle to take the rural hamlets away from the Viet Cong and return them to the Saigon government is gathering momentum. As of July 1, 1965, about 3,199 villages were reported "secure." By the end of June this year, an estimated 4,054 villages were considered secure. Put another way, an estimated 55 percent of the population is now considered secure, 24 percent is still under Viet Cong domination, and the remaining 21 percent is caught in the middle.

There are now in operation 431 "pacification teams" working to bring political and economic stability to the province villages. The training of new team members is being stepped up.

Roads are being improved and secured; new efforts are being made to establish law and order in rural areas; new agriculture techniques are being employed; education is being improved; and medical care is being expanded and improved.

Since 1962, the use of chemical fertilizer has more than tripled.

Since 1963, hog production has more than doubled, and the average weight has gone from 130 to 220 pounds per hog.

A rural electrification program has begun and rural water supplies have been improved.

About 6,400 new village classrooms have been built so far.

About 2.2 million textbooks have been distributed to elementary school pupils.

Agriculture and vocational training is being increased.

An average of 39,700 patients are being treated each month by our medical teams.

Some 90,000 Saigon elementary pupils have been immunized.

Thirty-two nations in the Free World have joined the US in this "other war." More than seven hundred teachers, technicians, and medical personnel from these countries are now in Vietnam. In the first six months of this year, they contributed more than $15 million in assistance programs. More than six hundred Vietnamese now are studying abroad at the invitation of foreign governments.

US officials admit that progress has been slow in some areas, but there has been progress. And the momentum is growing. The country is moving forward—even in the midst of a military war.

THANKSGIVING 1966

Thanksgiving in 1966 was a troubling time for Americans, as reflected in the tone of this newsletter.

It was also when I took my first trip overseas as a member of Congress, along with a small number of my colleagues from the House Foreign Affairs Committee, to meet with officials of other countries. We traveled by commercial airline, rather than on an Air Force plane, to the USSR and several Eastern and Western European countries.

I remember the extraordinary hospitality of the host countries, even the Russians. But I also remember that the meetings were tough, especially the meetings with our Russian counterparts. They would bear down on US policy. They knew a lot about our country, and would ask us to defend racial discrimination, segregation, unemployment, and more. The discussions were wide-ranging and thorough. I got a clear sense early on that dialogues with leaders of other countries would not be a cakewalk and that I had to be thoroughly prepared.

We had access to the top leaders, and I found the trip informative and valuable. Over the years I've been a strong advocate of travel for members of Congress, as it allows them to learn firsthand about a host of important issues and to see how policy in a given region is being implemented and how it is being received. Some congressional trips in recent years, especially those financed by private groups, have been rightly criticized as junkets. But many are serious business. On this trip we had no sightseeing, no touring. Just numerous meetings in government office buildings. People would later ask what I thought of Warsaw or Budapest, but I had to explain that I never really saw the cities. I only saw the hotels and the foreign ministry buildings, though I'm not sure they believed me.

November 23, 1966 (untitled)
Washington Report
Vol. II, No. 56

The Thanksgiving season is upon us, bringing us pause to reflect on those things for which we can be truly thankful.

Our first assessment brings us to the conclusion that much is wrong in the world on this Thanksgiving season.

We are involved in the Vietnam conflict, a tragic and sometimes confusing kind of war in an Asian land that has known little but war for nearly three decades.

And the other war—the Cold War—is still very much with us, making itself known in reports about missiles and anti-missile systems, nuclear testing and such.

New sounds of unrest erupt in China, creating concern not only in the free world, but among those nations aligned with China through Communism.

It is my belief that these hot- and cold-war tactics and the rumblings from China would be much more intense if it were not for our stand in Vietnam. It is our demonstration to the world that Communism will not be allowed to be propagated by force.

When families gather for the traditional meal of Thanksgiving, Vietnam will be in their thoughts and in their prayers. No one wants our young men faced with this kind of danger or have our country involved in this kind of conflict.

Yet the Communist world has not allowed us to choose what we want. They have tested us in the past and they will continue to test us. Our task is to show them that we are determined to preserve freedom in those countries which have asked us to help them.

And it was this restless yearning for freedom that brought those first Americans together for Thanksgiving many years ago. They were determined to live in a free society and to defend that society.

There was much wrong in their world, too. Not great global problems to be sure, but problems of surviving. It is still true today.

The preservation of freedom is the great, distinguishing characteristic of the American people.

I will be in Moscow on Thanksgiving day on a study mission for the House Foreign Affairs Committee. The purpose of the mission in Russia and in the Eastern and Western countries is to seek better understanding and areas of greater cooperation between our nations.

I suspect it will be alien and strange, thinking about Thanksgiving in a country which opposes our way of life.

Meanwhile, Nancy and I extend to all residents of the Ninth District our most sincere wishes for a happy Thanksgiving holiday.

LUNCHEON AT THE WHITE HOUSE

One of the initiation rites of every new member of Congress is the first official visit to the White House. The grounds, the security, the hospitality are all impressive—as are the presentations made by administration officials who know every aspect of their topic. My main thought on my first visit was that I was now in the big leagues.

During a luncheon and briefing at the White House in May 1967, I spent some time with Secretary of State Dean Rusk. I followed up by inviting him out to Indiana to meet some Hoosiers to discuss the administration's position on the Vietnam War. I was surprised when he accepted.

But he explained that he felt he was spending too much time in DC and wanted to experiment a bit and see what impact he could have out in the country. He viewed Indiana as the heartland, and thought it would have a good audience to reach.

It started out well. His first appearance was in the city of Columbus in the south-central part of the state, at a packed high school auditorium of perhaps four thousand to five thousand local people. Then we had a motorcade to Bloomington for his appearance at Indiana University. On the way we got word that protesters were in front of the building where he was to speak, so we decided to go in by a back door. In the auditorium, Mrs. Rusk and I sat in the front row, but the mood was volatile. When Secretary Rusk and IU President Elvis Stahr appeared onstage, they were greeted with boos all around and objects were thrown at the stage by students who opposed the war. President Stahr had a difficult time getting through his few sentences of introduction, which ended up taking fifteen minutes. Secretary Rusk tried to speak over the boos and shouts and kept saying, "I'm prepared to be your guest if you'll let me." But after a half hour he just gave up.

Indiana University was deeply embarrassed by the incident, and soon sent a delegation to Washington to apologize to him; I accompanied the delegation. The secretary was an appealing person: always a gentleman, unflappable, very bright and articulate, someone who never raised his voice. He was gracious about the incident, but he didn't forget it. For years afterward, whenever I would see him he would kid me that Indiana University was the only university that didn't allow him to speak.

May 1967 (untitled)
Washington Report
Vol. III, No. 18
Lunch at the White House . . . what is it like?

Certainly, it's a great departure from the hurried soup-and-sandwich breaks that make up most noon meals on Capitol Hill. On the other hand, it's not quite the many-splendored thing that most people think.

The recent luncheon I attended at the invitation of the president for General William C. Westmoreland, commander of the US forces in Vietnam, was unhurried and yet business-like.

Members of Congress who were invited were stopped at the East Gate of the historic grounds and asked to show their invitations before being allowed to enter. One was struck by the immaculate beauty of the grounds. The grass was manicured and spring flowers in the Kennedy Garden were blooming. And looking from the Portico, the view abounded with dogwood and magnolia.

In the great hall of the White House, the Marine Corps band played a lively piece. Military aides to the president approached, assigned luncheon table seats, and announced your name as you approached the president and the receiving line.

After greeting the president, he, in turn, introduced me to the guest of honor—in this instance, General Westmoreland. Pictures were being snapped continually as the luncheon guests moved down the reception line.

Once through the reception line, guests were served cocktails in the historic State Room where waiters moved through the crowd of cabinet members, governors, and members of Congress with trays of beverages of all varieties. The cocktail period was brief, however, and aides politely—but firmly—suggested that the guests move into the East Room where lunch was served.

Eight or ten circular tables were set up for eight guests each. The gold-rimmed White House china and gold-plated tableware were set for the occasion. Place cards and the menu, written in flawless script and embossed with the gold presidential seal, also were at each setting.

I was seated with Secretary of State Dean Rusk and Governor Winthrop Rockefeller of Arkansas. Conversation was both casual and serious, ranging from humorous incidents to discussion of matters of state. Dean Rusk remembered a similar luncheon earlier at which a woman asked him, "And what is your name?" "I'm Dean Rusk," he replied. "And where do you work?" "I'm associated with the State Department." "How nice."

President Johnson acted as the master of ceremonies, introducing first Miss Martha Raye, the actress and comedienne who has distinguished herself as a nurse and entertainer in South Vietnam.

He also introduced Dean Rusk, who reported on the US Vietnam peace feelers, and General Westmoreland, who reported on the US military progress in Vietnam.

And, as a final touch, as each guest left, his name was discreetly broadcast to a parking area and his car was waiting as he arrived at the drive near the South Portico.

VISIT TO THE CIA

I've always had high regard for the intelligence community—for their expertise and professionalism—and I've had close ties to that community for almost fifty years. They strive to be accurate, and they have a tough job: trying to get information from people who don't want to give it to them. Their predictions are not flawless. But I've found their briefings—starting from my first, in June 1967, and continuing through the years when I was chairman of the House Intelligence Committee—to be well done and helpful in analyzing foreign-policy problems and issues. The briefings as well as their reports were beneficial to me throughout my career in Congress. I would even at times take on the task of defending the CIA in debates on college campuses—not a winning side to be on for most college audiences, but I felt it would help balance out what they were hearing elsewhere.

While I am supportive of intelligence professionals, I did become wary of political appointees in the CIA and other intelligence agencies. They are appointed by the president, are sensitive to his needs, and tend to be selective and give him the information he wants—the basic problem of the politicization of intelligence. I can recall very few times in the Oval Office when I heard someone tell a president something he didn't want to hear.

June 19, 1967 (untitled)
Washington Report
Vol. III, No. 24
Recently, I was among a small group of Congressmen who were briefed by the Central Intelligence Agency (CIA) on subversion in Latin America.

If the project conjures up images of a James Bond type "filling us in" at some dimly lighted hideaway, let me quickly dispel those thoughts.

We were picked up in a car on Capitol Hill and driven eight miles to the agency's Langley Falls (VA) headquarters. The drive, out

George Washington Parkway, affords one of the best views of the panorama of the historic Potomac River and the quiet, lush Virginia Hill country to be found in the area.

The driver turned off the busy parkway at an unmarked exit for the mile-long drive to the CIA headquarters building. Other government buildings along the parkway are announced by turn-off signs and driving directions. The only clue to the CIA turn-off is a Bureau of Public Roads marker.

The headquarters, an eight-story, U-shaped structure surrounded by a high, chain-linked fence, came into view shortly after the turn-off. At the gate, a uniformed guard carefully checked the driver's identification badge, then asked us to state our business and to identify ourselves.

Only after the guard had verified our appointment and identity did he allow us to pass. We were driven to the main entrance of the building.

In the light and airy main lobby we were "checked out" once more by a guard and our escort met us and stayed with us every step of the way. As we waited, I noted the CIA seal and a number of American flags in the lobby. On one wall of the spacious, marbled room was inscribed the Biblical adage, "And ye shall know the truth, and the truth shall set you free."

The escort led us to a special elevator to the director's office. We stopped at the seventh floor, the operations center of the huge building. Here, we were led down a carpeted corridor, past doors labeled "Director" and "Deputy Director," to a spacious conference room. A massive table, surrounded by twenty or so high-backed leather chairs, dominated the room. A pad and two pencils were at each setting.

As coffee was served, I noted a number of maps on the walls, each dealing with some aspect of this country's security operations. Projectors and screens were also in this room.

CIA director Richard M. Helms, fifty-three, a tall, slender, graying man, conservatively dressed, entered and greeted each of us individually. We were seated and he announced the agenda, introducing some of the top intelligence people who were to brief us. We were invited to question them at length. Mr. Helms then excused himself.

The agents, who looked and spoke more like college professors, began an informal but astoundingly intricate briefing on a number of Latin American countries and their present-day political and economic status. They spoke knowingly of political leaders in these countries—even down to the results of their latest physical examinations.

It soon became apparent that these men were genuine experts who pored over countless reports, news stories, speeches, and statistics to acquire the expertise with which they spoke. Their presentations lasted for about an hour and they then fielded our questions with ease and competence for another hour.

At the conclusion of the briefing we were once more escorted back to the main lobby. I was told that no visitor goes unescorted through the building.

The car was waiting at the front entrance and we began the drive back to the Capitol. We were quieter, perhaps a little overwhelmed by the facts and figures with which we had been bombarded.

From time to time we hear harsh criticism of the CIA. Without passing judgment on that—it is reassuring to see the competence and skill of the CIA experts.

PRESIDENT JOHNSON OFF THE RECORD

Informal get-togethers with colleagues are an often overlooked but important part of a member's time in Washington. And meetings that involve a president can be particularly valuable, allowing a glimpse of a side of him they might not otherwise see.

In President Johnson's case, he proved to be much more personable and engaging than the somewhat wooden person seen giving speeches on television, and he could be relaxed and open when there were no reporters around taking down his every word. He could also be uncouth and a bit rough around the edges, but he had a very refreshing candor about him. You always knew exactly what he had in mind and what he wanted to do— as well as what he wanted you to do for him.

I found the president to be a bright person—not in the sense of being book smart, but in his learning from talking to people and remembering long after points they had made. He also had enormous respect for his wife. She was a gracious person, and I sometimes wondered how she could handle all the various sides of his personality. But his respect for her opinions was clear, and he greatly valued her political instincts. I often heard him say, "I want to check with Bird on this."

I enjoyed being around President Johnson, in a variety of settings. In 1966 he came out to the Ninth District to help support me in my reelection effort. They needed some reason for him to make the visit, so it was determined that he would give a beautification award to a local postmaster for planting a petunia garden in front of the Jeffersonville Post Office. In the excitement of the president's visit, hundreds of people trampled over the garden and it quickly looked like a plowed field. But the president didn't miss a beat and he delivered his congratulatory remarks with a straight face.

July 21, 1967 (untitled)
Washington Report
Vol. III, No. 29

The invitation, from Congressman Richard Bolling and Mrs. Bolling, said it would be a Sunday afternoon cookout. Dress would be casual, and there would be swimming and hot dogs and hamburgers.

It didn't say the president and Mrs. Johnson would drop in for a three-hour visit.

With Nancy and the children and I, there were about twenty adults and fifteen children at the Bollings' suburban Maryland home. The guests, which included congressmen, federal agency officials, and businessmen, were either in or around the backyard swimming pool when someone said in hushed voice, "It's the president."

Looking up from the pool, I saw walking in our midst a tall, smiling man in tan sports coat and slacks. With him was a beaming woman dressed in a bright pink summer dress. The president moved straight to the children, picked up and kissed the smallest, and introduced himself to the others with a handshake or a pat on the head.

He then walked to each of the adults at the pool, greeted them warmly, and eased himself into a lawn chair. He said he had spent most of the day conferring on the railroad strike and was looking

for something to do to relax when he remembered the invitation
from the Bollings.

For three hours he talked, occasionally sipping a diet soft drink
or biting into a doughnut. He reminisced, sometimes with obvious
nostalgia, about his Texas hill country and its people. He remembered earlier days in Washington and he recounted some of the
historic events of recent weeks in which he was a participant.

The guests sat around him, some in dripping swimming attire,
occasionally retreating to the grill for another hot dog or ham-
burger. Mrs. Johnson walked slowly around the spacious backyard,
chatting with the wives and children, then with the rest of us, and
listened while her husband "unwound."

He seemed to enjoy it immensely. The children continued their
play in the pool and around the yard. Dogs barked. There was the
hum of conversation, the laughter of children. It was like a thousand other backyard cookouts across the country on that Sunday
evening. . . . But here, in the mild and growing dusk, there was in
this group one of the most powerful men on earth, talking in an ani-
mated, sometimes folksy way, about some of the events which have
shaped world history.

About his summit meeting with Chairman Kosygin, he remembered the Russian leader as an extremely disciplined man, precise
in his conversation, intelligent and diligent to the Communistic way
of life. "I never studied so hard for anything in my life," he said of
his preparation for the meeting.

The president said he had been told that Kosygin talked with
his eyes fixed on his subject. The president decided he would do the
same. For ten hours, the two conversed, eyeball-to-eyeball, not even
letting their gaze wander while reaching for pens, pencils, glasses of
water, etc.

"I had to count to ten a couple of times," he remembered as the
Russian leader commented about war-mongering Americans, profit-
hungry capitalists, and the like.

The president seemed the most relaxed as he talked about
Texas, its people and the land. And he remembered vividly a great
number of acquaintances in Washington in his years as congressman, senator, vice president, and president.

He spoke quietly and movingly of Vietnam and of his desire for
peace. It was not the man you and I see on television. He was ani-
mated at times, pensive and sometimes forceful. It was the kind of
conversation in which the listener loses track of time.

The sun had set when the ever-gracious Mrs. Johnson suggested gently that it was time to go. It was the first mention of time,
and the president reluctantly rose to leave. The watchful Secret Service man, who had lingered in the background, moved up and they
walked to the limousine, parked with the other guest cars.

As they drove away, someone said, "The president sure turns
up in the darndest places." We were glad he had turned up where
he did.

URBAN RIOTS

I was part of the generation after World War II that was optimistic about
our country and its future. That permeated the political atmosphere—there
was no problem we couldn't solve. But that was prior to Vietnam and the
urban riots that shook American cities in the late '60s. In the summer of
1967, people were shocked by the violence and were asking how this could
happen in our country. The idea that seventy American cities were experiencing civil disorder was something that many of us from rural southern
Indiana could not easily grasp. I did a crash course on urban problems in
America, because I felt some responsibility to try to explain to my rural
constituents what was going on.

The riots were personally devastating to President Johnson, coming
just a few days after the passage of the Civil Rights Act. He established a
commission to analyze the causes of the violence and search for solutions.
Headed up by Illinois governor Otto Kerner, its report became known as
the Kerner Report. It was the work of a distinguished group of Americans
from both the public and private sectors, and I was quite impressed by it. It
helped many of us to better understand how complicated and diverse our
country was, and the extent to which many of our citizens did not have
even basic opportunities. One of its major conclusions was that America
was "moving toward two societies, one black, one white—separate and
unequal."

President Johnson largely rejected the report, because it didn't confirm
his suspicions about the causes of the violence and it called into question
his domestic policy accomplishments. But I believe it opened the eyes of a

nation to how serious these problems were and how difficult they would be to resolve. At the time I wrote that this would be a task for a generation. It has turned out to be a task for several generations.

August 5, 1967 (untitled)
Washington Report
Vol. III, No. 31

We in America are proud of our country, proud of its freedom, energy, and prosperity, and we are confident of the future. But the fiery, riot-torn days of past weeks have shaken that pride and deeply disturbed and perplexed us.

We read of sniper raids, fire bombings, lootings, and open disregard for law and order and we ask ourselves, "Can this be America?" Most of us, I think, associate violent civil outbursts with cities with nearly unpronounceable names in foreign countries. Now, however, the places are Newark, Detroit, and Milwaukee.

So far this summer, more than seventy cities—nearly fifty of them in the last two weeks alone—have experienced some measure of civil disorder. The toll: 73 persons dead, some 3,200 injured, about 8,000 arrested, and about $530 million in property damage. The cost in human suffering cannot be measured.

In the Ninth District, as across the nation, Americans are asking themselves "Why?" Some say recent Supreme Court rulings on criminal procedure paved the way for the outbursts. Others blame a Communist conspiracy. Some point to deplorable social conditions in the cities. Still others say the blame should be placed on criminal elements, while some point to militants such as H. Rap Brown and Stokely Carmichael as instigators of the outbreaks.

As the remarks of Ninth District residents suggest, there is no single or simple answer, and no easy, quick solution.

Our task in the days and months ahead is to focus on the central questions—What happened? Why? What must be done to prevent this from happening again?

Several points are clear, however:

1. Law and order must be preserved and asserted quickly and decisively to protect lives and property. William Pitt, one of history's great parliamentarians, said, "Where law ends, tyranny begins." The arsonists, the looters, and the snipers

must be brought to justice. It would be a mistake to be lenient with those who have openly defied our laws.

2. The response to rioting must not be the hasty expenditure of money. Massive expenditures do not assure progress. We should not reward cities where riots have occurred, and, in this way, encourage more disorders.

3. We must, however, see that law-abiding, responsible members of the strife-torn communities are clothed, fed, and housed.

4. We must bring together the best minds available to search for the causes of these tragic outbursts and to offer long-range solutions. This inquiry should be free and open, centered on such questions as, Why do riots occur in some cities and not in others? Why does one man break the law while his neighbor does not? Has there been any planning or organization to these outbursts? Why have some riots been contained effectively while others have not? How well equipped and trained are law enforcement agencies and State Guard units to handle riots? What is the background of those who took part in the riots? Who suffered most in the outbreaks? What is the proper public role in helping cities repair the damage done? What can the individual citizen, groups, and government do to prevent lawlessness?

These questions have been posed to the National Advisory Commission on Civil Disorders which was recently established by President Johnson. They need searching examination.

Partisan politics has no place in this search for answers. It should be the task of all levels of government and all elements of our society. The problem won't be solved in a year or two. It will be the task of a generation.

THE REGULAR ORDER

Nothing makes people's eyes glaze over more quickly in a public meeting than talking about congressional process and procedure. But it didn't take long for me as a new member of Congress to recognize the central importance of good process—that although it doesn't guarantee that we will always get a good result, it does significantly enhance the prospect that we will.

The regular order (as Congress's established, traditional rules and procedures are known) allows all sides to be heard and have some input and makes it possible for Congress to do its work. The more I learned about the regular order the more I respected the steps it lays out for the way Congress should conduct its business. But I've also been impressed by the hard work involved in trying to keep to the regular order as many members push for taking shortcuts around one step or another in the process.

It is striking that most of what I wrote in 1967 about regular order just doesn't apply to how Congress operates now. Congress has wandered far from its established and long-standing process for developing and passing the nation's laws—and that has been to its detriment. More on the regular order later.

August 26, 1967 (untitled)
Washington Report
Vol. III, No. 34

One cannot begin to understand the workings of Congress until he understands the role of the committee. Congressional committees are at the hub of the business of lawmaking in the nation's capital.

Many of you are familiar with city council or county commissioner meetings in which the merits of a community improvement are discussed and then voted upon. Because of the size of Congress (435 representatives and 100 senators) and the overwhelming number of bills proposed each session (22,843 in the 89th Congress), open discussion of each proposal is an impossibility.

On Capitol Hill, bills are channeled to committees for study—and in the case of the one in each one hundred which does come out of committee—to be hammered into the form and context most likely to be accepted by Congress as a whole.

By way of review: The House has twenty standing or permanent committees responsible for some two hundred areas of subject matter ranging from space exploration to the price of peanuts. Further, these standing committees have more than one hundred subcommittees which are assigned specific areas of study in each general area of subject matter.

For example, the House Foreign Affairs Committee, of which I am a member, has subcommittees on Africa, Europe, the Far East and the Pacific, the Near East, Inter-American Affairs, plus five more subcommittees dealing generally with foreign policy, foreign assistance, and foreign operations. I am a member of the subcommittees on the Far East and the Pacific, Europe, and Inter-American Affairs.

In most cases, committees serve as a hearing body for reports from the subcommittees. In effect, the subcommittee is the first of a number of tests to which proposed legislation is put.

The bill is introduced on the floor of the House and assigned to a committee by the Speaker of the House. The committee chairman to which the legislation is assigned may then forward the bill to a subcommittee for study and public hearings.

At the conclusion of the public hearings, the subcommittee may recommend amendments or changes to the bill. The full committee then reviews the legislation and may or may not recommend further changes before voting it out. The House then acts on the bill— approving it, approving it with amendments, or rejecting it.

If approved by the House, the bill is sent to the Senate where it undergoes essentially the same procedure. If the Senate elects to amend the House version of the bill, a conference committee is selected to fashion a compromise version suitable to both the House and the Senate.

Finally, the president must sign the bill before it becomes law. Now, perhaps it becomes easier to understand why the wheels of legislation turn slowly.

One of the most costly and time-consuming aspects of committee work is the hearing. A case in point: The House Committee on Education and Labor recently completed hearings on funds proposed for the Economic Opportunity Act programs. The hearings lasted seven weeks, during which 138 witnesses appeared and gave 4,514 pages of testimony. Cost of the hearings has been estimated at $46,000.

There are critics of this form of legislative procedure to be sure. They say the hearings do little to alter the opinions of committee members, that hearings are expensive, and that they are inefficient.

But efficiency is not the standard by which to judge legislative procedure. Public hearings perform one of the most basic functions of democracy—that of maintaining the individual's right to speak out for or against legislation.

It is, in a very real sense, a demonstration of freedom in meeting the problems of the nation—time-consuming and expensive as it may be.

THE US ROLE IN THE WORLD

Our nation's experience in Vietnam led me to better recognize the limits of military power and the extreme difficulty of nation-building—how hard it is to understand another nation and to change its behavior or government. It was the beginning of my interest in the question of what the role of the United States in the world should be. That is the fundamental question in American foreign policy, and it became the dominant question in my interest in foreign affairs, one that I would return to again and again.

Around this time I was beginning to give considerable thought to how to harness all aspects of American power—not just military but also economic, political, and diplomatic—to advance the interests of our nation.

My main thoughts about the US role in the world in 1968—about maintaining our military strength while assessing sustainability, avoiding overcommitment, expanding cooperation with allies, and working through multilateral organizations—are all points I would still agree with today.

January 20, 1968 (untitled)
Washington Report
Vol. IV, No. 3
What is the role of the United States in the world today? What should this country's global policies be?

The United States is, by any measure, a superpower and by necessity assumes a role of world leader. Yet, there is growing concern in this country that we are overcommitted and overextended. Critics of our foreign policy ask, "Where will these global responsibilities end?"

The range and scope of this country's foreign commitments is awesome. We have commitments in Africa, East Asia, Europe, the Near East, the Middle East, South Asia, Southeast Asia, Southwest Pacific, and the Western Hemisphere. These pledges of assistance range from the historic Monroe Doctrine of 1823 to the Manila Conference of 1966.

Senator Mike Mansfield, D-MT, said recently this count has more than forty-five commitments under present treaty organizations. Actually a commitment to help a foreign country ranges from such worldwide pacts as the United Nations, to geographic treaties such as NATO, SEATO, and CENTO, to written or verbal assurance of help to a small, emerging nation from the president.

Concern over the extent of these commitments has become increasingly strong since Vietnam. Because of the frustrations of that conflict, there is more and more sentiment for isolationism.

The answer to the question of whether or not we are overcommitted depends in part on how we view the Communist threat. If we believe the Communist threat has greatly diminished and is not as strong as it once was, we are more likely to argue that our responsibilities need not be so extensive. On the other hand, if we believe the Communist threat to be as strong as ever, we are more likely to argue that the United States must stand firm in its obligations around the world.

However, certain guidelines of policy suggest themselves:

1. The United States cannot be the policeman of the world. Even with our great resources, there are limits to what we can do. We must avoid overcommitment.

2. The United States could decide not to take on renewed commitments as the present ones expire without the most careful scrutiny. However, caution in avoiding overcommitment does not necessarily mean in every instance we should decline to become involved. For example, in the Middle East where the Soviet Union is establishing a very strong presence, there are renewed dangers for us.

3. The United States certainly must maintain its strength— militarily, economically, and politically. Even with the great changes in the world today, the United States still remains the bulwark of freedom and democracy.

4. We must encourage our allies to form and cooperate with regional groupings and to take on more and more of the responsibility for economic development and military defense.

5. We must also strive to improve international organizations for peace keeping. An effective, strong, international peace-keeping force could be a potent instrument for global stability.

With power comes responsibility and the United States has not shirked that responsibility. However, we continue to pay a heavy cost. Secretary of State Dean Rusk pinpointed the sentiment of many concerned Americans recently when he said, "We would all be isolationists if we could."

SENATE HEARINGS ON THE VIETNAM WAR

In 1968 the Senate held a series of hearings in which senators asked administration officials a host of questions about the Vietnam War that were increasingly on the minds of ordinary Americans. The hearings were particularly significant because they showed that Congress was beginning to reassert itself on questions of foreign policy, and they became the focal point for discontent with the war.

Congress will often take a back seat to a president on major issues, especially in foreign policy, so the fact that Secretary Rusk was being grilled by senators was an important signal of renewed congressional assertiveness. The Constitution divides power between Congress and the president in defense and international affairs, and Congress has the challenging role of being both a partner and a critic, providing an independent assessment of American foreign policy.

The system needs a strong presidential role, but it works best when there is also a strong congressional role—especially because Congress is the branch most closely in touch with the American people and no major foreign-policy decision is sustainable in the long run without their support.

March 23, 1968 (untitled)
Washington Report
Vol. IV, No. 12
Secretary of State Dean Rusk's appearance before the Senate Foreign Relations Committee was certainly one of the more popular

television programs here in Washington last week. From all indications, it had a wide viewing audience across the nation, also.

For ten hours over a two-day period, Secretary Rusk faced a blinding bank of lights and answered the questions of his interrogators. It was not the easiest or most comfortable spot to be in, to say the least.

Ostensibly, the hearing was called to review an administration bill authorizing some $2.9 billion for foreign economic and military aid for fiscal 1969. But the committee chairman, Sen. J. W. Fulbright, D-AR, quickly turned it into a forum on our commitments in Vietnam.

Very probably, no votes were changed as a result of the hearings. And there have been some rumblings that the hearings were something of a disappointment. There was much comment on Secretary Rusk's composure under pressure, but, by and large, the hearings seemed to be reruns of previous performances.

The theme of the secretary's testimony seemed to be that our objective in Vietnam is an organized peace and that we have a basic commitment to freedom which "requires an environment in the rest of the world in which freedom can survive and flourish."

Although he acknowledged that there was a component of a civil war in Vietnam, he said the United States does not accept the view that it is solely a civil war.

In reviewing our commitments in that country, he concluded, "I don't know what would happen to the peace of the world if it should be discovered that our treaties do not mean anything."

This is not to say that the senators did not have their day, too.

Senator Mansfield expressed the hope that there exists some way out of the difficulty in Vietnam because of the unrest and frustration that conflict is creating in this country.

Senator Morse spoke of an "incipient uprising in this country in opposition to the war." Senator Carlson asked for more facts for the people back home, and Senator Gore said that the policy in Vietnam needs a thorough reassessment.

Senator Symington spoke of his "increasing doubt" about the US course of action in Vietnam, and Senator Case said he was "more and more convinced that our course was wrong."

The hearing did point out to the country the concern of Congress that it be informed and consulted before any decision is reached to send additional troops to Vietnam.

The real impact of the hearings probably is the effort to make more effective the constitutional right of Congress to consult and advise the executive in foreign policy.

The senators want the right to be heard before any major decisions are made by the administration. Secretary Rusk did say that "if more troops are needed, we will, as we have done in the past, consult with appropriate members of Congress."

Hopefully, these hearings will lead to closer consultations between the administration and the Congress on Vietnam policy. No one expects that congressional advice will be heeded in every instance, but closer consultation will at least lead to broader understanding and defuse some of the harsh criticism made by the Congress of administration policy.

CIVIL DISORDER AFTER THE ASSASSINATION OF MARTIN LUTHER KING JR.

In my personal contacts with Dr. King—such as one time when I had an extended conversation with him at an airport while we were both waiting for our flights—he was unfailingly gracious, interested as much in talking about my family and how they adjusted to my political life as he was in discussing broader issues. I also saw him several times when he came to the Hill to meet with members of Congress, through meetings arranged by the Congressional Black Caucus. Sometimes there would be twenty of us in those meetings, sometimes seventy-five. I found him less impressive in the give-and-take discussions of those smaller groups than I did when he was giving formal speeches to large audiences, when his stirring oratory was persuasive and inspiring. He impressed me as a good man, but one weighted down with very heavy burdens. Sometimes he seemed to bear all the planet's grief on his shoulders: famines, massacres, wars, slums, cruelty, anguish. He was only thirty-nine when he was killed.

Lost over the years with the emphasis on Dr. King's civil rights work was his uncompromising opposition to the war in Vietnam. As a minister he felt mandated to seek peace. The bombs in Vietnam, he said, exploded at home, destroying the dreams and possibilities for a decent America.

King's assassination—like those of John Kennedy and Robert Kennedy—was a terrible setback for the country. So were the riots that followed his assassination—some reaching within blocks of the White House. Some parts of the cities hardest hit by the riots, including Washington, DC, still have not recovered.

April 22, 1968 (untitled)
Washington Report
Vol. IV, No. 16

The wave of civil disorder which followed the assassination of Dr. Martin Luther King Jr. has served to announce to the Congress the urgency for dealing with this domestic problem.

In its search for ways to correct the conditions which create civil disorders, the Congress must not lose sight of the fact that lawlessness—in any cause or under any banner—is inexcusable. Law enforcement officers must act promptly, with sufficient display of force to make clear their intent and capacity to suppress disorder and insure public safety.

The disorder in Washington, DC, has provided the Congress with some firsthand observations on civil disorder and the means to meet it. Officials in Washington gave my office this report:

The orders to police were to arrest all looters. Only during the early hours of the disorder was this practice not strictly adhered to. Officials said at this time police were so overwhelmed by the numbers of people in the street that to attempt mass arrests would have endangered the policeman's life and would have risked gunfire. Gunfire, in turn, would have endangered innocent bystanders and would have provoked even greater disorder.

Statistics indicate that the law enforcement agencies in Washington soon regrouped and began making mass arrests. From April 4, the evening Dr. King was assassinated, until midnight, April 13, when the disturbance had been quelled, 7,999 persons were arrested in the District of Columbia. About 6,000 of these arrests came in the first four or five days of the disturbance.

By comparison, in Newark last year from July 12 to July 17, only 1,465 arrests were made. In that city, twenty-three persons were killed—including one policeman and one fireman. In Washington, eleven persons were killed in the disturbance or in disturbance-related incidents, and fifty-one policemen suffered minor injuries.

In the much more severe Detroit riots, 7,200 persons were arrested and 43 persons were killed.

Of the 7,999 arrests in the District of Columbia, 4,714 were for curfew violations. Another 1,036 were for burglary. To date, all the felony offenders have at least made preliminary appearances in court. All will be prosecuted, say the Washington officials. Only a small percentage of the curfew violators have been processed, however.

Out of all the arrests, twenty-seven were employees of the federal government and fifteen were employees of the District of Columbia government.

The initial estimate of damage is $13.3 million. By comparison, Detroit has $45 million, Newark, $15 million.

The appearance of National Guard and regular army troops in Washington had the effect of quieting a situation which law enforcement officers were finding increasingly difficult to handle. Each soldier carried a card which included instruction for conduct in areas of disorder. Among the instructions:

- Do not discuss or pass on rumors.
- Unless impossible or impractical, let police make arrests. If you must make an arrest, turn over your offenders to civil authorities at the first opportunity.
- Provide medical aid wherever necessary.
- Do not load or fire your weapon without the express orders of an officer on the scene, or under specific instructions listed prior to taking your duty station, or in order to save your life.

In general, the response in Washington probably kept personal violence at a relatively low level.

THE ASSASSINATION OF ROBERT KENNEDY

Indiana was a critical state for Robert Kennedy in his 1968 campaign for the White House. He had done well in national polling and in primaries in eastern states, but the question in Indiana was whether he could win in the Midwest. I met him at the Columbus, Indiana, airport and accompanied him to his local appearances. Although in private meetings I found him to be introverted and aloof, even shy—not your typical outgoing politician— he was, as evidenced in his appearances that day, skillful in winning over a crowd. He won the Indiana primary by a solid margin over Gene McCarthy and Indiana governor Roger Branigin, who ran as a favorite son to control delegates at the convention. Less than a month later, Kennedy was dead, assassinated after winning the California primary.

Growing out of the King and Kennedy assassinations was an increasing sense of intolerance and discontent in the country. In my commentary to constituents I was trying to counter that feeling, explaining the demands that representative democracy makes on all of us—to avoid violence, to work within the system, to develop an attitude of tolerance.

To make this point, I used a quote from Learned Hand which I think expresses a lot about the attitude of tolerance we need when we participate in a representative democracy—the recognition that it's possible that I just might not be right, that not all the wisdom is on my side. I think it's a profound quote, and it's one that I've used numerous times over these past decades. But it's also one that people often don't like to hear, since it runs counter to how they think of themselves and their views.

> **June 15, 1968 (untitled)**
> **Washington Report**
> **Vol. IV, No. 24**
> Justice Learned Hand once said, "The spirit of liberty is the spirit which is not too sure it is right."
> It seems to me that observation by one of America's great judges is one of the lessons to leap out of the tragic series of events surrounding the death of Senator Robert F. Kennedy.
> Senator Kennedy apparently was gunned down by a young Arab nationalist who believed the senator was wrong in advocating US support of Israel in the Arab-Israeli conflict. News accounts tell us that the young man often flew into rages against Israel and the Jewish people, and was bitter about US policy in the Middle East.

He seems to have judged the world and its leaders in black-and-white terms on the single issue of Middle East policy. He was positive he was right, and equally positive that those who disagreed with him were blind, stupid, and even evil persons.

That one man could kill another just because he felt that another man's thinking was wrong seems incredible to us. But that young Arab nationalist's failure to understand the necessity of tolerance for the views of others illustrates a demand which is made of all of us today.

The democratic process demands that we act with conviction but recognize the possibility we can be wrong. We are required to accept the fact that our ideas, our proposals, and our solutions are not infallible.

The democratic system calls each of us to study the problems, decide what is the best solution, and act with a determined sense of responsibility to achieve that solution. But that process also requires each of us to have a decent respect for the opinions of others. We must be willing to submit our ideas and solutions and proposals to steady examination and criticism by others.

We must not be tolerant to the point of accepting any view, but we also must not be so intolerant that we reject all views save our own. The problem is: how do we strike a balance between determined, deeply felt conviction and a tolerance for the views of others?

When persons believe that those who differ with them are blind, stupid, evil persons, the democratic process breaks down and the spirit of liberty expires.

The young Arab nationalist who assassinated Senator Kennedy could not bring himself to be tolerant of the views of others, so he reacted in a violent manner. Many others, not driven to that extreme, are nonetheless persuaded that those who differ are blind and stupid, and they express their views with such rancor and disrespect that it is apparent they never really have understood the rigors of the democratic process.

But if we understand the spirit of liberty, as Justice Hand defined it, we hold firmly to our beliefs, yet know we might possibly be wrong. We therefore are more tolerant of the views of others.

Knowing the number and the appalling complexity of the problems we face, we recognize that our fellow Americans are wrestling with them, too. And just possibly, they are doing the very best they can to propose solutions.

So the democratic process asks us to recognize that we might not always be right. It asks that we enjoy—not just accept—the inconvenient fact that others may disagree with us. It asks us to fight hard for our convictions, but to yield gracefully.

Looking back on the Johnson administration, one thing that impresses me now about Lyndon Johnson is that of all the presidents I have known, he stands out, first, as someone who had a clear vision of where he wanted the country to go. He had no doubt about his agenda: attack racism and injustice, bring people out of poverty, expand opportunity, improve the lives of Americans. Johnson might be criticized for overreaching or maybe for being too idealistic. But unlike many other presidents, Johnson knew where he was headed. Second, he knew how he would bring it about, and that was with the federal government leading the way. For Johnson that was key, and the legislation he got through Congress, particularly during the early years of his presidency before he got overwhelmed by Vietnam, was transformational.

Congress also, in my view, gets fairly high marks on its legislative record during the Johnson years, particularly during the 89th Congress: it was seriously trying to address the nation's problems, and although the Democrats had large majorities in both the House and the Senate, legislation was generally developed in consultation with the Republican minority, trying to accommodate their views as much as possible. The result was that most of the major bills passed Congress with fairly broad support from both the Democratic and Republican sides, and, although amended from time to time, they have continued as the basic law of the land.

My initial years serving in Congress were not in any way during ordinary times. It was a turbulent period, as the nation was dealing with war, riots, and assassinations. Many Americans were shaking their heads in disbelief over what was happening in our country. Congress also had to wrestle with complex and divisive issues of poverty, health care, and discrimination. Overall I believe Congress acquitted itself well during a challenging time in our nation's history.

The Congresses from the 1st, in 1789–91, through the current 114th have been quite a mix. Some produced landmark legislation, many were mediocre, others have been notable only for their partisan bickering. No Congress has been without its flaws, but a handful stand out above the rest in terms of producing important legislative accomplishments, being able to put aside partisan differences and work together for the common good, and enjoying strong public support. The 1st Congress would be in this category, along with a few others, but so would the 89th. It was a remarkable time for me to begin in Congress, and I felt fortunate to have been part of it.

TWO

THE NIXON YEARS
(1969–74)
Accomplishments amid Turmoil

MY PERSONAL TIE TO PRESIDENT NIXON WAS THROUGH HIS mother. She was born and raised near Butlerville, Indiana, and he knew I represented that part of the state. Every time I saw him he'd ask, "How are things in Butlerville?" He always spoke very highly of his mother, and his middle name—Milhous—was his mother's maiden name.

He used to joke with me about Indiana. He would say that whenever he ran for president he would sit down with a yellow legal pad and mark two columns—one with an R and one with a D—to get a sense of the likely electoral count. His very first entry in the R column, he said with a smile, was always Indiana. He must have told me that story three or four times. He liked Indiana not just because of his mother's background but also for its Republican leanings.

So once I invited him to come out to Butlerville. He was surprised by my invitation, and I was even more surprised when he accepted. So in June 1971, two years into his first term, President Nixon came out to rural southern Indiana. It was a quick visit—he was only in Indiana for part of the day—but it was a major event for people in that part of the state. He flew into Indianapolis and then took a helicopter to North Vernon for his speech. His speech was fairly general, covering a range of topics, and he ended by saying, "Thank you for reminding me why my mother loved this land so much"—which was very well received. On the way back to Indianapolis he didn't stop in Butlerville, but he did have his helicopter fly over the town. My time with the president that day was limited, but the visit clearly had an impact on him. It was an emotional trip for him, a homecoming of sorts.

Nixon had become president in January 1969, and his relations with Congress were strained from the start. Democrats had been running against Nixon for years. They thought he was highly partisan and didn't like his negative campaigning. On top of that he was the first newly elected president in more than a century to begin his presidency with a Congress under the control of a different party. So a different dynamic was operating from the beginning, and a more difficult task lay ahead for both the president and the Congress.

His first inaugural address was well done and well received. It was positive and forward looking, and seemed to express an openness to working with Congress. He talked about how in this country, "We cannot learn from one another until we stop shouting at one another—until we speak quietly enough so that our words can be heard as well as our voices." Yet in his dealings with Congress there was generally a tension on both sides. The House Democratic leadership had a gut feeling about Nixon that he couldn't be trusted and they didn't much like him. For his part, Nixon tended to be suspicious of other people and mistrustful, and he had the mindset that others were out to get him. It all seemed headed for a disaster and major legislative gridlock.

So it was surprising how much important legislation was passed during the initial years of the Nixon presidency. It was a solid, politically moderate set of legislative accomplishments. Nixon had run against the Great Society, yet he showed more moderation on policy than was expected and his presidency ended up on the side of those who believed that government could do some good things. During the 91st and 92nd Congresses, the House and Senate passed and President Nixon signed into law the National Environmental Policy Act, the Federal Water Quality Improvement Act, the Clean Air Amendments, the Occupational Safety and Health Act, the Federal Election Campaign Act, the Consumer Product Safety Act, the Title IX education amendments, and more. And both the president and Congress supported the Twenty-Sixth Amendment to lower the voting age and the

Equal Rights Amendment, which were sent on to the states for ratification. In contrast to the gridlock we have seen in Washington in recent years, it was a good example of Congress and the president—despite their different parties and different perspectives—being able to pass meaningful legislation benefiting the nation.

During his second term, relations between Nixon and Congress became much rockier as Watergate unfolded, and some of the major legislation Congress passed before he resigned attempted to rein in presidential powers—in particular the War Powers Resolution and the Budget and Impoundment Control Act. Yet even in those trying months, some of the most difficult in our nation's history, the 93rd Congress passed and President Nixon signed into law the Federal-Aid Highway Act, the Trans-Alaska Pipeline Authorization, the Endangered Species Act, the Legal Services Corporation Act, an overhaul of the farm subsidy program, and an increase in the minimum wage.

Unlike the Johnson years, the legislative successes during this time were not due to easy and open communication between the president and Congress. My sense is that success was due much more to the strong working relationship between the Democratic and Republican leaders in Congress. They knew each other very well, and their relationship was marked by civility, even friendship. They were solid professionals, and the flow of information among them—as well as their staffs—was remarkably smooth. The ability of Speaker Carl Albert and Minority Leader Gerald Ford to work together was particularly strong. There were obviously political and policy differences between the two sides, but they sensed the turbulence of the day and they all wanted to move legislation forward for the good of the country.

Even though Nixon was not personally popular among House Democrats, they did respect his intelligence, energy, and focus—and they found a way to make things work with him. But Nixon was more respected than liked, and a reservoir of good will that he could draw upon when troubles emerged was not there.

The 91st Congress: Key Facts

· January 3, 1969, through January 2, 1971, during the first two years of the first Nixon administration
· House of Representatives controlled by the Democrats, 243 to 192
· Senate controlled by the Democrats, 58 to 42
· 695 bills enacted
· Major accomplishments included passing the Tax Reform Act of 1969, the National Environmental Policy Act, a reduction in foreign military assistance, the Federal Water Quality Improvement Act, the right to vote for eighteen-year-olds, the Postal Reorganization Act, the Organized Crime Control Act, the Occupational Safety and Health Act, the Legislative Reorganization Act, the Comprehensive Drug Abuse Prevention and Control Act, the Clean Air Act Amendments, and an expansion of the food stamp program; and Senate ratification of the Nuclear Non-Proliferation Treaty
· Support for President Nixon's position in the House: Democrats 60 percent, Republicans 72 percent; in the Senate: Democrats 56 percent, Republicans 74 percent

The 92nd Congress: Key Facts

· January 21, 1971, through October 18, 1972, during the last two years of the first Nixon administration
· House of Representative controlled by the Democrats, 255 to 180
· Senate controlled by the Democrats, 54 to 44 (2 other)
· 607 bills enacted
· Major accomplishments included passing and sending to the states the Twenty-Sixth Amendment to lower the voting age and the proposed Equal Rights Amendment; passing the Economic Stabilization Act Amendments, the Federal Election Campaign Act, the Rural Development Act, the Federal Water Pollution Control Act Amendments, the State and Local Fiscal Assistance

Act, the Marine Protection, Research, and Sanctuaries Act, the Consumer Product Safety Act, and the Title IX Education Amendments; and Senate ratification of the US-USSR Anti-Ballistic Missile Treaty and the Strategic Arms Limitation Talks Treaty
· Support for President Nixon's position in the House: Democrats 55 percent, Republicans 77 percent; in the Senate: Democrats 50 percent, Republicans 77 percent

The 93rd Congress (First Part): Key Facts

· January 3, 1973, through August 9, 1974, during the second Nixon administration until the president resigned
· House of Representatives controlled by the Democrats, 239 to 192 (4 other)
· Senate controlled by the Democrats, 56 to 42 (2 other)
· 368 bills enacted
· Major accomplishments during the Nixon part of this Congress included passing a prohibition of funds for US combat activities in Southeast Asia, the Agriculture and Consumer Protection Act, the Domestic Volunteer Service Act, the Federal-Aid Highway Act, the Endangered Species Act, the War Powers Resolution, the Trans-Alaska Pipeline Authorization Act, an increase in the minimum wage, the Federal Energy Administration Act, the Congressional Budget and Impoundment Control Act, and the Legal Services Corporation Act
· Support for President Nixon's position in the House: Democrats 45 percent, Republicans 69 percent; in the Senate: Democrats 43 percent, Republicans 68 percent

CHRISTMAS AT THE NIXON WHITE HOUSE

Informal get-togethers across party lines are an important part of how Washington works—getting to know your colleagues and their families, establishing contacts, learning about common interests. These social events

are especially important in politics, where so much of the day-to-day in-
teraction is adversarial, and I began to appreciate such amenities more
and more.

President Nixon liked to engage in substantive policy discussions but
he was less comfortable in social settings. He was not your typical easygoing, backslapping politician, and there was an artificiality to his presence
in social situations. It was a tribute to his driving ambition that he stayed
in politics and was able to reach out in gatherings that could be awkward
for him. At this particular event, during his family's first Christmas in the
White House, Nixon was in a comfortable environment and I thought he
and his wife were gracious hosts.

December 22, 1969 (untitled)
Washington Report
Vol. V, No. 49

Like perhaps no other holiday, Christmas is a time for gathering
and storing memories of home and family. Because the White House
is this country's symbol of home and family, the Hamiltons would
like to share with you a visit to the White House for a Christmas
service.

The invitation to the Sunday service was a telephone call from
one of the president's secretaries. The service, to be in the East
Room, would include selections from George Frederick Handel's
Messiah, the president would make a few remarks, but there would
be no sermon. Guests would be seated by 11:15 a.m. The service
would begin at 11:30.

The White House, one of Washington's most impressive buildings, gleamed especially white in the brisk morning air as we
approached the large iron gates to the South Lawn. The uniformed
guard checked our identification very thoroughly—not exactly the
normal beginning to a Sunday service.

We entered the White House at a ground-level entrance at the
South Portico and were greeted by a military aide, a Marine in full-
dress uniform. We were told to wait a few moments in the basement
oval-shaped reception room while the choir completed its rehearsal.
We took advantage of the time to inspect the displays of presidential
china, particularly those used by Lincoln, Benjamin Harrison, one
of the Hoosier presidents, and by John F. Kennedy.

We were then ushered upstairs, past the striking White House Christmas tree, to the East Room, which was decorated with poinsettias, greenery, and a life-size crèche. We were taken to our seats in the second row to await the arrival of the president and his family. We learned then that even presidential functions have last-minute problems as we watched a harried aide scurry about the choral platform, setting up microphones, arranging wires, and searching for outlets. His frantic exercise was completed at precisely 11:29.

At 11:30, President Nixon, Mrs. Nixon, and David and Julie Eisenhower entered and took the seats directly in front of the Hamilton family. The president turned to the 150 or so guests and said the service was to be a musical one, adding that members of Congress in the gathering had probably heard enough talking anyway.

The president then introduced the forty-voice New York Avenue Presbyterian Choir, which assumed its place on the choral platform. I could not help but reflect that their church was the one in which Presidents Lincoln and Franklin Roosevelt attended services and in which the famed minister, Peter Marshall, took the pulpit each Sunday.

The choir sang eight sections from Messiah, closing with the immortal and majestic "Hallelujah Chorus." The president rose again, thanked the members of the choir, and invited all to coffee and pastries in the Oval Room.

The gathering was informal and each guest had a moment or so of quiet conversation with the president and Mrs. Nixon. They were most gracious and expressed their pleasure at seeing the Hamilton children at the service.

The president and Mrs. Nixon left for their private quarters after chatting with each guest, leaving the guests to look over the Christmas decor of the formal rooms of the White House.

The White House Christmas tree, a perfect nineteen-foot fir from Ohio, dominates the foyer. It is adorned with fifty eight-inch velvet and satin balls embossed with the flower of each of the fifty states. Fireplaces are banked with stately poinsettias and mantels are adorned with fir and holly. Columns are entwined with greenery, and green wreaths and candles hang in the windows facing Pennsylvania Avenue. Small, decorated trees stand on tables everywhere.

With echoes of Christmas greetings still lingering in the halls, the guests departed, taking with them the memories of an inspiring musical service and the hospitality of the president.

CHANGING THE HOUSE SENIORITY SYSTEM

During my years in Congress constituents would sometimes ask me why I decided to get involved in so many congressional reform efforts and commissions over the years. My interest started with the 1970 attempt to reform the House seniority system. Something so seemingly routine and arcane as deciding the procedure in the Democratic Caucus for selecting who would chair various House committees in fact had a huge impact on our nation.

The seniority system that operated during my early years in Congress meant that the most senior member of a committee would be the automatic choice to be chairman. There is something to be said for experience, but this practice meant giving enormous power to conservative Democrats from southern states who had safe districts and would easily get reelected. Yet their views, particularly on civil rights, were out of step with those of rank-and-file Democrats as well as those of most Americans.

Howard W. Smith, the wily, powerful chairman of the House Rules Committee, was the main target of the reformers, but by no means the only one. As a segregationist he had used his position as chairman to successfully bottle up most civil rights legislation for several years. Known as a master obstructionist, Smith a few years earlier had attempted to kill the Civil Rights Act of 1964 by tacking on an amendment to include women under its provisions. Instead of dooming its passage, the bill plus amendment passed, and Smith, ironically, became a key figure in advancing women's rights.

Looking back on it now, this newsletter was, for me, a surprisingly blunt statement about the drawbacks of the seniority system, about how it could result in "the selection of mediocre, senile, or otherwise incompetent chairmen." To the older committee chairmen it clearly put me on the side of the reformers, and they started to look at me—then only in my third term—with suspicion.

March 9, 1970 (untitled)
Washington Report
Vol. VI, No. 9

There is a compelling need to make the Congress more responsive to the will of the majority of its members. One of the most pressing needs is the modification or the elimination of the iron rule of
seniority.

The seniority system in the Congress means simply that the
member with the longest uninterrupted tenure in office is accorded
a position of power—as a committee chairman or floor leader, or
choice committee assignments. There are no requirements of health
or intellect, expertise or integrity, party loyalty or convictions—
only that he achieve longevity.

Ironically, the seniority system has no legal or constitutional
basis. It is neither a law nor a rule of the House. It is only a custom
which has become absolute in recent years—primarily since World
War II. It is a custom which no other state or national assembly in
the world follows as absolutely as does the US Congress.

No one argues that seniority is unimportant in determining the
leadership of the Congress. It assures the country of experienced
leadership, and it establishes the ground rules for the younger,
newer members of the Congress to achieve that leadership.

A cardinal defect of the seniority system is the "automatic"
achievement of a committee chairmanship. Long life and a "safe"
congressional district virtually assure a member of a committee
chairmanship, regardless of his interests or capabilities. At times
the absolute rule of seniority results in the selection of mediocre,
senile, or otherwise incompetent chairmen.

Obviously, such a system allows chairmen to be unresponsive
to the nation, the Congress, the committee, and their political party.
They can obstruct, distort, emasculate programs and policies with
impunity.

The system virtually guarantees committee chairmanships to
members from "one party" districts who are reelected with regularity. This is true, particularly, of Southern Democrats or members
from machine-dominated big-city districts. Southern Democrats
chair some of the most powerful House committees, yet few of them
profess to be "national Democrats" and they seldom vote with their
Democrat colleagues from the North.

Additionally, the system has resulted in a steady increase in the age of committee chairmen. Despite the fact that the nation is sending younger congressmen to the House, its chairmen are getting older. Today the average age among House chairmen is seventy. One hundred years ago, it was in the forties. We now have only three House chairmen under sixty; eight are in their sixties, seven in their seventies, and three in their eighties. The workload and the responsibilities of committee chairmen demand full vigor. At a time when one-half of the people in the nation are under thirty years of age and when American corporations, colleges, and other institutions are turning leadership over to younger men, the leaders of Congress are getting older. If the ordinary retirement rules operating the nation applied to Congress, all but five of the present chairmen would be forced to retire—some of them ten to fifteen years ago.

Among the several proposals for changing the seniority system I find attractive these:

1. Use the seniority system to nominate chairmen, subject to majority approval by the party caucus. Should the most senior member fail to get the approval of the caucus, the next most senior member would be considered, and so on.

2. Have the caucus select committee chairmen from among the three most senior members, permitting a selection based on the fitness and acceptability of the prospective chairman.

3. Authorize the Speaker of the House to nominate chairmen subject to approval by a majority of the party caucus. Should the caucus reject one of the Speaker's nominations, he could continue to make nominations until an acceptable chairman is found.

Additionally, I would support the setting of an age limit on committee chairmen, to assure the selection of members physically able to take on the duties of the position.

MEETING WITH STUDENT PROTESTERS

Some of my colleagues were dismissive of the college students who came to Washington in the spring of 1970 to protest our nation's continuing involvement in the Vietnam War, and they refused to meet them. But overall I was impressed by the students. They were intensely disillusioned with the war and the politicians who got us there, yet they were still willing, even eager, to engage in a constructive dialogue with members of Congress without hostility and without being disrespectful.

They forcefully got across their point that Congress was passive and not stepping up to its constitutional role in war making, leaving too many of the decisions about the Vietnam War to the president and not scrutinizing what was going on. What they had to say and the manner in which they conducted themselves had a big impact on me, and I started to have a series of meetings on college campuses in Indiana to continue the dialogue with young people about the war. The meetings varied considerably in size and format—the most unusual was at Indiana University, where several members of Congress were stationed at different locations in a central outdoor commons area, and students could wander around and talk to any of us—but the message from the students was always clear and consistent: Get us out of Vietnam.

In all my meetings with young people about the war I felt keenly the fundamental strength of their perspective: those of us who were older were in Congress making the decisions and staying in the comforts of home while they were the ones being called on to do the fighting and dying.

May 25, 1970 (untitled)
Washington Report
Vol. VI

The politics of confrontation, with the techniques of demonstrations, moratoriums, sit-ins, lockouts, strikes, and in some instances riots and violence, has become familiar to the American scene.

Recently, seventy-five thousand young people from college campuses across the nation poured into Washington to protest US involvement in Indochina. There were some uneasy moments as the rally produced the usual inflammatory rhetoric, the usual invectives, and the usual call for stepped-up confrontations.

But, in my view, the most significant and encouraging aspect of the protest was the apparent decision of the young people to work within the system to seek redress of their grievances, proceeding in a manner familiar to any lobbyist pleading his case with the legislator or partisan seeking the election of a candidate.

All week long, students and faculty lobbyists sought out members of Congress to express their anguish with the war and to seek legislative proposals to limit the conflict.

The young people were not the radicals, rebels, rioters, and extremists so often depicted in the news media. They were bright, articulate, concerned, discontented Americans. They are persuaded that the nation is off course, and they are eager to help set it steady again. They are worried about their political impotence, and they want to be heard. Some were bearded, some barbered, some dressed in flamboyant styles of youth, but most were in conservative dress. Many came from fine middle-class homes of middle America.

The central theme of their plea was that this war must stop. Some pleaded from almost encyclopedic knowledge of the Vietnam conflict, some stressed the illegalities of US involvement, others talked of what was being rejected at home because of the money spent for war abroad, others spoke of personal tragedies and heartache.

Many expressed concern that Congress had not played an adequate role in the development of this nation's foreign policy, and specifically, has let the war-making power slip beyond democratic control and rest in the office of the presidency alone. They are very much concerned that the constitutional powers of the Congress in war making have been very seriously eroded.

Generally, I think the students received a courteous and attentive hearing on Capitol Hill. Most members of Congress made every effort to clear their schedules so they could meet with the young people.

Congressmen know that whatever currents are affecting the atmosphere of the colleges and universities today will, in due time, spread beyond to the larger society, and that it is important that we listen to their views—as we would to any interest group.

It is my plan to participate in as many meetings with Indiana students and faculty as my legislative work and Ninth District schedule will permit. We need a dialogue in this country to keep open the line of communication between the great majority of our bright, idealistic young people and their government.

I finished my week of twenty meetings with young people more encouraged than worried. The conversations and dialogue had been worthwhile—the process of open exchange had proved its worth. But, most of all, I felt a sense of relief because they had come forward with their deeply felt protests within the system. They had turned to rational discourse and inquiry, not violence and intimidation.

One of the great changes in American political life is the involvement of young people. With their concern, intelligence, mobility, and energy, they are having a profound impact on national policy in many areas, from Vietnam to the environment.

REDUCING THE VOTING AGE

Out of the several thousand votes that I cast while in Congress, one that I've always wondered about was lowering the national voting age to eighteen. I have long emphasized the importance of getting people more civically involved, and that certainly includes young people. The argument made at the time was compelling—that it was simply unfair to require eighteen-year-olds to go off to fight in Vietnam but not allow them to vote.

So, with my support, in June 1970 Congress passed legislation lowering the voting age to eighteen. But the Supreme Court held that Congress had the power to do this for federal elections but not state and local elections, so we then passed and sent to the states for ratification a constitutional amendment to extend the law to cover all elections. It took only three months for three-fourths of the states to approve it, and on July 1, 1970, it became the Twenty-Sixth Amendment to the Constitution.

What impressed me was how quickly this proposal became the law of the land. The idea of lowering the voting age had been around for a long time, but in just about the span of a year, Congress passed the initial act, the Supreme Court ruled it unconstitutional, Congress passed the proposed constitutional amendment, and thirty-eight states ratified it. Our system can act quickly—even to amend the Constitution—when the right factors converge.

Yet I have always been disappointed with the outcome of this change. Young people have not stepped up to this new opportunity—and responsibility—as their voting rates have typically been quite low. Not only does the country lose by their poor participation, but so do they as a group. It is no coincidence that older people get a disproportionately large share of federal spending. The voting turnout rate of seniors is high, and members of Congress are sensitive and responsive to that.

June 22, 1970 (untitled)
Washington Report
Vol. VI, No. 22
The Congress has passed an historic voting rights bill, which

1. Limits to thirty days the state residency requirements for US citizens to vote in state, local, and national elections;
2. Imposes a nationwide suspension of literacy tests as a requirement to vote;
3. Extends the Voting Rights Act of 1965 for five years; and
4. Reduces, after January 1, 1971, the voting age to eighteen.

The eighteen-year-old vote has gained widespread, bipartisan acceptance and support. Presidents Eisenhower, Kennedy, and Johnson publicly supported lowering the voting age. President Nixon has, too. Both major political parties, in their 1968 conventions, called for an eighteen-year-old vote. Nationwide public opinion polls continue to show heavy support for lowering the voting age to eighteen.

That attitude is reflected in the substantial margin by which the Congress approved the Voting Rights Act of 1970. However, debate on the issue has pointed out a sharp division over whether the eighteen-year-old vote should be granted by federal statute, or by an amendment to the Constitution. The question is whether or not the Congress has the authority to alter the voting regulations established by the states.

Opponents to the statutory route to lowering the voting age argue that the Supreme Court will declare Congress's action unconstitutional. Although the issue is a close one, I believe the Congress has acted within its constitutional prerogative. I believe the present law, which denies eighteen-, nineteen-, and twenty-year-olds the right to vote, represents a denial of equal protection under the law, and I believe the court will sustain that view.

In 1966, the Supreme Court ruled that Congress has the constitutional authority to make its own determination of what constitutes a denial of equal protection, and to pass legislation to correct it. That kind of precedent would indicate, at least, that the court will sustain the judgment of Congress in this case—if the court is convinced that Congress has acted on a reasonable basis.

One of the root feelings of young people today is that they are called upon to bear the responsibilities of citizenship—including the burden of military service—but are not permitted to participate in the political process. Eighteen-, nineteen-, and twenty-year-olds pay taxes and they are treated as adults under the criminal laws of our land, yet they have no voice in the selection of those who create and administer the laws.

Furthermore, young people today are capable of making intelligent voting decisions based on education and political awareness. For example, 79 percent of today's eighteen-to-twenty-one-year-olds have high school diplomas, while only 17 percent of their counterparts in 1920 had graduated from high school. While 47 percent of today's eighteen-year-olds attend college, only 18 percent were in college in 1920.

Opponents of the statute also argue that equal protection under the law should be confined to preventing voting discrimination against minorities. While they cite the equal protection test as the basis for supporting the literacy test ban and the residency requirement change, they are inconsistent, it seems to me, in not applying the same logic to the eighteen-year-old vote.

And finally, they argue that the Supreme Court could not rule on the constitutionality of the eighteen-year-old vote statute in time to prevent confusion in upcoming elections. A number of recent decisions by the court indicate that it is willing and able to reach a quick resolution of constitutional issues affecting election procedures.

In passing the Voting Rights Act of 1970, the Congress has responded to a suffrage issue of some two hundred years in our history. We have expressed our intent to bring some twelve million disenfranchised young Americans into the political process of their nation.

SETTING UP OUR SYSTEM OF GOVERNMENT

A frequent theme of mine when talking to various groups from school age on up was that the individual lies at the center of our system of representative democracy. People need to better understand how the democratic process works, its many challenges, how they can have an impact on the process, and the burden our system places on each one of us as individuals.

I often wrote commentaries like this around July 4 that put in a good word for America—reminding people from time to time of the important system of government we have inherited, but also that a great system doesn't matter unless individuals carry it on.

June 29, 1970 (untitled)
Washington Report
Vol. VI, No. 23

When the Continental Congress adopted the Declaration of Independence on July 4, 1776, the stage was set for a series of events which created a nation of incomparable energy and wealth. As we approach the two hundredth anniversary of that historic event, we still draw inspiration from the Declaration of Independence and sustenance from the Constitution.

When the Founding Fathers drafted the Constitution, they were determined to create a government which guaranteed

- the right to life, liberty, property, happiness, and free conscience;
- the freedom of speech, press, assembly, and petition of grievances;
- the principle of consent, which is the key to the political obligations on each of us.

Most impressive, perhaps, was the fact that they were able to agree at so many points on the structure and the function of government. The Founding Fathers, made up of liberals and conservatives, Northerners and Southerners, East Coast urban residents and frontiersmen, agreed:

- Whatever the form of government, it must preserve the maximum liberty and equality of the persons under it.
- Government should be as plain, simple, and intelligible as possible.
- Government should be kept near the people, with frequent elections.
- Officeholders should be the servants of the people, not the masters.
- Government must be constitutional, that is—of law, not of men.
- A representative government is essential, but that system must be restrained by a separation of powers and checks and balances.

Just as importantly, they knew it would take more than an agreed set of principles and a plan of government to preserve order and liberty. They saw that in order to make our constitutional system work, people had to understand what the democratic process required of them as individuals.

The democratic process puts the individual at the center of things, but much depends upon the kind of individual. For government—for ordered liberty—to succeed, there must be a moral basis to government. The maintenance of freedom depends upon the quality of the individual's life.

As individuals, we must possess an attitude of tolerance, exposing our ideas, proposals, solutions to the analysis of others. We must adopt an attitude of confidence in our fellow man, since our government is founded on the belief that each is given responsibility for his own destiny and his own community.

The democratic process also requires us to adopt an attitude of trust. We assume the other will obey the law. We don't police everyone, assuming each will fill out his income tax correctly, stop at the stop sign, obey the speed limit.

But our system also requires us to respect the rules. Using the ballot, not the bullet; fair expression, not slander or libel; and peaceful redress of our grievances, not violence.

If our system is to continue to work, enough of us must meet these qualifications. We must possess the wisdom to discern, and the virtue to pursue, the common good.

We may not have succeeded in every respect in meeting the goals set by our Founding Fathers, but we have come closer to the ideals of freedom and liberty than any nation in history.

America is not an achieved state or resting place. It is a building and a making, a process, a living tissue. And we must build with it.

REPORTS ON TRIP TO WAR ZONE

In 1970 I was asked by Speaker McCormack to serve on the Select Committee on US Involvement in Southeast Asia. The lessons from my visits to Vietnam and Cambodia during the war were several, but one in particular was what a horrendous job the combat soldier has, and what an enormous physical and mental burden we as a nation place on twenty-year-olds. The soldiers I met with were hot, stressed, and constantly on edge from the ordeals of battle. They told me they slept fitfully, and their tobacco-stained fingers were chewed to the quick. All seemed old beyond their years. During our discussions they would constantly shift their gaze to be on the alert for an attack from a machine gun that might be only a few yards away. It was a harrowing, stressful experience, and many didn't make it back.

Although I had come to Congress supporting the war, during my various visits I got the clear sense that we had done what we could do: we had given the South Vietnamese a chance to survive; the war was not winnable—at least at a price we were willing to pay; and it was time to get out. As I struggled with what to say to Ninth District families who had lost sons in the war, not wanting to make it sound like our withdrawal would mean their sons had died in vain or that we had been defeated, that is what I would tell them—we had done what we could.

An orderly withdrawal would eventually take place. Yet there would still be three more years of fighting after the time these newsletters were written until US combat troops finally left Vietnam.

July 6, 1970 (untitled)
Washington Report
Vol. VI, No. 24

EDITOR'S NOTE: Congressman Lee H. Hamilton has just returned from a fact-finding mission in Southeast Asia. He was one of twelve selected by the Speaker of the House to make a report to Congress on the US involvement in Southeast Asia. This report, which will deal with US policy, will be covered in future releases.

The following is an account of a visit with American units in Cambodia, prior to the US pullout on June 30. With Congressman Hamilton on the Cambodian inspection tour were Congressmen C. V. Montgomery (D-MS) and Howard W. Robison (R-NY).

The helicopter which carried us into Cambodian territory flew at about five thousand feet, well above its normal flying altitude, to keep out of the range of small arms fire from the enemy. Lower, and at each side of the craft, gunship helicopters cruised with us, watching for signs of the enemy.

When we reached an American base camp in the Cambodian jungle, the helicopter made a swift, vertical descent into the clearing of some four hundred yards in diameter. While the gunships circled overhead, we landed just outside two barbed-wire defense rings and we were escorted into the camp area, which was ringed with sandbag and earthen defense works.

The fortified clearing was the center of operations for several American companies, and most of the men had spent the last month or more in the jungle, serving on patrols and enduring mortar attacks on the base.

Among those with whom I talked at the base camp was Lt. Ray B. Hersman, son of Mr. and Mrs. Ernest R. Hersman, New Albany. All with whom I talked appeared tired, but proud of the work they had done. They had been carrying the brunt of the Cambodian operations, searching out hidden stores of enemy supplies and equipment, and making almost daily contact with the enemy during the patrols.

Found in their search were food, ammunition, bicycle and bicycle parts, medical equipment, and weapons. Bicycles, I was told, were the primary carriers of supplies in the jungle area, laden with as much as six hundred pounds of supplies, and wheeled along jungle trails by the enemy. An American medical officer told me the medical supplies which had been unearthed were as sophisticated as his own.

After lunch with the men—beef stew, mashed potatoes, peas, and grape drink—we departed for a clearing in the jungle some twenty to thirty miles, to visit the site of recently discovered caches of ammunition. There, we visited an American company which had been exposed to consistent enemy attacks in recent weeks. Nearly half the men had been killed or wounded.

I noticed immediately the tension and fatigue in their faces. Most were shirtless in the hundred-degree, airless jungle heat. Most were bearded and grimy since baths were not available in this forward area. The commander, a Negro captain of about twenty-five, said the unit had been under nightly attacks and had been skirmishing with the enemy almost daily on patrols. Despite the fatigue and the tension, however, they were genuinely pleased to see somebody from the "outside."

The captain escorted us to the site of a cache which had been found just a few hours earlier. This one consisted of three bunkers, each about fifteen by fifteen feet, which were filled with ammunition. They had been found by an alert soldier, who, after sensing how spongy the ground was underfoot, probed down about two feet and found one of the storage areas. As we inspected the caches, they were being charged with explosives, to be detonated before the American pullout.

We left the area, where the temperatures are stifling, where the enemy can conceal himself within a few feet, where any movement in the foliage is cause for alarm, with a deep sense of appreciation for what these young men are called upon to do. Most of those with whom I talked were nineteen to twenty-two years of age.

July 13, 1970 (untitled)
Washington Report
Vol. VI, No. 25

EDITOR'S NOTE: The following are excerpts from Congressman Lee H. Hamilton's supplemental report to the Congress on the US military involvement in Southeast Asia. The Ninth District congressman was one of twelve picked by the House Speaker for the fact-finding mission, and he filed a separate report to that filed by the committee as a whole.

You will find in Vietnam evidence to support the view you had before you arrived. The complexity and variety of the scene is such that the "hawk" and the "dove" will each observe, investigate, and leave assured of the wisdom of the view he had when he arrived.

I came away from Vietnam with a keen appreciation of what we cannot do. In a word, we cannot build a nation for the South Vietnamese. By the expenditure of enormous resources, we have given South Vietnam a chance to survive, and that's probably the best we can do. Their severe political and economic problems can only be solved by them. We can do our best to assist them through economic and technological aid, but much as we would like to, we cannot assure their security, their prosperity, or their democracy.

The United States must consider Vietnam in the context of Asian policy. I believe we should downgrade the US interest in Southeast Asia, and certainly subordinate it to our interest in Japan. We should be interested in the long-range development of the nations of Southeast Asia, but our immediate, vital interests are limited.

A key to our future Asian policy is to recognize our limitations in bringing about development in Asia. The United States should do all it can to encourage and support an Asian collective security system, supplying economic and technical assistance, but we should be most reluctant to commit American troops. We must look, instead, to the nations which are threatened to provide the manpower.

An important step in the future of the United States in Asia is to end, in an orderly way, our involvement in Vietnam. This will be a task calling for the utmost skill. The nervousness of friendly Asian leaders about the US role in Asia is apparent. They genuinely fear that the United States will desert them. They accept the fact of US disengagement reluctantly.

One of the things I tried to do in my conversations with South Vietnamese citizens was to persuade them that the United States is withdrawing. Although they invariably nodded their heads in assent, I wondered whether they actually believed it with the still-massive American presence all around them.

We are in better shape in Vietnam than we have ever been before, and after five years of major combat, we have done about all we can do. We ought to accelerate withdrawal if at all possible, being careful to protect the US forces, and to encourage the safe return of American prisoners of war.

The American prisoners of war create a special problem. Pressure must be kept up by the Congress to push at every conceivable opportunity for the identification of all prisoners, the establishment of regular communication between them and their families, the prompt repatriation of the seriously sick and wounded, the observation and inspection of prisoner-of-war camps by impartial observers, and the eventual release of all prisoners of war.

I returned less optimistic than many of our officials. North Vietnam is a highly organized, patient, disciplined society and South Vietnam is a highly inefficient, fragmented society. The United States can give—and indeed has given—the South Vietnamese a chance to survive. As the United States withdraws from South Vietnam, we must be very firm—even tough—with the South Vietnamese in order to give them an opportunity to survive.

THE PENTAGON PAPERS

I viewed the unanimous 1971 Supreme Court decision to allow the publication of the Pentagon Papers—the secret Pentagon study detailing the history of our involvement in Vietnam—as a victory for good government. I recognize that there may be at times good reasons for keeping some government information secret, but I am concerned about the damage that occurs to our country when fundamental policy papers are not publicly available. In a representative democracy like ours, public debate gives us better policy. So my bias is on the side of more information, not less, with those who want to keep a document secret needing to demonstrate strong reasons for doing so.

As a politician I was getting a clear sense that the nation was changing its mind about the war. In almost every trip back to the district during this period, I would meet with constituents who would not present fancy arguments against the war but instead relay the horrible impact that the war had on their families, through the loss of a son or close relative—always with the question, "For what purpose?" I would listen by the hour as they talked about their pain and suffering, and that made a lasting impression on me. Members of Congress were getting a better view of the war not just from documents, but also from the American families who bore the burden.

The release of the Pentagon Papers also had a broader national impact, as Nixon's concerns about the leak of classified materials would be a major factor leading to the Watergate abuses and the downfall of his presidency.

July 5, 1971 (untitled)
Washington Report
Vol. VII, No. 27

In recent days, the nation has been wrestling with a question of historic importance: can the courts stop the publication of documents which the government asserts will damage national security?

The issue grew out of the decision by several newspapers to publish portions of a forty-seven-volume, seven-thousand-page Pentagon study of the Vietnam War. The action created a legal conflict between those claiming freedom of the press, and the government asserting its right to maintain national security.

While Washington discussed the impact of the study on Democrats and Republicans . . . on former President Johnson and President Nixon . . . on future presidential candidates, a more serious consequence was being overlooked. The real victim may be the American people's confidence in the integrity of their government.

I agreed with the Supreme Court's ruling that the documents could be published. While the government argued that irreparable damage would come from their publication, in my view, greater damage would result from continued secrecy. The Pentagon Papers deal with some fundamental questions which need answers if we are going to avoid future Vietnams: What went wrong in Vietnam? How did we get involved? How did we lose our way?

The task before us is to learn from the Pentagon Papers. Several lessons already are apparent:

1. We must improve the decision-making process in this country. While our policymakers were involved in raging debates over the Vietnam conflict, very little of it surfaced. The American people, who had the most at stake, were given little or no opportunity to understand the stakes, the difficulties, or the options.

   The vital process of policymaking must be improved by raising the quality of debate, assuring that fundamental questions are continually reassessed and that the whole process is open and responsive to the people. My own bias is that policy which is held up to public debate tends to be better policy, and we must do all we can to open up the process.

2. The government classification system is inadequate, and in some instances, absurd. We need a more rational system, with the chief aim of making far more information available to the public, assuring us that relevant documents on any crisis, including Vietnam, are made available. This means establishing regular procedures outside the executive branch of the government for examining and deciding on the release of documents.

3. The Congress must become more effective in the foreign-policy process, serving as a counterweight to the executive. I served on the Foreign Affairs Committee during several of the years covered in the Pentagon Papers, and I am concerned about the amount of information which was kept from the Congress.

4. The experts deserve more respect. The one government agency which emerges from the Vietnam debate with honor is the CIA. It consistently provided accurate assessments of our position in Vietnam, and was just as consistently ignored.

5. Our policymakers must have time to examine the fundamentals of policy, and not become exclusively involved in the implementation of policy. The Pentagon Papers reveal that the Vietnam debate was concentrated upon the best means of achieving policy objectives, and not what our policy should be. There appears to have been little discussion of the vital question: is Vietnam in the national interest?

6. It would be a grave mistake for the nation to engage now in a search for scapegoats. The fact is that most of our top leaders since World War II shared in the decisions which led to Vietnam. Nothing is to be gained, and much is to be lost, in picking out villains among them.

The Pentagon Papers have shown us the government did not act in a manner in which to earn the confidence of the people, but there is another side to the issue. The people must act in a way to earn the confidence of government, to be informed, and not to react by instinct to complex questions, or engage in careless rhetoric and name calling.

NIXON'S TRIP TO CHINA

I was a member of the House Foreign Affairs Committee when President Nixon began to open up US diplomatic relations with China in the early 1970s, but I first learned about his upcoming trip in the newspapers, just like everyone else. It was kept secret not only from Congress but also many in the White House and the administration, as the president kept a close circle of confidants and said he was concerned that advance publicity would have given opponents time to undermine the effort. But that was the preferred approach of the president and Henry Kissinger over the years, and not just on this occasion: acting in secret and telling Congress as little as possible.

At the time of the president's trip, there was a debate in the country about the wisdom of the opening to China and who would win and who would lose. But most historians have since concluded that it was clearly worthwhile. It was one of the most important foreign-policy initiatives during my tenure in Congress, and Nixon deserves credit for it.

Nixon had a much stronger interest in foreign policy than in domestic issues, and his primary focus was on China and the Soviet Union. Despite having been a firm anti-Communist for many years, his approach to these two countries as president was for the United States to seek stable relations with them.

March 20, 1972 (untitled)
Washington Report
Vol. VII, No. 62
To understand the significance of the president's historic trip to China, it is essential to understand why the trip was made.

A change is taking place in the relationship among the big powers in Asia. The Soviet Union and China are at odds. Japan has become a major power. The United States is reducing its military presence in the area. The British have departed. And the SEATO grouping of nations is losing its viability.

Taking place is a reordering of power, especially among the dominant forces in Asia: China, the Soviet Union, Japan, and the United States. The relationship between and among them must be worked out, and the meeting between President Nixon and the leaders of mainland China served the purpose of both nations in beginning a dialogue to work out the relationship.

It will take time to work out an accommodation among the four dominant powers in Asia. The US requires a relatively stable relationship with China to lower its posture and yet maintain its influence in Asia. China, worried about the massive presence of Soviet troops on the Chinese border, obviously is hoping that a "live and let live" relationship with the US will cause the Soviet leadership concern about a possible collusion between the US and China.

Balance-of-power politics, of course, is a dangerous area. The Soviet Union could get its back up if it believed such a collusion were taking place. The US hope is that a fairly stable relationship among the four powers will emerge, including arrangements to defuse trouble spots such as Korea and Vietnam.

President Nixon and Premier Chou concluded nearly a week of meetings by issuing a joint communiqué which included (1) a pledge for a gradual increase in American-Chinese contacts through trade, science, culture, sports, news media, and frequent diplomatic contacts, and (2) the US acknowledgment that all mainland Chinese maintain that "Taiwan is a part of China," and that it is our desire for a peaceful settlement, reached by the Chinese themselves. It also affirmed as an ultimate objective the US withdrawal of the eight-thousand-man military contingent on Taiwan, "as tension in the area diminishes."

After twenty-two years of no contact and much hostility between the two countries, the communiqué was an acknowledgment of both the common interests of China and the US, and of their disagreements, such as diverse ideologies and Taiwan. More important than any agreement or disagreement was that a dialogue was begun on the future structure of the Pacific. Just as important as the carefully worded and balanced communiqué is that the meeting took place with great publicity, cordiality, and expression of respect.

Quick conclusions about the results of the summit—who won or who lost—should not be made. More significant is the kind of communication which will continue from this point on. The meeting did bring to an end, in a dramatic fashion, the historic containment-of-China policy which the US has followed, sometimes with an evangelical fever, for more than two decades. It would be foolish to pretend, however, that all of the fundamental differences between the two countries have been, or will be, resolved quickly.

Some say the president's concession to China on Taiwan was a US surrender. The language of the communiqué contains many loopholes and escape hatches, however, in the event that the future China conduct is disappointing. For example, we pledge to withdraw US forces from Taiwan as an "ultimate objective, contingent upon the reduction of tension in the area," which is a vague phrase the president can interpret as he pleases. There simply is no other way for the US to begin any kind of accommodation than by dealing with the question of Taiwan.

Not the least significant aspect of the president's widely publicized China trip is that it opened a whole new world to many Americans, who probably learned more about China and its 750 million people in those few days than they had ever known before. It reopened communications, started some candid talk between Washington and Peking, and cut away many of the illusions which have hampered US-China relations in the past.

EVALUATION OF THE APOLLO PROGRAM

The 1961–72 Apollo program to land the first human on the moon was a stunning achievement, and the American people took enormous pride in it.

I went down to Cape Canaveral with a group of members of Congress to see the 1969 launch of Apollo 11—the launch that took Neil Armstrong to the moon. It was the first time I had been to Cape Canaveral, and I was impressed by the extent of the NASA facilities and the expertise of the people involved.

One of the early Apollo astronauts, Gus Grissom, was from the small town of Mitchell, Indiana, which was in my district. That generated a lot of pride in the area. But it also meant a lot of pain when he died in a launchpad accident in 1967. Purdue University became known as the university of astronauts, because many, including both Grissom and Armstrong, were Purdue graduates. So Indiana had both a personal and an institutional connection to the program. I participated in several assemblies in southern Indiana high schools with the astronauts. When these national heroes in their immaculate uniforms with rows of military award ribbons on their chests spoke about their exploits, the students were simply in awe.

It may be difficult for people nowadays who did not grow up with the space program to understand its impact on the nation. It was a huge undertaking by the federal government, and we have not seen a unifying national effort of this magnitude in all the years since.

December 11, 1972: "Evaluation of the Apollo Program"
Washington Report
Vol. VII, No. 95

The spectacular launch of the Apollo 17 moon shot signaled the end of a great American enterprise—an effort costing $25 billion over eleven years, sending nine crews to the moon and landing six crews on the moon's surface. While it will take many years for the significance of the Apollo program to unfold, an immediate evaluation is in order.

This decade will be remembered in history as the time when man broke his earthly bounds and placed his footprints upon the moon. This stunning technical achievement, sixty-nine years after man first flew in a heavier-than-air machine, has given Americans a badly needed shot of confidence and inspiration as an example of what man can achieve when he sets his mind to a task. It revives our faith in the idea of progress itself.

Curiously enough, our moon trips have enabled us to see the earth more clearly, its finiteness, its uniqueness. This new perspective has sharpened our appreciation of our environment and increased our sense of oneness among all people and the need for better stewardship of our fragile planet. The poet Archibald MacLeish said it best: "To see earth as it truly is, is to see ourselves as riders on the earth, brothers in that bright loveliness in the eternal cold."

Historian C. P. Snow observed that this turning inward toward earth comes about with the realization of how gigantic the solar system really is, and this may be the most important impact of the Apollo projects.

As people the world over have watched the moon walks on television we have sensed that we were witness to events of profound importance, but we have only dimly perceived what they might be. The moon explorations have been one of the most scientifically prolific ventures in history. Scarcely one-tenth of the information and material brought back from the moon has been fully evaluated, and probably won't be for years to come.

The Apollo program has enabled man to take his first steps in space, even if he does not know where they will lead him. Man will not cease to explore, and in the decades to come, he will surely build and enlarge upon the knowledge and techniques gained during the Apollo missions.

In a more practical sense, the question now is, "Where do we go from here?" James C. Fletcher, the administrator of the National Aeronautics and Space Administration, said, "We turn from space exploration to space exploration for practical purposes." We seek a more rational use of space, a period of space exploration aimed at more practical purposes and at less cost.

The post-Apollo programs include a global inventory of our natural resources, enabling us to manage more efficiently our planet's limited commodities; improved communication satellites to assure expanded and less expensive world communications; and new weather satellites, to help us understand the forces which create our weather and perhaps to reduce the violence of our storms.

The 1970s also will see the first rendezvous of American and Soviet spacecrafts, demonstrating the potential of international cooperation in space, and hopefully fostering other international projects to ease world tension. In the late 1970s, a US space shuttle program is to get underway, utilizing a "returnable" spacecraft to carry payloads into earth orbit.

In the 1980s, with an experimental base established, the application of solid practical technology is to begin. Interest is being shown in the production of new metal alloys, true metal castings, new fiber compositions, and even super-pure vaccines in the airless, germless vacuum of space. We also will become more familiar with the solar system through orbiting telescopes viewing Mars, Jupiter, and the outer reaches of the universe.

INAUGURATION 1973

Several of my Democratic colleagues in Congress boycotted Nixon's second inauguration, and throughout the city there were counterparades and demonstrations. Yet inaugurations do play an important unifying role in our nation—particularly in difficult times. They give us a sense of hope, a willingness to put clashes behind us and move on.

In his inaugural address, the president repeated the conservative themes of personal responsibility and a reduced role of government that helped him win reelection, but he devoted more of his speech to peace than any other topic. He emphasized the "Nixon Doctrine" on foreign policy: "The time has passed when America will make every other nation's conflict our war, or make every other nation's future our responsibility. . . . Just as we respect the right of each nation to determine its own future, we also recognize the responsibility of each nation to secure its own future." A notable emphasis on restraint in foreign policy had entered Nixon's remarks and it was a significant change. It's a position that many members of Congress today would agree with.

> **January 29, 1973: "Inauguration 1973"**
> **Washington Report**
> **Vol. VIII, No. 5**
> Inauguration Day in the nation's capital is a strange mixture of solemn ceremony and exuberant celebration. It is a festival of democracy, a celebration of unity, and a time of national renewal. For those who take part, it is also a time of hectic personal schedules, massive crowds, and frustrating traffic jams.
>
> While a number of my colleagues in the Congress boycotted the ceremonies, I did not. In the rhythm of our national life, a new administration marks a resurgence of hope and a renewal of energy. So many divisions and differences exist in the nation, forces which pull us apart, that these inaugural observances are needed. An inauguration is a time to begin fresh and to strengthen our confidence in our institutions. We need to be reminded that, although our problems are mountainous, so are the talents and resources we can bring to bear to meet them.

Although the president is chosen through a party system, and stands pledged to the principles of that party, he nevertheless is president of all Americans. The inauguration ceremony symbolizes the essential, underlying unity the nation requires to endure.

The swearing-in ceremonies and the president's inaugural address are the most important events of Inauguration Day. President Nixon took only a minute to recite the thirty-five-word oath of office, and at that time he became one of only twelve men in our history who have more than once been elected president.

His second inaugural address stressed reliance on self-help, the disengagement of government, and a limited American involvement abroad. His address, which was thoroughly conservative in philosophy and orientation, made no bows to the liberals, and was clearly directed to the constituency which had elected him.

The festivities surrounding this brief ceremony include about four days of parties, exhibits, entertainment extravaganzas, receptions and dances preceding the inaugural, a parade, inaugural balls with as many as twenty-five musical groups, and a Sunday worship service following the event.

Those who come to Washington for the festivities find them to be expensive affairs. Tickets for all of those events easily total $500. Boxes (and breathing room) at the inaugural balls cost $1,000. Tickets to the inaugural parade range from $5 to $50. A souvenir of the occasion can range from $1,250 for a gold plate, to a dollar or so for a pennant or a lapel button.

There is, however, surprisingly little grumbling, either about the cost or the crush at the affairs. The five inaugural balls staged this year were not so much dances as wall-to-wall humanity—stifling, confusing, and loud. At one reception, arranged to accommodate 1,500 persons comfortably, 15,000 showed up.

Celebrities are everywhere to be seen. Forty of the nation's governors were on hand, entertainers Bob Hope and Frank Sinatra, Miss America, prominent members of Congress, cabinet members, and, of course, the supercelebrities, an ebullient president and his family.

The inaugural parade was a "superparade," with entries from practically every state marching by in a two-hour procession which included the largest-ever marching band—nearly two thousand musicians in a single unit. About three hundred thousand persons lined Pennsylvania Avenue to watch, enduring thirty-degree temperatures and a biting, twenty-five-mile-an-hour wind.

There were protesters, too, and they staged their own inaugural concert, which was attended by some three thousand who could fit in the stately National Cathedral, and twelve thousand who listened outside to a program of music directed by Leonard Bernstein. About seventy-five thousand marched in their own antiwar inaugural parade from the Lincoln Memorial to the Washington Monument on Inauguration Day.

In all, the city handled the celebration with apparent ease. The police restrained the rambunctious crowds and the swearing-in ceremony and the parade came off on schedule. Within five minutes after the inaugural parade was over, street cleaners were hard at work. By Sunday morning, Pennsylvania Avenue was all cleaned up. The celebration was over and the hard tasks of running the government lay ahead.

THE COSTS OF THE VIETNAM WAR

President Nixon's first strategy to try to end the war—escalating the fighting and the bombing in order to get the North Vietnamese to negotiate—had limited effect. So he combined that with a second strategy: improving US relations with China and the Soviet Union so they would reduce their support for the North Vietnamese, increasing the pressure on them to negotiate. That was more successful, and on January 27, 1973, a week after Nixon's second inauguration, the Paris Peace Accords were signed by all parties at war in Vietnam. However, that proved not to be the final chapter of our involvement in Vietnam, which finally ended during the Ford presidency.

The war was the most significant force in politics during the 1960s and 1970s, and my approach to foreign policy was to a large extent shaped by the Vietnam experience. I became much more wary of our commitments to other countries, and began to scrutinize all of those commitments very carefully. To this day I wonder if we learned the lessons of the limitations of military power.

Vietnam made it clear that the actions of the military cannot be sustained without the support of the American people. I often hear people say that their voice doesn't matter. But it was the voice of the people that brought about the end of the war in Vietnam.

February 12, 1973 (untitled)
Washington Report
Vol. VIII, No. 7

The Vietnam War has been a searing experience for Americans. It has cost at least 1.3 million lives over the last decade, according to US figures, including more than 56,000 American combat and noncombat deaths.

We dropped over seven million tons of explosives from aircraft on both North and South Vietnam. That's three and a half times more than the total dropped in World War II, and it adds up to 289 pounds of explosives for every man, woman, and child living in the four nations of Indochina.

Some economists estimate the total cost to be $400 billion, including the costs of benefits to veterans in the decades to come, plus the economic loss of the contributions those who died would have made. If one takes into account inflation, unemployment, the diversion of public resources, the failure to meet our domestic needs, and the social divisions at home, the war may have been the most costly in American history.

The true costs, of course, are incalculable because they include wasted lives and resources, the anguish and heartache of the surviving relatives, the loss of credibility of government leaders, and the erosion of the Constitution itself. Our confidence in our political institutions was strained because of the secrecy and deception of the war; our respect for justice was diminished because of the way we manned the armed services; and the respect of our allies was weakened by our conduct of the war and our failure to resolve it quickly.

The impact of the war on the American military was another cost of the war. In the words of former Vietnam commander General William Westmoreland, Vietnam was "a traumatic experience." The US Army was, in a sense, a major casualty, hit with drug problems, disregard for authority, and violence. A Pulitzer Prize–winning reporter said that the army was saved from ruin by the president's decision to pull out of Vietnam.

It should be said that the military fought the war in the most difficult circumstances with no clear military objectives, a failure to declare war and mobilize for it, a lack of moral imperative at home to support the fighting, and the length of the conflict. One lesson of Vietnam is that the US cannot successfully fight a war that way. We need clear objectives, victory or defeat, and in the long run, our military cannot exist without the good will of the people.

Although we have paid heavily for our Vietnam experience, the United States emerges from the war having learned important lessons. We should know now our limitations in shaping the future of areas as remote as Southeast Asia, and we will be much more reluctant, if not unlikely, to intervene with military forces in foreign countries.

Other nations will see us as less sure of our international course, less predictable, and close association with us will be less attractive to them.

Some say the US will swing back to isolationism. I do not expect that to happen and I hope it does not. If the Vietnam War causes the American people to turn their backs on their genuine national interests in the world, that would be unfortunate, and could be disastrous for world peace.

The Vietnam settlement leaves the balance of power in Asia relatively stable and the prospects of a major clash between the big powers has been reduced. The US role in Asia will be more restrained, with our trade expected to increase sharply, but our strategic presence in Japan, Thailand, and Taiwan diminished.

In the post-Vietnam world, economic power may become the most important element of national influence and prestige, and military power will become less important.

The war is behind us now, and I hope we have ended our involvement in Indochina except for limited economic and military assistance.

THE VICE PRESIDENT'S RESIGNATION

Vice President Spiro Agnew's resignation in response to charges of extensive corruption was an extraordinary event, generating a wide variety of emotions at the time. But at its core it was another serious blow to the public's trust in their elected officials.

Public cynicism and the view that "they're all a bunch of crooks" undermine the very essence of our system of representative democracy, which depends on the confidence of the people that their elected officials are working for the common good rather than trying to enrich themselves. I have often been asked about the best ways to reform Congress and improve public confidence in the institution. I always put maintaining high ethical standards for members among the top items on my list.

October 24, 1973: "The Vice President's Resignation"
Washington Report
Vol. VIII, No. 39

In another stunning development in the most tumultuous year in modern American politics, Vice President Agnew's resignation, after he admitted evasion of federal income taxes, startled and saddened the nation.

My first reaction to this unprecedented personal and national tragedy was compassion for the former vice president and his family, regardless of the actions which caused his resignation. There is no joy and no cause for celebration in seeing a man crash down from the nation's second-highest political office to a convicted felon.

In my view the vice president's action was appropriate. It avoided the peril to the nation of having a vice president under indictment and involved in lengthy court proceedings, and as Mr. Agnew has acknowledged, the American people deserve a vice president who commands their unimpaired confidence and trust. The forty-page summary of evidence against Mr. Agnew prepared by the Department of Justice describes a decade of activity by Mr. Agnew, from county executive in suburban Baltimore County to vice president of the US, during which he received cash in envelopes, kickbacks and payments from engineers and businessmen who wanted government business. The settlement of the Agnew case may not be a triumph of justice, but it represents an acceptable solution to an unprecedented case, in which the claims of justice, politics, and the Constitution were inextricably mixed. The vice president avoided jail, which the federal judge in the case acknowledged would be the ordinary sentence for the crime, but the public interest of removing a vice president under criminal indictment was served, as was the political interest of the president.

The news of the vice president's resignation also gave me a sense of depression. At a time when the American people have experienced so many disappointments and disillusionments that their confidence in their political leaders and institutions is at a low ebb, Mr. Agnew's resignation is yet another staggering blow to millions of decent, honest, and much put-upon Americans who want desperately to believe in the integrity of their high officials. Whether you agreed with Mr. Agnew or not, many Americans did believe in him, considered him their champion, and saw in him an extraordinary politician, purer and better than other politicians. Their cynicism and suspicion of American politics can only be reinforced by the fall of the man who was the preeminent American spokesman for law and order and attacker of permissiveness.

His resignation raises all sorts of difficult questions. Did he receive favored treatment and avoid a jail sentence because of his high office? And if he did, will Americans believe that the law falls with equal application on the powerful and the powerless? What about the process by which vice presidents are selected? How is it possible that the process failed to reveal so obvious a pattern of corruption? Do all politicians, as the cynics insist, really take payoffs? How can we really remove the taint of money from the political process? Can we really believe any politician?

I am hopeful that the former vice president's resignation will prompt further efforts in the Congress to improve campaign practices and procedures for selecting vice presidents, and provide all of us in government with a new determination to give the people integrity in government. It is that quality, above all others, that I think the American people now want in their government.

The immediate task of the Congress is to act with care and dispatch in confirming the president's nomination of Congressman

Gerald Ford of Michigan as vice president. Under the Twenty-Fifth Amendment to the Constitution, the Congress has an obligation to examine fully Mr. Ford's competence, not only for the responsibilities of the vice presidency, but for the more important ones he would assume if he became president.

Although I experienced some misgivings about the festive spirit surrounding the president's announcement of Mr. Ford, and thought that since it followed immediately upon the tragedy of the resignation, the occasion demanded a serious and restrained atmosphere, Mr. Ford is a popular choice in the Congress, and, barring unforeseen developments, I expect to join a majority of my colleagues in confirming his selection.

THE HOUSE JUDICIARY COMMITTEE AND IMPEACHMENT

Going into the Nixon impeachment hearings in the summer of 1974, it was not at all clear whether the House Judiciary Committee and its new chairman, Peter Rodino of New Jersey, would be up to the task. Moreover, the committee's proceedings would be televised, something that was rare in those days before C-SPAN. It was a time of testing for Congress, and the question was whether it would rise to the occasion.

Many Americans—including many members of Congress—were restless and wanted quick action against Nixon on the charges outlined in this commentary. Yet impeachment is a profoundly serious matter. Taking steps to remove a president should be done only with utmost care. The committee took its role seriously, and proceeded in a careful, deliberate way. I was quite proud of how the committee conducted itself, and its actions helped gain respect for the deliberative process in Congress.

Shortly after this commentary was written, the transcript of the "smoking gun" tape was released, which revealed the president's involvement early on in the cover-up of the Watergate break-in. At that point all was lost for the president, and he resigned on August 9, 1974.

August 7, 1974: "The House Judiciary Committee and Impeachment"
Washington Report
Vol. IX, No. 31

For the first time since 1868, and only the second time in American history, a committee of the House of Representatives has recommended the impeachment of the president. This historic action of the House Judiciary Committee captivated the attention of Americans as they watched the proceedings on nationwide television.

The consensus in Washington is that the House Judiciary Committee's six days of meetings were marked by the dignity and responsibility that the occasion demanded. There were mistakes, of course, but, all in all, the Judiciary Committee's performance was reassuring no matter how one felt about the final result. The committee helped restore confidence in the political process, especially the United States Congress, and deepened our understanding of the Constitution.

The members of the Judiciary Committee spoke with intelligence, debated with spirit, demonstrated their anguish, and conducted themselves sensibly and conscientiously. These members of diverse views and personalities rose splendidly to the high occasion and proved that the House can act responsibly as it tackles perhaps the most difficult assignment in the practice of self-government. The televised sessions of the Judiciary Committee served to contradict the charges that the committee is a kangaroo court or a lynching party.

The performance of individual members of the committee was impressive. They were articulate, low-key, moderate, and frequently eloquent. They were able men and women, not engaged in a partisan plot, but obviously struggling with an unpleasant, even sad, duty.

The committee debate, which gave Americans an extraordinary view of a congressional committee at work, was alternately inspiring and tiresome. It illustrated the characteristic wrangling of the legislative process over words, procedures, and politics. After the high-blown rhetoric of each committee member's opening statement, the committee debate refined the issue of impeachment. The charges relating to impoundment of funds, the secret bombing of

Cambodia, campaign funds, tax deficiencies, and improvements on San Clemente faded, and the issues of abuse of presidential power and the cover-up of Watergate misconduct emerged as the crucial issues. The articles of impeachment, as finally adopted by the Judiciary Committee, contain the central charges.

Broad areas of agreement surfaced during the committee debate. With few exceptions, the members accepted the standard that only "grave offenses" of a kind "definitely incompatible" with the Constitution, whether criminal or not, would justify the removal of a president. The committee members also agreed that the evidence must be "clear and convincing," a tougher standard of proof than "probable cause," but not so rigid as a jury verdict in a criminal case that requires an individual to be found guilty "beyond all reasonable doubt."

Moving through uncharted territory, members of the committee divided on fundamental questions. What is the definition of "high crimes and misdemeanors," specified in the Constitution as the basis of impeachment? Did the evidence show that the president had committed an impeachable offense? Will removing President Nixon from office be good or bad for the country? The opponents of impeachment demanded specific facts to support the charges, and the pro-impeachment congressmen, after a slow initial response, elaborated at length the facts they believe support impeachment. Opponents of impeachment, seeking to divide the proponents, complained about the lack of direct evidence against the president and the piling of "inference upon inference" to build a case against the president. Pro-impeachment committee members had avoided specific points of evidence in their early statements, but as the debate wore on they elaborated specific points to support impeachment. Working to unify their forces, they reworded the articles of impeachment to broaden support for them.

It is important that Americans have respect for the impeachment proceedings. Through television they can judge for themselves whether these proceedings are being conducted seriously and fairly. Many congressmen have been fearful of televising any part of the impeachment proceedings, but after the televising of the committee proceedings this past week, more congressmen now recognize that television performed an important civic function, and it is reasonable to expect the House to vote soon to have the full House impeachment proceedings televised. Television can assure that the greatest possible number of Americans understand the how and the why of the impeachment proceedings.

As a result of the committee action, the momentum toward impeachment has significantly strengthened. The Minority Leader has urged the president to take his case on national television as the only step that can save him. Officially, close associates of the president were expressing confidence that the president would avoid impeachment, but the reality of the events of the week was breaking through to them, and they were obviously deeply concerned about the president's future. The leaders of the Senate began gearing up for the trial of the president and guesses about the margin on the vote by which the House will approve impeachment kept increasing.

AFTER WATERGATE

In this commentary I was giving some thought to some of the overall lessons from the Watergate experience.

Much of my thinking about government in general took shape in the Watergate and post-Watergate periods—the problem of concentrating too much power in the president, the need to revitalize and strengthen Congress, the problem of the president's isolation from the people once in office, the problem of too much government secrecy, and the need for greater national focus on consensus and compromise.

One of the main lessons from Watergate is that it could happen again, and that all of us as citizens need to be vigilant. It was my hope at the time that citizens would respond to Watergate by resolving to get more involved rather than just become cynical about our political system. It turned out that many citizens did get more involved. But by and large Watergate only added fuel to the fire of cynicism.

Some of the key lessons of Watergate were not well learned. The problem of concentration of power in the presidency and the passivity of Congress that I focus on here was one that I would be talking about three decades later during the George W. Bush presidency.

April 24, 1974: "After Watergate"
Washington Report
Vol. IX, No. 17

After a year of Watergate many thoughtful Americans are beginning to come forward with healthy responses. Rather than focusing on the abuses of Watergate, they are suggesting the direction for change which will make future Watergates less likely and improve the quality of government in this country. These persons believe that more important even than Watergate is how we react to it, what we learn from it, and what we do about it.

One of the responses is to encourage a presidency that is open, accountable, and constitutional. In recent decades the American political system has concentrated more power in the hands of the president than the Founding Fathers intended or democratic government requires.

There are many reasons for this concentration of power, including the passivity of the Congress, but whatever the reasons, the results are apparent and disturbing as presidents assert executive privilege to keep information from Congress, claim the right to set national priorities by themselves through impoundment of funds, and commit American troops abroad without consultation with the Congress.

Based on a feeling that governmental power should be jointly possessed, a careful reassessment of the institution of the presidency is underway. Respect for the office of the president is obviously necessary, but with it must come a decline in awe and a determination to examine a president's proposals with care, intelligence, and healthy skepticism. Along with that, the presidency must be kept open to the public, the Congress, and the press. A president must be surrounded by a strong cabinet and advisors of the ablest people in America, who represent a broad philosophical base, and who have an appreciation for the essentials and the demands of the political process. No one is suggesting a weakened presidency, but rather a strong presidency under the Constitution, and a presidency, not insulated or isolated, but always exposed to the political pressures of the day and operating with a firm understanding that the decisions of government should be shared decisions.

Another emerging response to Watergate is the necessity of a revitalized Congress, a Congress meeting its responsibilities and dealing with the chief obstacles to responsive government. Congress may not be able to provide the kind of dynamic, comprehensive leadership necessary to quickly restore the people's confidence in government, but it can take the lead in bringing greater openness to discussion and criticism and greater candor to the conduct of the public's business, and it can be more effective in keeping an eye on the executive branch. It can proceed to reform itself by passing two of the bills now pending in the Congress that may become the most significant, even though unpublicized, reforms of the Congress in this century. The two reforms are designed to keep spending under control and to redistribute more equitably the workload and the power among the committees of the Congress.

Congress can also take a whole new series of steps to protect the integrity of American elections, including limitations on the size of gifts and expenditures, complete reporting of contributions and expenditures, tough enforcement, and the use of public financing, perhaps to match private contributions.

Strangely enough, a new appreciation for the role of the politician in society may also emerge as a result of Watergate. As John Gardner points out, worthy groups want mutually incompatible things in a country as big and diverse as America. Without the constant exercise of compromise and accommodation, which is the stuff of politics, this country would come apart at the seams. The role of the politician is to make the country work, providing stability, accommodating different points of view, developing a consensus, and meeting the needs of the people. People may come to better understand that although the political process does not provide perfect answers, it does provide suitable answers for a free people.

In the post-Watergate period, with people more aware that neither government nor governmental officials have a monopoly on information or wisdom, our commitment to freedom of inquiry and publication, and the value of the free press, may be reaffirmed, and the news media may become a more vigorous constraint on the abuse of power.

Citizens may also have been stabbed awake and aroused to action. Although there is much discussion today about people dropping out of politics because of their cynicism and despair, I find just the opposite reaction: a feeling that the vote and participation in the electoral process is more important than ever before. People are increasing their understanding and respect for the principles of a democratic system of government and beginning to understand more fully the demands it makes upon them.

There is, of course, no assurance that all or any of these suggestions will come to pass, and no fail-safe mechanism to forever ensure honesty in government. We should not expect miracles, but we can take confidence from the healthy responses that are emerging from the tragedy of Watergate, and perhaps even give them a boost.

Richard Nixon was a fascinating individual, the most puzzling president in my experience. He was a man of complex emotions and personality traits, a bundle of contradictions. He was the leader of the free world yet socially awkward; a leading anti-Communist who improved and stabilized relations with China and the Soviet Union; a conservative who signed into law many liberal initiatives and helped advance civil rights; someone who could do creative and strategic thinking in the development of policy but who made a series of remarkably poor decisions that brought about a constitutional crisis and ended his presidency. He was elected president and then reelected by large margins, yet he became the first president to resign and he severely tarnished the reputation of the White House.

On the one hand Nixon could be insecure, deeply suspicious of other people, and vindictive. Yet he was also smart, capable, and ambitious—and extremely resilient. From the beginning to the end of his political career he was moving from one crisis to another, yet he kept bouncing back, moving forward so he was able to face new opportunities. In the later years of his life, after all he had gone through, his advice was being sought by President Clinton, his books were national bestsellers, and he was appearing on the lists of most-admired Americans, which is an astonishing testament to his resilience.

Congress during the Nixon presidency gets high marks. Here was a situation in which the Republican president and the heavily Democratic-controlled House and Senate had different priorities and different political agendas. They had frequent clashes, and Nixon vetoed many bills and impounded funds that Congress had appropriated. Yet to a surprising extent they were able to put aside their differences and produce a solid set of legislative accomplishments. Even in the 93rd Congress, as tensions between Congress and the president were at their highest over Watergate, they still were able to agree on important legislation. The result was a set of legislative accomplishments during the Nixon years that far outstrips those of recent Congresses.

Making all of this possible was the excellent working relationship between the Democratic and Republican leaders in Congress. Legislators do not make the political environment in which they must work—the voters do. Their job as legislators is to make the system work, whatever the balance of power they are given and whomever they must work with. Despite the strained relations the Democrats had with the president and the increasing turmoil of his presidency, the leaders in Congress of both parties recognized their responsibility to work together on national legislation for the common good. Their accomplishments were a bright moment in the history of Congress.

THREE

THE FORD YEARS
(1974–76)
A Needed Respite

CONGRESS WAS OPTIMISTIC AS GERALD FORD'S PRESIDENCY BEGAN. Our tough Watergate years were behind us, and in the White House we had a president who was widely liked and respected by both Republicans and Democrats. In his brief remarks to the nation after being sworn in, President Ford said, "Our long national nightmare is over," and, "There is no way we can go forward except together." His sensitive speech resonated in the country as well as in Congress.

In my commentary at that time I noted that the new president was expected to have an extended period of good relations with Congress, since—having previously served twenty-four years in the House—he was viewed as "one of ours" and was promising to "consult and compromise" with Congress. Yet two years later I was observing that "the 94th Congress and the president slugged it out for two years on economic issues with no clear winner," and pointed to only modest legislative accomplishments. The Ford years turned out much differently than we expected in Congress. It was the reverse of the Nixon years, which had low initial expectations yet significant legislative accomplishments.

Decisions by the president as well as developments in Congress had quickly changed the overall dynamic. First was Ford's decision—after less than a month in office—to give Nixon a complete pardon for Watergate before he was even convicted of anything. The pardon was a major surprise, and it was not viewed positively by the public or the Democratic-controlled Congress. Even Ford's successor in the House, Minority Leader

John Rhodes, spoke out against it. Ford's popularity in the polls plummeted, and in a matter of days his honeymoon with Congress was over.

Two months later came the 1974 elections in which the voters, fed up with Watergate and the Nixon years, sent a large new class of Democrats to Congress. Throughout our nation's history most presidents have faced Congresses that were controlled by their own party. Ford faced a Congress that was not only controlled by the other party, but controlled by one of the most lopsided margins ever—with the Democrats holding a huge 291–144 advantage in the House and a 61–39 advantage in the Senate. Congress was becoming more assertive after the Nixon years anyway, but with their large majorities the Democratic-controlled House and Senate were not willing to give in to President Ford very much.

At the same time, Ford took several steps that did not go over well with conservative Republicans in Congress, including choosing Nelson Rockefeller as his vice president and not being as conservative as they would have liked in his judicial and other appointments. That eroded his normal Republican base of support in Congress.

The key overriding factor in all of this was that the American people at that time were not particularly receptive to new government proposals and initiatives. Americans had Washington fatigue. They felt they had been through a wringer for several years and they were not clamoring for an activist government. The modest accomplishments of Congress during the Ford years were largely a reflection of the times.

Those years were, however, significant as a time of national healing after Watergate, a task Ford's background made him well suited to lead.

Ford came to Congress sixteen years before I did, and became the House Minority Leader the day I was sworn in as a freshman member in January 1965. I've known few people in politics who were nicer. Everyone in Congress liked Jerry Ford. He had solid midwestern values: easygoing, modest, straightforward, and confident of his course. And down-to-earth—as he said, he was a Ford, not a Lincoln.

I got to know him fairly well. He lived a few blocks from me in northern Virginia, and Betty Ford and my wife became good friends. Ford was an ardent Michigan Wolverines fan, and he followed the teams closely. Often when he was in Congress I'd run into him in the hall and as we walked together he'd point out in a good-natured way—though sometimes in considerable detail—a recent Michigan victory over Indiana University. Fortunately my turn would come during basketball season, when IU would typically best Michigan. He was a pleasant person to be around, and he connected well with members of both parties.

As Minority Leader he was always on the go, traveling around the country on the weekends to speak at Republican gatherings and raise money for the Republican Party, starting the pattern that others would follow. He was a solid conservative and his main legislative priority, as I recall it, was defense spending. He was passionate about defense spending and he always wanted the maximum amount of funding for the military. He was effective in meetings and had a solid grasp of politics. But he was not considered an innovator or an imaginative thinker. He was recognized above all else as a loyal Republican, holding tight to the party line. That was clear in his defense of Nixon, which continued right up to his resignation.

The Speaker of the House during the Ford years was Carl Albert, a politically moderate Democrat from Oklahoma. He had worked with Ford for many years in the House, and he got along with him well. Like Ford, Albert put a heavy emphasis on compromise and seeking consensus, and was known for his fairness and integrity. I remember Carl telling us always to respect our colleagues in the House, no matter their party, ideology, or political background, and never to forget that each of them served in Congress because he or she was duly elected by the American people to do so. Coming from a border state Albert tried to bridge the differences between the Northern liberal and Southern conservative Democratic factions in the House, a gap which was basically unbridgeable. He retired at the end of the 94th Congress, saying he was tired and wanted to go home.

Albert was a gifted orator, one of the best I've heard. Once he came out to Indiana to appear at some events for me and Andy Jacobs, a congressman from the Indianapolis area. Albert gave a great speech in Seymour to a large crowd of Ninth District Democrats. As he closed his speech he surprised me by saying, "No state has ever sent a finer congressman to Washington than your sending Lee Hamilton." I thought that was very gracious of him to say, and, I'll have to admit, it puffed me up a bit. Our next stop was a meeting closer to Indianapolis. Another great speech, which he ended with, "No state has ever sent a finer congressman to Washington than your sending Andy Jacobs." I took leadership praise a little less seriously after that.

The 93rd Congress (Second Part): Key Facts

- August 9, 1974, through December 20, 1974, the remainder of the Congress during the Ford administration
- House of Representatives controlled by the Democrats, 245 to 187 (3 other)
- Senate controlled by the Democrats, 57 to 41 (2 other)
- 280 bills enacted
- Major accomplishments during the Ford part of this Congress included passing the Housing and Community Development Act, the Employee Retirement Income Security Act, the Energy Reorganization Act, the Federal Election Campaign Act Amendments, the National Mass Transportation Assistance Act, the Emergency Jobs and Unemployment Assistance Act, and the Trade Act of 1974
- Support for President Ford's position in the House: Democrats 48 percent, Republicans 59 percent; in the Senate: Democrats 45 percent, Republicans 67 percent

The 94th Congress: Key Facts

- January 14, 1975, through October 1, 1976, during the last two years of the Ford administration
- House of Representatives controlled by the Democrats, 291 to 144
- Senate controlled by the Democrats, 61 to 37 (2 other)
- 588 bills enacted
- Major accomplishments included passing the Tax Reduction Act of 1975, the Education for All Handicapped Children Act, the Energy Policy and Conservation Act, the Federal Election Campaign Act Amendments, the International Security Assistance and Arms Export Control Act, the Energy Conservation and Production Act, the Government in Sunshine Act, the Tax Reform Act of 1976, the

Toxic Substances Control Act, and the Resource Conservation and Recovery Act
· Support for President Ford's position in the House: Democrats 38 percent, Republicans 69 percent; in the Senate: Democrats 50 percent, Republicans 75 percent

THE PARDON

The September 1974 pardon of Nixon "for all offenses against the United States which he, Richard Nixon, has committed or may have committed" was the defining decision of the Ford presidency. Ford maintained steadfastly that he gave the pardon in the national interest to put Watergate behind us and that there was no deal with Nixon. But it was widely criticized at the time, and congressional and public support for the president dropped sharply. It may well have cost Ford the 1976 election.

The merits of the pardon could still be debated today. But over time some of those who were the harshest critics initially—including journalist Bob Woodward and Senator Ted Kennedy—changed their views and came to support it. A few years before he died, the John F. Kennedy Foundation gave Ford its "Profiles in Courage" award for his decision to pardon Nixon.

This commentary reflects my ambivalence toward the pardon at the time. I thought that Nixon should be held accountable for his actions and that a broad pardon before conviction was premature, but I also recognized that a lengthy trial could well set the country back. In retrospect I am still ambivalent but I do better understand the benefits that flowed from Ford's decision.

> **September 25, 1974: "The Pardon"**
> **Washington Report**
> **Vol. IX, No. 37**
> At a time when things seemed to be calming down, President Ford's decision to pardon former president Nixon and to consider pardons for all alleged Watergate conspirators ignited fresh controversy.
>
> The decision caused President Ford's approval rate in the public opinion polls to plummet from 71 percent to 49 percent. After

only thirty days in office, his press secretary resigned in protest, he said, "as a matter of conscience." The decision to pardon met a largely hostile reaction from the nation's press, and from most members of Congress. It interrupted, if not shattered, a period of good feelings, reactivated partisan division, and raised questions about the president's credibility. At the second press conference of his administration, fourteen of twenty-one questions dealt with the pardon. Even the president has acknowledged surprise at the popular reaction to his decision.

In my view, the reasons for the general public disapproval were several. Americans, who have a natural sense of justice, perceive the law as the means by which justice is achieved. This sense of justice was fortified by the experience of Watergate, which prompted a new and powerful concern for justice among Americans and a desire to see the law administered impartially. Their attitude, as I understand it, is that the truth about the misdeeds of the former president should be determined in a court of law by the same procedures that apply to all other Americans. In their view, equal justice under the law requires that the processes of the law run their course. It offended their sense of equity to see one kind of justice dispensed to the agents of the president and another kind to the former president, and it offended their desire for a conclusive determination to have a pardon leave unresolved the question of whether any or all criminal charges against the former president could be made to stick. They want and deserve to know the full Watergate story and the role of Mr. Nixon in it. If allowed to run its course, the law would have established his guilt or innocence.

Another reason for the reaction to the pardon decision was that President Ford did what he implied he would not do. At a time when the nation had been repeatedly dismayed by acts of intrigue and deceit, the people rejected what they perceived to be the politics of secrecy and surprise. When asked a year ago, then vice president–designate Ford indicated to Congress that the public would not stand for a pardon for President Nixon. In his news conference a week prior to the pardon, President Ford, although not ruling out the ultimate exercise of a pardon, said he would let the legal processes run their course before he made a decision. President Ford certainly did not invent the politics of presidential secrecy, but for the present, his decision has undermined his own reputation for candor. Already he has acknowledged that he will seek wider consultation in the future. The speed and manner of this decision, coupled with the fact that it controverted his previous statements, made it appear that the decision was made impulsively and without adequate consultation.

Another aspect of the pardon which contributed to the reaction was the agreement with former president Nixon on the handling of the tapes and papers accumulated during his presidency. The agreement abandoned control and access by the government and the public to these materials. In response to strong objection from many sources, President Ford has apparently suspended the agreement and is considering it further. The initial agreement struck with President Nixon was based on the assumption that the records of the presidency are the president's personal property to keep, donate, and dispose of as he likes, and there is ample precedent for that view. But such an agreement could result in the destruction or suppression of important parts of the historical record. My view is that public papers of elected United States officials should be the property of the government and should not be taken away at the end of a term of office. The public's interest in these materials is paramount and apparent.

Former president Nixon, of course, has acknowledged misperceptions and errors of judgment, but he has not stated that his actions were either wrong or illegal. Obviously he rejects the unanimous view of the House Judiciary Committee members that he violated his Constitutional duty faithfully to execute the office of president and obstructed the administration of justice.

President Ford called the evidence of former president Nixon's guilt of an impeachable offense "very persuasive," but he has vigorously defended his pardon of the former president because it would end the "turmoil and divisiveness in American society." He also pointed out that President Nixon has suffered enough and that a fair trial would be difficult to achieve.

Any new president comes to office with a reservoir of good will, and he must use it sparingly. President Ford has spent much of his good will with the decision to pardon. My hope is that he has learned his lesson and that he will scrupulously respect the people's sense of justice and law, that he will seek wider consultation before making major decisions, and that he will not use the politics of secrecy again.

AS WE LEAVE VIETNAM

In early 1975 Congress denied President Ford's request for additional funding to continue the fighting in Vietnam. A few months later, South Vietnam fell and we saw vivid scenes on television of South Vietnamese desperately fleeing Saigon before the Viet Cong arrived.

Both parties were uneasy about the possible political fallout. The Democrats were concerned that by denying Ford the requested funds they would be labeled the party that lost Vietnam. On the other hand, the Republicans were uneasy because the mood of the country had changed and now was clearly against the war.

In the end, the changed mood of Americans came to entirely dominate the debate, as only 17 percent of Americans supported continued US involvement. So the Republicans let up on their criticisms of the Democrats, and the Democrats—and the country—moved on to other things. The Vietnam experience was a case of Congress and the American people getting it right before the president did, a case of our system of representative democracy functioning as it was meant to. The divisive national debate about Vietnam was finally over.

During the war, a major concern was that our withdrawal would profoundly impact our position in the world for decades to come. I never agreed with that view and it did not turn out to be true. America's world leadership has continued unabated.

> **April 30, 1975: "As We Leave Vietnam"**
> **Washington Report**
> **Vol. X, No. 18**
> The American involvement in Southeast Asia is at long last about over, and all of us feel a variety of emotions: sadness as we see the collapse of a country we have supported for over a decade; relief that the end has finally come; sympathy for the human suffering; and depression that the United States ever got involved in Vietnam and that we spent so much in men and money. Most of us are drained from the Vietnam experience, and we want most of all to forget about Indochina. A few observations may be appropriate as we close a tragic chapter in American history.

The events in Indochina give us an opportunity to reconsider what really are the national interests of this country and to evolve policies which support them. We should emerge from the tragedy of Vietnam with a clearer understanding of this nation's world role and a healthier realism about the limits of American power. Surely the end has come to the era of American omnipresence and the idea that we can control events everywhere. Among other things, this means we should not make massive commitments of American prestige and power in situations where the national interest of the United States is not vital, and it means we should focus our efforts instead on the mainlines of American interest in Europe, the Middle East, and Japan. It also means a role as something less than the world's policeman, something less than bearing every burden and fighting every foe in defense of freedom, but something more than a retreat into fortress America and the isolationism of the past. Out task is to avoid excessive commitments without swinging toward a dangerous withdrawal from our responsibilities in the world. The United States must of course remain militarily strong, but it should rely less on its military strength and more on the attraction of a free, open, and prosperous country that is strong enough and confi-dent enough not to impose its will upon others and to allow diversity in the world's political and economic systems.

There just is no reason for Americans to feel a sense of defeat-ism because of the events in Indochina. Although some commen-tators think that the United States is in danger of collapsing as a world power, the world prestige and stature of the United States is not entwined in the fate of Cambodia and Vietnam. The collapse of Cambodia and South Vietnam may be a defeat for our allies, but it was not a defeat for the United States. We did all any friend could reasonably be expected to do in support of an ally. In the final analysis, we could not save Vietnam for the South Vietnamese. Only they could do that. Although battered, our political system emerges from Vietnam intact, and our national priorities, long distorted by the war, can be reestablished. Our overall power continues without challenge, and we remain the only military superpower in the non-Communist world. The bulk of US diplomatic relationships continue on a normal course, and there are no immediately threatening crises. Neither the Soviet Union nor China has been tempted to ex-ploit the deterioration of American authority. Our economic power is awesome and will be enhanced as we end the drain of resources to Indochina. Likewise, our cultural power has established an influence in the world of the arts, theater, and publishing that is as pervasive as it is underrated. In short, Americans have no reason to lose confidence.

So I disagree with those who contend that the failure in Indochina is a sweeping setback for American foreign policy. The United States does not really have any vital interest in Southeast Asia, and other nations will not conclude that because we are refusing to continue resistance there we will not resist in other areas of the world where we do have vital interests.

This is not the time to search for scapegoats or to engage in a fruitless debate on who lost Indochina. Frankly, I have been disappointed by statements of President Ford and Vice President Rockefeller encouraging that kind of discussion. The vice president has suggested that Indochina will be a political issue in 1976, and the president has consistently suggested that the Congress has frustrated efforts to meet our commitments. The impact of these words is to politicize the failure in Indochina and to downgrade confidence in America's dependability and strength. My view is that the Congress in recent years has understood the American national interest better, and certainly more realistically, than recent presidents. The Congress has also better understood that no foreign policy will work unless the American people understand and support it.

How we leave Vietnam is important. We should acknowledge our responsibilities and our mistakes—in the initial involvement in Indochina, in the continuation of the war in the face of staggering human and material costs, and even in the events since the Paris Accords. We can claim that we did the best for an ally that we could. We should do all we can to bind up the wounds of war. Hopefully, we will be willing to learn from our errors, shake off any sense of defeatism, put Vietnam behind us, and move on with even greater striving toward the ideals of the nation which have made us both a strong and compassionate people.

Now is the time to begin to restore perspective on the real American national interests and to revive confidence in American ability and will.

THE MIDDLE CLASS

Ten years after the Johnson War on Poverty the focus of Congress shifted from what could be done to help the poor and the least fortunate among us to what could be done to help the struggling middle class. This attention to the middle class stuck, and it has been a key refrain of politicians ever since. It has become impossible to imagine a president today placing at the center of his domestic policy a war on poverty.

Middle-class families during the Ford years were being hit particularly hard by the economic problems of high unemployment, poor economic growth, and high inflation, with consumer prices increasing at double-digit rates. It was a toxic mix of problems—given the new name "stagflation"—and trying to shore up the economy became a major preoccupation of policymakers during much of the Ford years.

> **May 21, 1975: "The Middle Class"**
> **Washington Report**
> **Vol. X, No. 21**
>
> Middle-class Americans are having a tough time these days.
>
> They are squeezed by inflation, recession, and high taxes. They feel that they are the forgotten persons of American politics. They point to the broad range of subsidies available to low-income families which are unavailable to them but are paid for in large measure by their taxes. They earn too much to benefit from federal programs and too little to pay for what they need. They also know that the well-to-do often benefit from inflation and receive all kinds of tax breaks.
>
> They watch apprehensively as their financial position slowly erodes, and they are wondering just how much longer they can continue to pay their bills. One symptom of the growing squeeze is that a number of middle-class citizens have been applying for food stamps, even though they may be uncomfortable in doing so. More than half of all food stamp recipients hold part-time or full-time jobs and receive no other public assistance. The financial security of middle-income Americans has dropped dramatically in recent years, with net assets at the end of 1974 only 64 percent of what they were at the end of 1972.

One characteristic of middle-class Americans has always been their expectation for a better standard of living, but they are losing their traditional optimism and are beginning to question whether things really will be getting better for them. Their hopes for a better future have been deflated, and they wonder what can happen to them next.

Middle-class people constitute the largest and most important group in our society. More than half of the nation's fifty-five million families are in the middle class, with much of the increase over the last two decades a result of significantly higher family incomes. Their income levels run from $10,000 to as high as $35,000 in high-cost-of-living areas. Most people tend to consider themselves a part of the middle class, or act as if they were, and membership has been expanded to include blue-collar workers. The economic impact of middle-class Americans is tremendous since they buy 80 percent of all cars and roughly three-fourths of most major appliances.

Home ownership is slipping beyond their grasp. Owning a house has traditionally been one of their most important goals, but rising home costs, high interest rates, and soaring utility bills have combined to price many middle-income families out of the single-family housing market. The median cost of new homes in 1974 was a staggering $41,300. A family must have an income of about $23,000 a year to make the necessary payments on a new home, but the US median family income is only about $12,051.

The promise of a better education is fading for many middle-class people. Higher education costs, which cut deeply into family savings, are approaching $6,000 per year in some cases, and even the least expensive college education, at a two-year public college for a student who lives at home, will cost more than $2,000 a year by September. Only limited financial assistance is available to middle-class students and their parents, who are wondering if they can stand the expense. At today's rates, the cost of a college education can place a heavy burden on savings and retirement money.

To make the squeeze even worse, middle-class Americans bear a heavy tax load, and inflation has substantially increased the burden. Inflation reduces the real value of the personal exemption and standard deduction and pushes low- and middle-income taxpayers into higher tax brackets, which are narrower than those at higher income levels. So the middle class is seeing a greater proportion of its income go for taxes. Last year payroll and income taxes for families with average incomes rose from 17.8 percent to 19.5 percent of their family budgets, with the higher tax payments representing the single biggest family expenditure. From 1973 to 1974, for a family with an income of $14,466, personal income taxes rose by 26 percent, even though its standard of living stayed the same. That same family's Social Security taxes rose 21.6 percent.

The significance of the financial squeeze on middle-income Americans cannot be exaggerated. The squeeze is bound to influence their thoughts and actions and test their mettle, perhaps as much as they have ever been tested before. Already changes in their views are emerging. They are more cost-conscious and conservation-minded. As consumers, they are shopping hard for product quality. Their political sensitivities are sharpening, and their suspicions of government are growing. They question more intensely than they once did whether politicians are really doing anything for them. No longer do they unquestioningly accept the promise of constant progress, and their values, moral standards, and dedication to work are undergoing changes.

For those of us in government there is a clear lesson. We must remember that it was the stability of Americans, largely middle-class Americans, which enabled the nation to endure the shocks of Vietnam and Watergate, and it is vital to the health of the nation that their good sense of tempered optimism about the future continue. We must never ignore the central importance of middle Americans to the welfare of the nation. It is they who sustain it and give it strength, and our policies and our statements must be sensitive and responsive to their needs. Among other things this means we had better begin to give special weight to the impact of our actions on middle-class Americans.

THE QUIET REVOLUTION

The decade of the 1970s was a time of major advances in the women's movement, and Congress, through some of the measures mentioned in this commentary, played a significant role.

While women have made great strides since then, one area in which they still lag far behind men is in the number of women elected to Congress. New Hampshire's delegation to Congress recently was made up entirely of women, but in all the other states men outnumber women, usually by large margins. Their numbers have increased steadily since 1975, but they still make up only about 20 percent of the total membership—far below the levels in other democratic countries in which women hold 40 percent of the seats or more.

Women members of Congress have enriched the political discourse in our country and have brought a different tone and context to our politics. Initially their impact was on family issues—and soon all members of Congress were talking about the family—but quickly their influence broadened to all policy topics. I thought their numbers would increase more than they have. Who serves in Congress is up to the voters in the fifty states, but from my perspective the women coming to Congress have had a positive impact on the substance and civility of the discourse in Congress, as well as the willingness to build consensus and find common ground. They have softened a lot of rough edges in our politics.

June 18, 1975: "The Quiet Revolution"
Washington Report
Vol. X, No. 25

A quiet revolution is underway in America. It may not be spectacular, and it may have escaped your notice, but it is changing life in America in dramatic, if even quiet, ways. The revolution is in the impressive progress women are making toward full achievement of their rights.

This progress gained new momentum this past week as the House and Senate passed legislation that would allow women to enter the US service academies and new regulations were issued by the federal government to require equal treatment for women in the nation's schools and colleges in vocational training, athletics, financial aid, and faculty hiring.

Although most of the attention in the area of women's rights has focused on the ratification of the Equal Rights Amendment, which now requires approval by four more states before 1979 to become a constitutional amendment, a number of less noticeable, but significant, changes are taking place.

Women comprise approximately 40 percent of the nation's workforce, and they are entering a number of occupations which were once open only to men, including such traditionally male jobs as carpenter, police officer, and locomotive engineer. Women are also entering professional schools in unprecedented numbers. From the mid-'60s to 1973, the enrollment of women in law schools jumped from approximately 2,500 to over 17,000, and the percentage of women receiving medical degrees rose from 6.5 percent to 10 percent.

In higher education as a whole, enrollment of women rose by 120 percent from 1963 to 1973. In 1974 about 40 percent of master's degrees, up from 34 percent in 1966, and 15 percent of doctor's degrees, up from 11.6 percent in 1966, were earned by women. The number of women teaching at colleges and universities, although far below the number of men, has also increased noticeably. We are moving toward a time when intellect, talent, and skill will be recognized and rewarded, regardless of the sex of the persons concerned, and the country will certainly benefit.

Many state legislatures are dealing effectively with problems confronting women. Legislation intended to protect women, but actually protecting jobs for men, has been challenged in over half the states. Indiana has made several changes in state law to remove sex distinctions which had previously denied women the full benefit of the law and, like other states, has passed legislation to encourage women to report rape incidents by protecting their personal lives from unnecessary public disclosure. The chief aim of the changes in the laws concerning rape is to encourage women to seek police help in arresting their attackers and to enhance the chance of convicting them.

Women are also playing an expanding role in politics and government. More than 1,200 women ran for state or national office in 1974, and, as a result, the nation has 19 congresswomen, 1 governor, 1 lieutenant governor, and 466 state legislators who are women. These women are bringing fresh perspective and new vitality to the search for solutions to a whole range of state and national challenges.

In spite of these gains, pervasive sex discrimination continues to exist. Although women constitute 51 percent of the population and a growing share of the workforce, they hold most of the lower-paying jobs in the economy and lag behind men in pay, earning approximately 60 percent of what men earn, and whatever the type of job, women earn less than men on the average. The average woman with a bachelor's degree who works full time earns about the same median income as a man who is a high school dropout. The female unemployment rate today is nearly two percentage points above the male unemployment rate.

There are a number of other sources of discrimination against women. Social Security discriminates against women both in terms of contributions and benefits. Women also have greater difficulty obtaining credit than men, and they face higher insurance costs for basic health, medical, and income disability coverage. In some states, women's rights to establish independent businesses or to be a guarantor or a surety are restricted. The criminal laws of some states discriminate against women, for example, by making a sentence for a woman harsher than a man's sentence for the same offense. The admission policies of colleges and schools often require higher standards for women than for men. Even in government employment, women are crowded in the lower grades of the civil service and rarely found in the highest grades.

So the struggle for the fundamental dignity and individuality of each human being goes on, and more is happening and still needs to happen in the area of women's rights than most of us realize. These may be the times that try men's souls, but, no matter, because the quiet revolution cannot be turned back, and life in these United States will never be quite the same.

POLITICIANS

This was another of the "good word for America" commentaries that I wrote around the Fourth of July, this one on the importance of politicians. It was an important commentary for me, laying out some of my basic thoughts on the key role that politicians play in our country. These are still basically the same points I make today.

Over the years I took on the role of saying something positive about politicians to all kinds of groups, and actually became fond of doing so. It went against the grain for most people because it was not at all what they expected or wanted to hear. But getting them to understand better the role of the politician in our system of government was essential for a more productive relationship between voters and public officials. A representative democracy in a large country like ours simply cannot work without the core process of listening to diverse views and then trying to find acceptable common ground. And that, in a word, is the role of a politician.

July 9, 1975: "Politicians"
Washington Report
Vol. X, No. 28

Given the deep mistrust of politicians, anyone—and especially a politician—who takes pen in hand, or opens his mouth, to defend politicians as a group should probably be prepared to duck fast. But I believe the defense needs to be made, so I'll ignore my own advice and give it a try.

You don't need to tell those of us who are politicians that we have a bad name and that people have become extremely cynical about us. Attacking politicians is, of course, a national sport, played enthusiastically year-round, in good weather and bad, in or out of doors.

What, then, can be said in defense of politicians? Believe it or not, a pretty good defense can be made, and it goes something like this: the role of the politician is to make the country work. John Gardner reminds us that in a country as big and diverse as America, worthy groups want mutually contradictory things. Without the aid of politicians in creating consensus and accommodation, the country would come apart at the seams. The politician promotes stability, accommodates different points of view, develops a consensus, tries to meet the needs of the people, and strives to achieve justice. On any scale to values, these are not unworthy tasks.

Most politicians are knowledgeable about competing pressures in the country, and they learn to mediate among them. They know the flashpoints of contention on most subjects, and they try to work their way through conflicting arguments and pressures to workable solutions. Politicians are necessarily students of what will work and of what will keep all sides in a conflict, if not satisfied, at least not too unhappy. They will often blur the stark line between victory and defeat by making gracious overtures and even concessions when they win, and by putting the best possible face on defeat when they lose.

People often have exaggerated expectations of what politicians can accomplish. They want instant satisfaction, and when they don't get it they experience instant disappointment. They often overestimate the ability of their favorite politician to solve a problem and they underestimate the difficulty of the problem itself. They become too quickly frustrated and disenchanted with the political process when politicians do not make the progress they think should be made. In fact, politicians often accomplish more than people realize. Too often people become so transfixed by the daily charges and countercharges, as the news media focus on personalities, differences, and generalities, that they miss the progress made and the problems avoided.

Basically, politicians struggle for power; that is what their business is all about. In this country this struggle is out in the open, in a system in which politicians try to take the competing interests, the frustrations and desires of 215 million Americans and mold them into some kind of national policy. Politicians play an indispensable role in this vital process, although, admittedly, it is sometimes done rather crudely.

In a big, tough, sometimes cruel world, the politician also serves as an important buffer between individuals and their government. Any congressman can tell you that he and his staff spend much time in obtaining Social Security benefits or unemployment compensation for constituents, and in many other ways politicians are able to make a harsh environment a little kindlier for individuals who encounter the sometimes appalling indifference of massive government bureaucracy.

The politician's efforts to build a majority or a consensus are also essential in forging national unity. The forces of sectionalism are very strong in this country. We rightly pride ourselves on the diversity of class, race, creed, and region, but these things do have a divisive thrust, and on many questions the country needs all the unifying forces it can muster. Fence-straddling, backslapping, frustratingly ambiguous politicians may deserve more credit than you think for softening the rough edges of America's fabulous diversity. In the long view, the unity of the country is more important than winning or losing a particular fight over policy.

This defense of the politician may be a little one-sided, but the other side is heard so often that I hope it is in order. To paraphrase a prominent political scientist: there is no America without democracy; there is no democracy without politics; and there can be no politics without politicians.

DEMOCRACY AND CAPITALISM

In the mid-1970s there was growing pessimism around the world about the future of democracy and capitalism. The aim of this commentary was to give some reasons why the outlook might not be so bleak. And in decades since there has actually been a global resurgence of democracy, capitalism, and economic freedom. They have had their ups and downs, but the overall situation today is more positive than what many leading thinkers were expecting a few decades ago. Contrary to former West German chancellor Willie Brandt's dire prediction in the 1970s quoted in this commentary that democracy in Europe might last only twenty or thirty more years, there have instead been advances in democracy globally in recent decades. Today more than half of the world's population now lives in a democracy, although many of those countries are struggling to provide good governance.

> **July 23, 1975: "Democracy and Capitalism"**
> **Washington Report**
> **Vol. X, No. 30**
> Democracy and capitalism, two key institutions greatly cherished by Americans, are in serious trouble in the world.
>
> One almost gets the impression that democracies are disappearing. Recently a group of experts on government from Europe, Japan, and the United States decided that democracy is on the decline and that democratic governments face a bleak future. Willie Brandt, the former chancellor of West Germany, suggested that "Western Europe has only twenty or thirty more years of democracy left in it." India, the world's largest democracy, has veered sharply from its democratic course; Italy is going broke under a weak democratic coalition; and antidemocratic forces rule in most of Africa and Latin America. Leaders of free nations everywhere, confronting serious and complex problems, are on the defensive.
>
> Democratic governments are having major economic problems as well as political ones. Great Britain, the parent of our own democracy, for example, is struggling with a 25 percent inflation rate which is straining its social contract. Ten years ago capitalism in the United States, Japan, and the countries of Western Europe was riding high and seemed to be on the verge of producing permanently

affluent societies, but economic problems have now engulfed these countries as inflation and recession have struck simultaneously.

Inflation-recession has become the major problem, not just for capitalism, but for democracy, too, threatening the survival of both. Grimly and painfully the capitalist countries are trying to deal effectively with their problems and struggle out of an economic slump, well aware that the future of democracy and the future of capitalism are closely intertwined.

It is, of course, a little early to sound the death knell of democracy or capitalism. They have survived wars, depressions, and changes in government, and even their most severe critics acknowledge that their downfall is not imminent. They have shown themselves to be marvelously adaptable to change.

But neither is it time for complacency. Most of the people of the world have had no experience with capitalism or democracy. Both institutions are constantly under attack, always threatened and never secure, and, if history is a guide, we must all be pessimists about the future of either one. Economic progress and personal freedom are not forever assured, even to Americans.

It is always interesting to note, despite all of our problems in America, how much our friends from abroad look to us for the answers to the crisis of democracy and capitalism. They may be critical of us for a variety of reasons, but they also want to know what America is going to do about the crisis and when. They recognize America's promise of prosperity in freedom.

There is encouragement to be gained from what Americans are doing about the crisis as they search for ways and means to achieve that promise. Several leading national magazines have run articles about the search for new approaches toward making the economy work better. A spirit of openness to change and reform marks the attitude of the proponents of capitalism and democracy. There may be some confusion, and more than normal disarray, but thoughtful persons are everywhere engaged in the search, and our hope rests on the belief that free men and women can respond to this challenge as they have responded to other serious challenges in the past.

The struggle to improve and maintain democracy and capitalism one with the other is never-ending, and the promise of prosperity and freedom may be presumptuous, but we have come close enough to fulfilling it as a nation that we know that if our will and energy do not fade, we can continue to achieve it, no matter what.

For most of us, there simply is no alternative to capitalism and democracy. They have served us well, bringing most of us abundance and liberty, and, despite their woes and faults, we see a better world for ourselves and others if they prosper and spread.

BIG GOVERNMENT

The appropriate role of government again became a major issue during the Ford years as the president believed that cutting federal spending and trimming back government would be important for turning around the weak US economy. That connection between federal belt-tightening and economic growth has not been quite as clear as proponents might claim.

But the basic question of the size and scope of the federal government is one of the enduring questions of American politics, and it was a topic I returned to in commentaries several times over the years. My view early on came to be that our goal should be a limited government that performs well.

I also put a lot of emphasis on federalism—that there were many responsibilities being handled in Washington that could just as well be handled by state and local governments. And I put a particular emphasis on the basic importance of this sorting-out process. It is an ongoing one. We will always be debating what the role, scope, and responsibilities of government should be.

It should be noted that some progress has been made in recent decades to rein in the size of government. Since this commentary was written, total federal government employment has dropped by 16 percent, and this was during a period when the US population increased by almost 50 percent.

January 21, 1976: "Big Government"
Washington Report
Vol. XI, No. 3
One feature of the two-hundredth-birthday celebration is that Americans are not happy with their government. In a few words, many Americans view their government as inefficient, intrusive, and just too big and expensive. How to transform the mood of doubt and disillusionment with government which now exists in this

country and restore an affirmative attitude toward government
will be an important issue in the 1976 elections.

The complaints about government are familiar: the proliferat-
ing, but seemingly ineffective, programs to deal with real social
problems; the long arm of government regulation which stifles
competition and increases prices to the consumer; and the tentacles
of red tape and paperwork which threaten to strangle us. These
complaints, supported by the sheer size of government (14.6 million
people in federal, state, and local workforces) and cost ($523 billion
on all levels), are the bases for government's low public esteem.

It is really not difficult to see how government got so big. For a
good many years we have followed a fairly systematic approach to
solving our social problems. Once a problem was perceived we established a program and an agency to solve it. If the problem proved
intractable, we threw more federal dollars at it and expanded the
size of the agency. Government did not grow big by accident. It was
nurtured and inflated by real problems, ever-increasing demands
from interested people, and the visions of elected leaders. Whatever
the successes or failures of this approach, many students of government are now saying we must try new approaches.

This antigovernment mood can be easily overstated, however.
No one really wants the government dismantled and everyone ac-
knowledges that government has a positive role to play in defense,
in restraining the excesses of the economy, and in providing a floor
of economic security. A politician learns that not everyone who
decries big government really means it. Some people want better,
not smaller, government. Many may be against big government in
general, but they howl and protest when a government service that
benefits them is reduced or abolished. Many who denounce excessive government regulation are the first to appear in Washington to
urge the Congress to reject proposals to deregulate their industry.

So, as we enter our third century as an independent nation, it is
apparent that we are still debating the basic question of the government's role in the life of the nation. This debate has gone on for two
hundred years and it is likely to continue.

Just what we should do is by no means clear. There is agreement on one point: it will not be easy to find the solutions to the
problems of big government. We have reached the point where we
must redefine what we want government to do and what we want to
pay to get it done.

To accommodate this mood of Americans toward government, it seems to me that certain adjustments are essential. There is no reason to alter the goals we have sought of national and economic security and of a just economic and social order. But our approach to these goals does need to adjust. Our new agenda should concentrate on making government work better, including a ruthless examination of the effectiveness of all federal programs and regular checks on how each department is operating, how effective its job is being done, and what improvements can made. Government reorganization should be given far greater emphasis to bring better management to the whole governmental process. Major problems, now under government direction and control, could be transferred to autonomous agencies run like private businesses. An example is COMSAT, which has successfully operated the international communications system beamed through space satellites. Expiration dates of programs and performance standards should be written into legislation.

Major attention should be given in Congress to strengthening its oversight of government programs, with particular emphasis on performance review and evaluation. Emphasis should be placed on increased productivity and efficiency among government workers. The entire regulatory structure of government should be overhauled to eliminate duplicate expenses and services. A large number of the 1,250 federal advisory boards and commissions should be eliminated. Federal categorical grant programs should be consolidated, and block grants and revenue-sharing programs used. Moves should be made, where possible, to return authority to state and local governments. Every effort should be made to encourage private decisions before resorting to government action. And whenever government acts, it should try to use the private sector as much as possible without depending upon bureaucrats.

Much else could be said, but the key directions are indicated by the words deregulation, competition, consolidation, decentralization, and efficiency.

Basically, what is needed is a lowering of everyone's expectation of what government can do, a more modest approach, and a knowledge that the ability of government to satisfy demands is limited and that those limits are in view. This is not a call for no government at all, but a call for a better appreciation that government should do what it can do well and not do what it does poorly. It means that at a time when we recognize the limitations on government's ability to solve problems, we must make choices about the tasks government should tackle.

CONGRESS AND FOREIGN POLICY

During my thirty-four years in Congress I devoted more attention to foreign affairs than to any other area. But when I started out in Congress I had asked to serve on the Public Works Committee because I thought that would be particularly helpful to my district. The Democratic leadership instead assigned me to the Foreign Affairs Committee. Despite my limited background, two senior members of the committee took a special interest in me: Thomas Morgan of Pennsylvania, the committee chairman, and Ross Adair, an attorney from northern Indiana. Both were equally gracious and supportive, both equally willing to lend a hand to guide me along the way and to kindle my interest in foreign affairs—which has continued to this day. What would strike people today is that one was a Democrat and one was a Republican. But that's the way Congress worked then.

After the Vietnam experience and resurgence of Congress post-Watergate, there was a lot of hope in the early 1970s that Congress would play a stronger role in foreign policy in the years ahead. The record of Congress in the decades since then has been mixed—not as strong as I would have hoped.

For its part, Congress must take proactive steps and show that it can properly balance its dual roles of being both a partner and a critic of the president on basic foreign-policy questions. All House leaders recognized the importance of their consultative relationship with the White House and struggled to get it right. At the same time, the president, as the chief actor in the federal government, needs to be more aggressive in seeking out meaningful advice from Congress. As explained in this newsletter, each branch needs to respect the other and take various steps that could improve the partnership. I've never felt that this consultative relationship between the president and Congress has been worked out satisfactorily. There were some notable successes, such as by Carter on the Panama Canal Treaty and George H. W. Bush on foreign aid after the fall of the Soviet Union, but overall no one president stands out on this. Consultation needs to be more than episodic and to occur more often than just during crises; instead it needs to be sustained and regularized.

February 25, 1976: "Congress and Foreign Policy"
Washington Report
Vol. XI, No. 8

In recent days, a national debate over the role of Congress in the making of American foreign policy has heated up.

This debate recalls the observation of a great constitutional scholar, Edward Corwin, who said that the United States Constitution is an invitation for the president and the Congress to struggle for the privilege of directing American foreign policy.

Today most members of Congress would concede that the president should play the principal role in the foreign-policymaking process, but they would also suggest that the United States has, over the last several decades, gone too far toward putting too much power, including the war-making power, in the hands of one man. In their view, unrestricted presidential power in foreign-policymaking is neither necessary nor tolerable in a free society.

The president and Congress, who both acknowledge the need for a new national partnership in the conduct of foreign policy, are now engaged in an effort to correct that imbalance. Both agree that corrections are needed, but there is little agreement over what correctives are essential.

Congress itself has aided the emergence of the president as the chief foreign-policymaker by its disinterest in decades past over many foreign-policy issues and its occasional outright abdication of powers to the president.

Congressional initiatives in foreign policy—including efforts designed to control the use of American armed forces abroad, to limit military aid and US commitment overseas, to obtain greater access to foreign-policy information, and to specify policy toward particular countries—have produced mixed results, primarily because of Congress's limitations in dealing with foreign-policy issues.

Congress's approach to foreign policy is often sporadic and eclectic, and tends to focus on immediate hot spots, the headline issues with which politicians must grapple. As a whole, Congress tends to lack an ongoing or sustained interest in or commitment to pursuing key foreign-policy trends.

Congress often sees complex foreign-policy issues in terms of a single aspect of a larger problem. For example, on the issue of aid to Turkey, instead of focusing on the totality of our interests and needs throughout the eastern Mediterranean, many members of Congress saw a narrow issue (Turkish opium policy, US-Greek relations, US intelligence facilities in Turkey) and cast their votes accordingly.

In Congress there is no dominant voice in foreign policy. Congress has 535 foreign-policy spokespersons at any given point in time and it is difficult to determine who speaks for Congress on foreign-policy matters. Often Secretary Kissinger doesn't even know whom to call on specific issues. In such a process our greater interests can be easily and quickly lost.

Congress's available instruments to shape foreign policy are blunt and imprecise. The arms, money, and credit taps for foreign states can be increased, slowed, or stopped. These levers, however, do not easily or readily weave into the delicate fabric of diplomatic relationships between governments.

Congress has been unable to determine what its individual or collective responsibility is in handling sensitive material and state secrets provided it by the executive branch. Ex–CIA director William Colby recently said that "almost everything that's been reported to the Congress has been exposed in the press." I do not know whether he is right or not, but the question persists concerning the responsibility of members in the handling of what is considered by some to be confidential information.

These shortcomings of Congress raise serious questions about its ability to help formulate and legislate an effective foreign policy. Nonetheless because of the strong interest of members of Congress in foreign policy, it is safe to say that Congress will continue to be active in foreign affairs.

In the months ahead, there must be greater sensitivity in Congress to its deficiencies in trying to legislate foreign policy, and in the executive branch to the need not to simply touch base with members, or to placate them, on foreign-policy issues. The executive must develop respect for the role of Congress in the formulation of foreign policy and engage in a genuine dialogue with the members of Congress. And Congress must realize that the executive branch needs flexibility in the day-to-day execution of foreign policy.

Hopefully, during this year neither campaign rhetoric nor short-term political need will keep us from progressing toward a more balanced formulation of American foreign policy.

The legislative accomplishments of Congress during the Ford years were modest. Congress got its basic work done, but not much more. The large and more assertive Democratic majorities in the House and Senate often had their own priorities and a different sense of the direction the country should go in. The relations between Congress and the president were civil, but not particularly productive. In less than three years, President Ford vetoed sixty-six bills, far more than Nixon vetoed in his five years in office and almost as many as Reagan did during eight years in office. Despite Ford's intimate knowledge of how Congress works, it was overall not a time of cooperative give and take, working through differences, and finding common ground.

The three years of the Ford presidency were more significant as a time of national healing, when the country, recovering from the trauma of Vietnam and Watergate, was less interested in an activist government than in a respite from too much Washington and too much national drama. Ford generally governed in a nonpartisan, evenhanded way, and he helped bring about a healing of America. Those of us in Congress had a special personal fondness for President Ford, with both Democrats and Republicans pleased that he had succeeded in turning the country around and leaving an important legacy—a system that not only survived but prevailed.

Despite various battles with Congress over legislation, President Ford's affection for the Congress remained undiminished. After the inauguration of his successor was completed and Ford was leaving Washington for the last time in an official capacity, he had his helicopter fly over the Capitol rather than the White House, because he always considered himself a man of the House.

FOUR

THE CARTER YEARS
(1977–80)
Intraparty Discord

THE CARTER PRESIDENCY SHOWED THAT THERE IS A BIG
difference between campaigning and governing, and between coming up
with ideas and getting them through Congress.

Carter was a marvelous campaigner, and he struck just the right tone
as the country was coming out of the Watergate years: lack of pretense,
down-to-earth, a new kind of leader more attuned to average Americans,
even to the point of carrying his own briefcase and luggage. He came across
as someone with strong values, independent, an outsider, not your typical
politician. He had a strong element of integrity about him.

Once elected, Carter was never comfortable with the political process
of Washington. He had campaigned against it when running for president,
emphasizing that he was not part of the system. But once he was there, it
became clear that insider skills—like those possessed by Lyndon Johnson—
are needed to make the system work and get proposals through Congress.

He liked to analyze issues carefully, thoroughly, and comprehensively
with the highly organized mind of a nuclear engineer—which he was. But
he was less skilled at working with Congress. He thought the strength of
his ideas would carry the day, but the 535 members of Congress and especially the powerful committee chairmen, many of whom had decades of
experience and expertise in working on major national and international
issues, felt that they had much to say about the challenges facing the nation.

So one of the most distinguishing features of his presidency was that
it was marked by surprisingly tough relations with Congress, even though
both the House and the Senate were controlled by the Democrats, and by
large margins. No president since has enjoyed margins as large. When

Carter took office in January 1977, Democrats outnumbered Republicans in the House 292 to 143, and in the Senate 68 to 31. Certainly, the country thought, significant accomplishments would be possible.

But with major differences in temperament, background, and legislative priorities, the ties between the Carter team from Georgia and the Democratic leadership in Congress started out poor and didn't get much better over time. Carter was intellectual, driven, ambitious, with a touch of arrogance—if you didn't agree with him you were wrong—while Tip O'Neill was a complete political pro: personable and pragmatic, operating by instinct, superb at networking members. Carter had run his campaign against the Washington establishment, but Tip didn't like that, since he *was* the Washington establishment. Carter's White House staff of Hamilton Jordan, Frank Moore, and Bert Lance just didn't click with Congress. Tip thought they didn't understand how Washington worked, and he didn't particularly like meeting with them.

In the meetings I attended at the White House during this period, it was not that the Carter-O'Neill relationship was antagonistic; it just wasn't a comfortable one. Tip still supported Carter overall and sometimes he would take major steps to come to his rescue, such as using an unusual procedure—an ad hoc committee to circumvent the regular committee review process—to get his energy policy through Congress. But it seemed that Tip was upset about one thing or another with Carter and his team from the first day to the last, and in many ways he had a better working relationship with President Reagan over the years than he had with Carter.

Compounding the difficulties for the president was the fact that since Watergate the office of the presidency had been weakened and the Congress had become more assertive and independent.

Perhaps it was due to the White House's recognition that the president needed to reach out more to members of Congress that I was invited one day to have lunch with him in the Rose Garden. At the time it was not quite clear to me why I was invited, and fairly soon into our lunch it became apparent that the president wasn't quite sure why I was there either. We chatted for a while without much focus, so I decided to ask the president what could be done about inflation, which was raging at that time. He paused, thought about it for a while, then finally said, "It's a bitch." And then we went back to our small talk.

The 95th Congress: Key Facts

- January 4, 1977, through October 15, 1978, during the first two years of the Carter administration
- House of Representatives controlled by the Democrats, 292 to 143
- Senate controlled by the Democrats, 68 to 31 (1 other)
- 634 bills enacted
- Major accomplishments included passing the Tax Reduction and Simplification Act, the Surface Mining Control and Reclamation Act, the Foreign Corrupt Practices Act, the Nuclear Non-Proliferation Act, the Civil Service Reform Act, the Agricultural Trade Act, the Airline Deregulation Act, the Ethics in Government Act, the National Parks and Recreation Act, the Energy Tax Credit Act, and the National Energy Conservation Policy Act; setting up the Department of Energy; and Senate ratification of the Panama Canal Treaty
- Support for President Carter's position in the House: Democrats 68 percent, Republicans 43 percent; in the Senate: Democrats 76 percent, Republicans 53 percent

The 96th Congress: Key Facts

- January 15, 1979, through December 16, 1980, during the last two years of the Carter administration
- House of Representatives controlled by the Democrats, 276 to 157 (2 other)
- Senate controlled by the Democrats, 58 to 41 (1 other)
- 613 bills enacted
- Major accomplishments included passing the Trade Agreements Act, the Emergency Energy Conservation Act, the Chrysler Corporation Loan Guarantee Act, the Depository Institutions Deregulation Act, the Energy Security Act, the Wind Energy Systems Act, the Privacy Protection Act, the Motor Carrier Act

(deregulation), the National Aquaculture Act, the Comprehensive Environmental Compensation and Liability Act (Superfund), and the Paperwork Reduction Act; and setting up the Department of Education
· Support for President Carter's position in the House: Democrats 71 percent, Republicans 41 percent; in the Senate: Democrats 73 percent, Republicans 51 percent

SOME IMPRESSIONS FROM THE INAUGURATION

An inauguration is always a significant time in the rhythm of our national life—a refreshing event that moves past the division of a political campaign to a time of optimism, hope, new energy, and new people. The incoming administration is the start of that change, the start of our national cycle of renewal.

The country was optimistic at the beginning of the Carter presidency. He was a fresh face and had solid values; he was someone the country hoped could get things done and make Washington work for average Americans. His Inauguration Day walk with Mrs. Carter all the way down Pennsylvania Avenue to the White House captured our imagination, and made us think that we had a president who during the next four years would really connect well with the American people.

February 2, 1977: "Some Impressions from the Inauguration"
Washington Report
Vol. XII, No. 5
Numerous impressions from the inaugural ceremonies remain vivid . . . the sea of faces, estimated by crowd experts at 150,000, stretching from the east steps of the Capitol across Capitol Hill to the steps of the Library of Congress and the Supreme Court . . . the proud high school bands strutting along Pennsylvania Avenue for the parade . . . the delight of the crowd of 350,000 as the Carter family walked the entire route of the parade . . . the optimism and good spirits of the people attending the inaugural functions . . .

the striking rendition of "The Battle Hymn of the Republic" by the Atlanta University Center Chorus . . . the particular jubilance of the Georgians celebrating the inauguration of a native son . . . the elaborate plans of the Army to destroy the snow with shovels, trucks, wedges, and even flamethrowers . . . the peddlers with their Jimmy Carter T-shirts, buttons, banners, caps, and peanut key chains and necklaces . . . the crush of people at the inaugural ball at the Mayflower Hotel trying to catch a glimpse of President and Mrs. Carter dancing for a few seconds.

I kept thinking during the inaugural ceremony what a marvelous thing it is that power can pass peacefully from an old to a new president in this country with such a simple and dignified ceremony. For the first time in sixteen years a new president took office without the pain of rejection, resignation, or assassination.

The brief inaugural address by the first president from the Deep South in more than a century was not a political program or even a rallying cry, but a sermon, a call to the American spirit, an appeal for decency and unity. President Carter spoke of his own mistakes, preached of the limitations of the presidency rather than its powers, and rejected offering a new dream, but urged fresh faith in the old dream.

I liked what I heard in his address about fighting wars against poverty and injustice, being aware of the limits of our own resources, being strong but peaceful, strengthening the family, restoring respect for law and government, and seeking arms control.

The theme of his address was that the future of the nation lies in the principles of the past. One senses that his religion is at the center of his life. He wears it naturally. One wonders, however, how these noble principles he annunciated in the address will be applied to the specific problems that await him. I suppose it was not among the more eloquent inaugural addresses, but there were a few phrases that we may remember: "fresh faith in the old dream," "if we despise our own government we have no future," and "a new spirit among us all."

During the inaugural ceremony, I also thought about President Carter's path to the presidency. For two years prior to Inauguration Day he had crisscrossed the country speaking of competent government, outmaneuvering an army of Washington politicians who sought the same job, recognizing better than all of the others the distrust and disillusionment with government which he made a central issue of his campaign, and emphasizing everywhere he went that it was time for healing and the restoration of faith in the simple virtues, the old values, and the basic goodness of the American people.

It was a bittersweet day for President Ford and his family. He had to bite his lip to hold back the tears as President Carter thanked him for all he had done to heal America. He also had to fight his emotions on his last visits to the Oval Office in the White House and to Capitol Hill where he had spent twenty-eight years of his life, and during the brief farewell ceremonies as he departed from Andrews Air Force Base for California. He must also have known that the American people appreciated what he had achieved during the two and a half years of his presidency.

The walk by the Carter family down Pennsylvania Avenue was clearly the highlight of the day. You could just feel the pleasure of the crowd at seeing a president walk among the people, and all the world seemed to stop when the Carters buttoned up Amy's coat. Everywhere people talked about the walk. It was a symbol of the new spirit, a feeling that there was nothing to fear, and that a troubled period in the nation's history had been closed.

But easily the most memorable recollection of the day for me will be the feeling of reconciliation and the extraordinary good humor of the people on Inauguration Day 1977.

HUMAN RIGHTS

President Carter made treating all people decently a centerpiece of his foreign policy, elevating it as no other president had done. His efforts made an important contribution to American foreign policy, and every president has talked about human rights since.

Where human rights fits into American foreign policy remains an enduring question. For Carter it was a top priority. Yet our push for human rights needs to be kept in balance, as economic, strategic, and political considerations can also be important, depending upon each particular situation. And the issue of human rights needs to be raised with delicacy, sometimes with quiet diplomacy, so we don't appear arrogant. Pushing it aggressively can also invite a backlash.

I remember having meetings with Alexei Kosygin when he was premier of the Soviet Union in which he spoke at length about unemployment in the United States, the plight of blacks in America, and our nation's homeless. He had a detailed knowledge of the weaknesses and failures of our system, and skillfully pointed out America's various human rights failures as well.

I was able to make a few strong points about the severe shortcomings of the Soviet system and its repressive and even brutal government. As I reflected on the session, it was tough, civil, illustrating the large unbridgeable gap between us, but I felt that I had given as much as taken and found that I had enjoyed the whole session debating the Soviet Union's preeminent defender.

July 6, 1977: "Human Rights"
Washington Report
Vol. XII, No. 27

The advancement of human rights occupies a central place in President Carter's foreign policy. He has adopted "an undeviating commitment to human rights everywhere."

The policy of outspokenness on human rights is not without its problems. Should the United States make military aid to South Korea dependent on the release of opponents to President Park's regime? Should the United States tell President Marcos of the Philippines that it will not sign a new defense agreement until martial law is lifted? If the United States does not raise its voice against the Philippines and South Korea will it not appear hypocritical when it attacks violations of human rights in South America or South Asia? What steps can the US take to improve the well-being of a Soviet citizen and yet not create undue tension between our two countries?

The dilemma for the United States is to acknowledge that we cannot police the whole world, and that we cannot ignore the obvious power of the United States to improve the condition of people in some areas. In pursuing a human rights policy there are limits to what the United States can achieve and to what the United States can impose upon other nations. The question is really how far the United States can go in promoting human rights without producing undesired results. Americans want a foreign policy which contains a strong moral component, but it is necessary to distinguish which expressions of moral concern are useful and which are not. Americans want to pursue policies which will enhance human rights, but if the only action their government takes is to issue public criticism of other nations, the situation may not improve and could become worse.

The answer to this question involves linkage, that is, the resolution of one issue depends on progress toward the resolution of another. In the conduct of our foreign policy, can we link the help sought from the United States (aid, trade) to the record of the particular country on human rights?

Proponents of a human rights policy, led by the president, make several points. They emphasize the strong support of the American people for human rights. Americans are proud of their democratic heritage and they want to spread democratic values. Most Americans view the United States as a moral force in the world, and they are pleased when its leaders speak forthrightly about human rights and use leverage to advance those rights. Supporters of the president's strong stand on human rights also argue that his outspokenness will not adversely affect resolving most important international agreements. For example, they contend that the Soviets are not likely to allow their annoyance with the president's human rights campaign to deter them from reaching agreements on SALT and other important matters.

Opponents of this view contend that there are sharp limits to what the United States can accomplish by expressing publicly its concern for human rights. By doing so, the United States will only inflame emotion, create unfulfilled expectations, and in the end accomplish very little. They argue that the United States will retain influence in a country only if there is a minimum of confrontation. In their view the Soviets are apt to perceive the human rights offensive, not as an expression of America's moral values, but as a move by the United States to stir up trouble inside their country. They say that improvements in the lives of Soviet citizens are more likely to evolve from forces within the Soviet society under prolonged conditions of reduced tensions than from pressure from the United States for change.

It seems to me that although the president continues to express his concern about the issue of human rights, he has taken a quieter, more conventional approach to the human rights issue in recent weeks. Apparently he is swinging around to the view that more can be accomplished by quiet diplomatic pressures than by public criticism. More and more he seems to be reserving the right to speak out on the issue of human rights without criticizing violators of human rights by name.

My own judgment is that the best way to pursue the course of human rights is not loudly and ostentatiously, but quietly, discreetly, and persistently over an extended period. Certainly the promotion of human rights is a legitimate goal of foreign policy, but it has plenty of pitfalls, and if carried too far, it produces arrogance. If mishandled, it could hurt the US badly; if handled well, it could boost freedom around the world and lift the stature of the US.

So I applaud the policy and urge that we continue to pursue it, but with great care. The question of whether an official statement will improve the situation for repressed people is a hard judgment that has to be made on a case-by-case basis. In most circumstances my guess is that much can be accomplished through quiet diplomacy behind the scenes.

REORGANIZING THE FEDERAL BUREAUCRACY

My interest in reforming the federal bureaucracy began around this time. The federal government is incredibly pervasive and complex, but Americans deserve a government that is effective and efficient, something President Carter recognized well. He successfully reorganized the executive branch when he was governor of Georgia. Now he would tackle the federal bureaucracy.

Carter didn't think about an incremental approach or a partial solution. His engineer's mind didn't work that way. He went for a fundamental overhaul, from top to bottom. Of course, he ran into a political minefield. Reform sounds noncontroversial, but it doesn't take long to learn that it has many powerful opponents. Those who have a vested interest in the status quo, such as agency heads, interest groups, and members of Congress, will really dig in and fight hard against change. President Carter was able to bring about significant successes, including consolidating some agencies and reforming the civil service system, but his accomplishments fell far short of his goals.

July 13, 1977: "Reorganizing the Federal Bureaucracy"
Washington Report
Vol. XII, No. 28

The federal government is a maze of incredible complexity. Nearly everyone complains about its size but few people really realize how big it is. A few statistics are revealing. The federal government

· employs five million, or one in every forty-three, Americans;
· spends an amount equal to about one-fourth of the country's total output of goods and services;
· owns one-third of the country's land;
· occupies 433 million square feet of office space;
· administers over one thousand aid programs through 11 cabinet departments, 59 independent agencies, and 1,240 advisory boards.

Of course, big is not necessarily bad. Defenders of the federal government often point out that the number of federal employees today is not substantially larger than it was ten years ago and that the federal budget is about the same percentage of the gross national product as it was ten years ago. The impact of the federal establishment, however, cannot be measured only by these statistics. The federal government touches every aspect of American life. It manages the economy, provides for the national defense, operates as a global power in an interdependent world, promotes science, and responds to personal problems in thousands of ways by providing entitlements and services to the people.

The agencies and programs of the federal bureaucracy did not just spring up. They were created in response to demands for services from politically mobilized groups within the country. But once established, each agency and program tends to develop a potent constituency of support, composed of key congressmen who fight any effort to eliminate their pet projects, bureaucrats who fight to protect their jobs, and individuals who fight to retain the benefits of a particular agency's programs.

Efforts to control the federal bureaucracy date back to the turn of the century. Every president since Theodore Roosevelt has created a commission to recommend changes to improve the administrative structure of government. Hundreds of recommendations have been made and many of them have been implemented, but many have also been defeated. Attempts to change the system have taken various forms. There have been executive orders, statutes, internal departmental directives, and reorganization plans. Presidents have often succeeded in creating new agencies, but have generally failed to eliminate or consolidate existing agencies.

In light of these facts, the campaign promise of Jimmy Carter to make government reorganization the top priority of his administration takes on special interest. President Carter has promised to reduce the number of federal agencies to two hundred. Massive consolidation of government agencies worked in Georgia and the president thinks that it will work in Washington. The history of reorganization, however, entitles anyone to be skeptical. The problem, of course, is that citizens complain about big government but demand more benefits and services while politicians talk bureaucratic reform but support new programs.

The president's reform proposals include

- a wholesale consolidation of agencies and programs;
- mandated periodic performance reviews which would require government agencies to justify their continued existence;
- a reduction of government regulation, paperwork, and interference in the lives of people;
- a shifting of government responsibilities and functions to private enterprise or to state and local agencies; and
- an increase in revenue sharing and block grant programs to give states and communities greater discretionary power.

The president believes that a principal reason for his election was his campaign pledge to reorganize the executive branch of government. Congress has now given him the general legislative authority he needs to go ahead. My own view is that he, like previous presidents, will run into a political minefield when he tries to use that authority. The pressure against massive bureaucratic change will be great. But the president is proceeding. He has identified four major areas—law enforcement, local economic development, human services, and administration—within which to begin to make government work better. A comprehensive agenda for reorganization is expected to come from the president soon. Under present law the president's reorganization proposals will go into effect sixty days after they are sent to Congress unless either house of Congress disapproves them.

My inclination is to support reorganization proposals. I cannot pledge to support each and every proposal, but I am persuaded that the greatest need of modern government is efficiency. A major overhaul is necessary to achieve purposeful, manageable, and competent federal government. My guess, however, is that the president will require all the support he can get.

THE PANAMA CANAL TREATY

President Carter has often been criticized for not having been able to get much through Congress, but he did an outstanding job in getting Senate ratification of the two parts of the Panama Canal Treaty. He and key people in his administration, primarily ambassador Sol Linowitz, who helped negotiate the treaty, needed to turn around a lot of votes to get the necessary two-thirds, but they were able to get both parts ratified—by a one-vote margin.

The Panama Canal Treaty was not of great interest overall in my district, but it was important for a core set of people who viewed it as simply giving away the canal that we had built. But it was not a difficult question for me; I supported it from the beginning.

I remember one particular public meeting I held at a 4-H building in small Switzerland County at the time the treaty was pending in the Senate. It was a fairly small gathering, maybe twenty-five to thirty people, but I faced a firestorm of opposition to my position. Then a young woman stood up and spoke in favor of the treaty in a knowledgeable and persuasive way, putting it all in the context of broader Latin American politics, and she probably saved me from being run out of town. It turned out she had just returned from being a Peace Corps volunteer in Panama.

The decision to approve the treaty has turned out to be the right one. Our national security was not threatened and our relationship with Latin America improved significantly—as the young woman had told the group in Switzerland County it would.

September 28, 1977: "The Panama Canal Treaty"
Washington Report
Vol. XII, No. 39

The fight over ratification of the Panama Canal treaties may have taken on a symbolic value far more consequential than its intrinsic value. Nonetheless, there are many Americans who are expressing grave doubts and patriotic concern about the proposed treaties and they are entitled to a full, honest, and responsive answer.

Two separate treaties are involved. Under one treaty, which lasts until the end of the century, the United States will retain control of operations and defense, with Panama taking part in both activities. When this particular treaty expires, the United States will still retain important rights. Another separate treaty commits the United States and Panama to maintain the neutrality of the canal indefinitely. This treaty places no limitation on our ability to take such action as may be necessary in the event the canal's neutrality is threatened or violated, and ensures that no foreign country can operate the canal or station troops in Panama after the year 2000.

Under the terms of the treaties, the United States will pay Panama $40 to $50 million annually for revenue from canal tolls, with an additional payment if canal revenues permit. In addition there is a package of loans, loan guarantees, and credits, which are subject to existing statutory procedures. With one small exception, none of these arrangements will require appropriations from the Congress. The treaties will involve little, if any, additional expense for the American taxpayer.

The United States has two principal foreign-policy interests at stake in the fight over ratification of the new treaties: (1) the continued efficient operation, security, and neutrality of the canal, and (2) the maintenance of cooperative and productive relations with the countries of Latin America.

In my judgment a new treaty is the most practical way of protecting and promoting these American interests. If a new treaty is not negotiated, our interests will be jeopardized. The choice for the United States is not between a new treaty and the present treaty, but between a new treaty and the consequences if we insist on maintaining the status quo. Without a new treaty we run the grave risk of harm to the broad range of American political and economic interests in Latin America, including damage to, or even closure of, the canal.

The canal is not simply a problem between the US and Panama. The Panama Canal issue involves far more than our relationship with Panama. All of the countries of Latin America are urging a new treaty and they will judge the outcome of the negotiation as a test of our relationship with them. Without a new treaty which properly provides for the Panamanians' just aspirations and which takes into account our national needs, the US may well find itself in the position of having to defend the canal by force against a hostile population and in the face of widespread, if not universal, condemnation.

Several arguments against the treaties, and the responses, are as follows:

1. The new treaties signify a surrender of US sovereignty and ownership of the canal. The simple answer is that the US never had either sovereignty or ownership of the canal. Unlike the purchase of Alaska or Louisiana, the US in Panama was given certain rights "as if it were the sovereign." Obviously these words would not have been necessary if the US were intended to be sovereign.
2. The new treaties prejudice our national security. The greatest threat to our national security in the Canal Zone would be an insistence on maintaining the status quo. The canal is clearly no longer as vital or as useful as it once was. Our top military leaders have agreed that the new treaties not only preserve, but enhance, our security interests.
3. The new treaties will harm our economic interests. While the canal is still significant economically, its importance has diminished. Larger vessels cannot use it. Only 8 percent of US exports-imports pass through the canal each year.
4. We should not negotiate with the present government of Panama. The present government is fully supported by the people of Panama, and every government of Panama since 1903 has agreed with the present government's position, irrespective of any ideological differences.

The support for the new treaties is impressive. Four US presidents of both political parties have recognized that our nation's
interests require reform of the present treaty. The top military leaders, all the nation's diplomats, responsible conservative business
interests, and organized labor all support the treaties. In my judgment the new treaties ensure the efficient operation of the canal,
and enable the US to protect the canal and to guarantee its neutrality permanently. The new treaties also provide an economic settlement that is fair and reasonable, and establish a firm foundation for
long-term cooperation between the United States and Panama.

AN ASSESSMENT OF THE
CARTER ADMINISTRATION

Reflecting some of Carter's early struggles, the overall tone of this commentary was quite different from that of the one I wrote after Carter's
inauguration. Yet by the summer of 1978, the president was getting more
comfortable in office and was even having some successes. I supported his
major initiatives, and thought he was analyzing things well. He was even
starting to reach out better to Congress.

In this commentary I pointed out that Carter had been fortunate in not
having to confront a major crisis. That was about to change. Major crises
were about to arise over the next two years that would severely strain his
presidency.

**June 14, 1978: "An Assessment of the Carter
Administration"**
Washington Report
Vol. XIII, No. 24
Seventeen months after his presidency began, people are still
asking what Jimmy Carter is really like. Many view him as inexpe-
rienced and ineffective, a politician who flip-flops on the issues and
has difficulty delivering on his campaign promises. Others admire
his personal qualities—a lack of pretense, a willingness to work
hard, and an ability to admit mistakes—and believe that his basic
instincts are sound. My guess is that most people do not yet have a

clear picture of the Carter administration. They do not see where the government is headed. These perceptions may explain the president's low standing in the opinion polls.

Mr. Carter assumed the presidency at a time when that office had been weakened. Vietnam and Watergate had taken their toll in terms of esteem. The persuasive powers of the chief executive had declined and his word was no longer accepted as gospel. The role of the Congress had been fortified with the enactment of several special pieces of legislation. The War Powers Resolution and the Budget Act in particular had resulted in a loss of presidential influence.

American attitudes have also made the challenge of presidential leadership more formidable. The people do not seem to sense crisis in any domestic or international issue. The priorities on the national agenda are not ordered and few people are certain what they want their leaders to do. Lack of urgency and unclear priorities set limits on the president and make the Congress less responsive to his blandishments and more sensitive to political pressures and crosscurrents. The Great Society—with its singleness of purpose and its strong feeling of direction—is gone. The people recognize that there are unsolved problems, but there is nothing approaching a consensus on the proper solutions to them.

In the face of a weakened office and changing American attitudes, expectations have nonetheless remained high. The people want a forceful president and they tend to get baffled when he cannot make progress across the board. They encourage the president to break all political deadlocks and they petition his support for the many causes that interest them. They urge the president to defeat the proposals they do not like and they hold him accountable for failing to control 535 very individual members of Congress. Since the president is blamed for most of the things that go wrong, he has become responsible, in a way, for almost everything. But in our system of government it takes a long time to solve problems, and solutions are politically feasible or they are not solutions at all.

Much of Mr. Carter's difficulty stems from the fundamental characteristics of his presidency. To begin, he himself is a structural reformer with a keen eye for detail who does not like to deal with partial solutions or the superficialities of problems. However, his desire for comprehensive, detailed reforms may not be in tune with the mood of the country today. Though he may yet convince the people of the necessity of his legislative program, so far he has not communicated to them his sense of urgency about the problems he addresses. A second characteristic—the anti-Washington emphasis—was undoubtedly an important factor in Mr. Carter's election, but it has come back to haunt him. As an outsider uneasy with the ways of the capital, he has needlessly crossed swords with influential lawmakers and has been slow to realize that good ideas and honorable intentions are not enough.

I have a feeling that the president has been hesitant to use presidential power, but that he is now settling comfortably into the Oval Office. It seems that he is beginning to master the intricate relationships in Washington and to maneuver among them, as a president must if he is to achieve his goals. He has had a long "shakedown cruise," but he has been blessed with good fortune at least in the sense that he has not had to confront a dangerous crisis. He is now intervening boldly in legislative battles, tackling long-ignored problems, and having some success. After a full year of congressional haggling, the president has the energy bill moving again. He is getting tougher both in his fight against inflation and in his support of fiscal restraint. He is taking on every major foreign-policy issue in the book, regardless of the political consequences. His Middle East arms sales package, his sharp attack on Soviet activities in Africa, his attempt to lift the Turkish arms embargo, and his staunch advocacy of majority rule in South Africa are outstanding examples.

Many people believe that Mr. Carter is indecisive. He seems to be responding to that criticism by making the effort to define his positions, even if the political flak is heavy. There is speculation about a one-term presidency for him, but surely such talk is premature. Presidential historians advise us to watch the crucial third year of a president, and Mr. Carter is still several months away from it.

All of us are entitled to judge a president severely, provided that our judgment is tempered by an appreciation of the circumstances in which he governs and the limitations of his powers.

THE CONGRESSIONAL BUDGET PROCESS

The congressional budget process instituted in the mid-1970s was a significant reform. It increased the power of Congress vis-à-vis the president, and it required Congress to look at its total spending and revenue in a comprehensive way and set priorities, making sure that the individual spending bills would fit together under the overall budget cap, rather than just passing a series of measures and hoping they would add up.

That core idea is a solid one, and the budget process was a success initially. But it soon became clear that the process that developed over time was too complicated, with too many resolutions, deadlines, and votes. My colleagues would often grumble on the way over to the House floor that all we seemed to be doing was taking budget votes. The process overloaded the system. It was more than Congress could handle, and it largely collapsed. Today the congressional budget process is largely ignored, and no replacement is in sight.

At the same time, it's important to recognize that there are limits to what can be achieved through new budget processes and mechanisms. Members of Congress will often look for a procedural solution to a substantive problem, and talking about process reform is easier for members than specifying what programs they would cut. Reforming the budget process can be helpful, but it doesn't go to the heart of the matter. All of the talent and energy might have been better spent trying to resolve the substantive policy question.

October 18, 1978: "The Congressional Budget Process"
Washington Report
Vol. XIII, No. 42

The fourth year of the congressional budget process has been a good one. The process has strongly influenced congressional decisions on spending and taxation. It has made itself felt on the side of restraint and prudence, matching the mood of the people toward the government's management of its fiscal affairs. I have the impression that the process has worked better than most Americans expected.

In response to widespread criticism that legislators failed to take an overall look at government spending and revenue, Congress passed the Congressional Budget and Impoundment Control Act of 1974. Basically, the act set up a mechanism through which Congress could consider all money bills together. No longer would Congress pass all manner of spending and revenue bills, letting the president worry about how the bills added up.

The congressional budget process is fairly simple in outline. Early each year the legislative committees of Congress prepare estimates of how much spending they anticipate for the coming fiscal year. The House and Senate budget committees review these estimates and then draft a resolution establishing spending and revenue targets for each major area of government operation. The targets have to be approved by the entire Congress before May 15, and only then may appropriations bills be debated. The targets exert a powerful influence on all the appropriations and tax measures that are eventually enacted into law.

Once the initial targets are in place, the budget committees move on to the second phase of the process. By late summer they draft a second resolution which takes into account any changes in government policy or the economy that may have taken place since the beginning of the year. The entire Congress must approve the second resolution before October 1, the start of the new fiscal year. This resolution puts a cap on total spending and a floor under total revenue.

There is ample evidence that the process has made itself felt. Because of it a tuition tax credit bill was rewritten, impact aid to education was trimmed, and a farm bill was defeated. In addition, the president's urban policy was sidetracked and his welfare reform proposal was shelved. Also, spending for social programs was held down as a percentage of the budget. A few more bills will very likely feel the bite of the process before the year is out.

It is still too early for final judgments, but it seems to me that one positive result of the process will be modest growth in the budget. For fiscal year 1979 the president proposed outlays of $500.2 billion. Congress, however, will only allow outlays of $487.5 billion. A projected deficit of $60.6 billion will drop 36 percent to $38.8 billion, the lowest in five years. The significance of this slowdown in spending is difficult to gauge, but it could represent the end of government attempts to meet the demands of every special-interest group.

There are other positive results, too. Money bills are moving through Congress faster, and spending and taxation are being programmed more rationally. The process has had a restraining effect on legislative committees, has made members of Congress more thrifty, and has forced everyone to think about the budget as a whole. The process has also made it easier to assess the budgetary consequences of bills. There is much less confusion about cost estimates, the wisdom of programs, and the legislative alternatives that are available.

In spite of all these positive results, it would be premature to pronounce the process an unqualified success. It has had the advantage of taking hold at a time when the antispending mood is strong in both the Congress and the country. Behind this mood is rising anxiety about inflation, but should inflation abate and a severe recession occur the Congress could reverse itself and return to a less conservative policy of economic stimulus. For the time being, however, such a reversal is not likely. Congress will continue to respond to the people's demand for austere budgets and lower taxes.

Whether times are good or bad there is a continuing danger that the process will be undermined by popular pressure for spending. This pressure is always great, and the process does little to lessen it. The fact that Congress now reviews the budget as a whole will not stop thousands of special-interest groups from demanding the specific programs that suit their needs.

Tough fights lie ahead. There will undoubtedly be efforts to weaken or dismantle the congressional budget process. While it is no panacea for the ills of runaway government, the process is powerful medicine. Abandoning it now would be a serious mistake.

A GOOD WORD FOR AMERICA

This commentary captures and addresses the mood of discontent in the country at that time, which President Carter would speak about fairly soon afterward in his July "malaise" speech. His speech didn't go over particularly well. Some viewed it as blaming the nation for its problems and not offering leadership. He followed it up a few days later by dismissing several of his department heads, which contributed to the sense of disarray in his administration.

In broader terms, the president's speeches were on the pessimistic side and he was unwittingly setting the stage for Ronald Reagan, who would win the election the next year with his positive, "morning in America" approach, which the public greatly preferred to a pessimistic or even realistic approach. That was the chief impact of Carter's speech.

During my years in Congress I frequently wrote commentaries on the mood of Americans. As a politician I thought it was most important to know the overall mood of the voters, rather than just pay attention to what surveys were saying about their views on particular issues. This commentary also reflects my view then—and now—that despite its problems, America is still a great country, and I have repeated its last line again and again.

March 14, 1979: "A Good Word for America"
Washington Report
Vol. XIV, No. 11

There is a mood of discontent among the American people today.

The reasons for the mood are understandable: inflation surges ahead; the job market is tight; the family and other important institutions are under attack; a lack of confidence in public officials makes virtually every government action suspect; threats to our security and well-being crop up almost daily in some part of the world. Our seeming inability to cope with the difficulties that surround us leads some of us to believe that America is slipping. We have the sense that we have lost our bearings and no longer control our destiny.

No sensible person will deny that we have serious problems as a nation. Likewise, no sensible person can fail to have questions about our ability to cope with problems. We must realize that the preeminence of America among nations is not written in the stars. At the same time, however, we should be sensitive to the dangers of shortsightedness and misplaced emphasis. It seems to me that we should not ask what is wrong with our country unless we also ask what is right with it. As I survey the American scene, I am not persuaded that we are on a downhill course. There is a lot more right than wrong with America.

America has always had serious problems. The struggle to found a new nation, the Civil War, the early trade union movement, the Great Depression, World War II, the war in Korea, the civil rights movement, and the war in Vietnam are just a few episodes that sorely tried and tested the American people. In each instance the voices of gloom and defeat were raised, but the nation persevered and eventually prospered. Each episode had its costs, but the country drew on its experience and grew in knowledge and stature.

We have met grave challenges, survived them, and bettered ourselves in the process.

We need not wait for future events to renew our confidence in America. National accomplishments of great significance are all around us. We sometimes forget that, despite inflation and other economic problems, we are more prosperous than ever before. We forget too that, despite too much bureaucracy and occasional dishonesty, our government has done more than any other to protect the freedom of its citizens. Our military power is second to none, and we are better educated and healthier than we have been at any time in the past. I mention these things only to underscore the remarkable strengths that America has.

Many people have suggested that the mood of discontent is a sign of apathy or, what is worse, total disillusionment. Some have even called it a symptom of sickness. I understand what these people are saying, but I do not see things exactly as they do. To me, the discontent is mainly an indication that Americans are not pleased with the status quo. We perceive a gap between reality and hope, and we want to change the reality so that it will conform more closely to the hope. Such a desire for change is healthy. I like the idea that Americans will not be satisfied until achievement and expectation are brought closer together. I reject the diagnosis of America as an indifferent, disillusioned, or sick society. I would not want to live in a nation where the people did not restlessly search for a better life.

There are other reasons why I have confidence in America. First, I see that the motives of the people are generous and good. Americans are honestly grappling with the right questions. We are asking ourselves about the kind of nation we ought to have, how we can reconcile the sometimes conflicting principles of liberty and equality, and what our proper role in the world should be. More often than not we have defined America in terms of commitment to the less fortunate among us. On the whole we have done a good job of balancing personal freedom with equal opportunity. Traditionally we have acted as defenders of democracy and human rights in the world. The mistakes we make are of the head, not of the heart.

Second, America has an enormous advantage that cannot be easily measured by objective standards. No matter how much discontent there is, America is a nation where initiative and accomplishment are rewarded. In this climate the intelligence and vitality of the people have been released for productive purposes. I have never ceased to be impressed with our foremost natural resource: creative and alert individuals who are willing to work hard and make sacrifices on behalf of us all.

Finally, much of the discontent is due to a heightened awareness of problems. Communications technology is so advanced today that it bombards us with far more information than we can absorb. We just do not have the time to put all the data into perspective. Trouble and strife have always existed in the world, but they are much more apparent to us now. This heightened awareness of problems must be considered a good thing even though it can cause pessimism.

In sum, I conclude that America, in spite of its problems, is a pretty nice place to live.

REFLECTIONS ON THE GASOLINE SHORTAGE

Public meetings with constituents tend to be a time of fairly informal, relaxed give and take, but they were contentious, even angry, when the topic was the gasoline shortage in the summer of 1979. This crisis hit Americans hard, jeopardizing everything from their vacation plans to simply getting to work, and the emotions expressed in my public meetings were the closest thing I had seen to a panic.

To his credit, Carter from the start of his presidency clearly recognized that energy policy presented a major challenge for his administration, and he gave it high priority. But his plan was complex, with more than a hundred major provisions, and it took Congress until the final year of his presidency to pass the Energy Security Act. Carter put much of the emphasis on reducing consumption, but he also understood the importance of expanding traditional sources of energy as well as developing alternative sources, especially solar energy. Our energy problems were caused by many factors and needed to be solved in multiple ways and, unfortunately for Carter's presidency, over a period of many years.

July 18, 1979: "Reflections on the Gasoline Shortage"
Washington Report
Vol. XIV, No. 29

The gasoline shortage dominated nearly every discussion I had with Hoosiers during my recent week-long visit to the Ninth District.

In scores of meetings and conversations in all parts of the Ninth District, the number and variety of questions on the gasoline shortage revealed a level of frustration near the breaking point. Some people were angry, others puzzled, still others disbelieving. Confusion was rampant, and there were deep divisions of opinion as to why the United States should be caught in the grip of a serious supply squeeze. Some people saw the shortage as a hostile action against the United States by the oil-exporting nations. Others perceived an inept, bungling government at the heart of the problem. Still others blamed the news media for inciting panic. Then too I heard the rumors of conspiracy: oil trucks were sent back and forth across the country without unloading, oil tankers were standing idle in coastal waters or were dumping cargoes at sea, oil storage terminals were full to overflowing, and oil companies were plotting to push prices higher by further restricting supplies.

The uneasy mood of the people and the tough questions it prompts pose formidable difficulties for a member of Congress. A congressman has no more important task than to try to explain to his constituents his understanding of the complex factors in which our present problems, such as energy, are rooted. In one public gathering after another, I knew that I had my work cut out for me. The following are a few of the points I made as I attempted to give Hoosiers a clear explanation of the gasoline shortage.

The course of events that led to the gasoline shortage is fairly well understood. In 1978, oil companies began reducing their inventories of oil to avoid high carrying costs. However, they had miscalculated short-term supply and demand. The weather in the fall of 1978 was mild and resulted in more travel, while the winter was severe and caused heavy demand for home heating oil. The government was transferring oil to the strategic petroleum reserve, a process which put even greater pressure on supplies. On top of it all, oil companies were producing less from their domestic wells. Events abroad also had a major impact. A revolution in Iran first slowed and then halted that nation's oil exports, but other oil-exporting countries did not completely compensate for the loss. When the government failed to explain these disturbing circumstances, both domestic and foreign, the public reacted by panic-buying, tank-topping, and, in some instances, hoarding.

It is apparent that these events alone do not provide a satisfactory explanation of the gasoline shortage. A worldwide deficit of only 3 percent in oil supply should not cause the kind of dislocation and inconvenience that Americans have experienced. An additional factor behind the shortage has been the incompetent performance of the government. The allocation program, an effort to distribute a scarce supply fairly, created a huge class of "priority consumers" (in defense, farming, etc.), diverted gasoline from cities to small towns, and ordered big deliveries to vacation areas which were less crowded because of changes in travel patterns. In short, the allocation program put the gasoline where the people were not. Other government blunders made things worse. Jobbers took advantage of government regulations and sent gasoline to the spot market, where it commanded a higher price. Refiners were urged to stay out of the spot market, but then they were given the go-ahead. They were told to build up stocks of home heating oil, but then the emphasis was shifted to production of gasoline. Through it all, the government failed to release accurate information on what was happening and what it was doing.

The most painful aspect of the gasoline shortage, at least for the consumer, has been the steep rise in prices at the pump. The average price of gasoline has increased by one-third (up twenty cents a gallon) since the beginning of the year. Oil price hikes account for seven to twelve cents of the rise, and much of the rest is due to profit-taking allowed under government regulations. Without question, there has been some price-gouging. The Department of Energy estimates that roughly one-half of the retail dealers audited in recent months have overcharged their customers. For some people, the shortage has been a financial bonanza.

The events of the past few months have led me to several conclusions. First, our energy problem is real. Most available analyses show the worldwide oil supply about 1.5 million barrels a day below demand. The issue is how best to lessen the impact of the shortfall. Second, the gasoline shortage will not be painlessly resolved. There will be no simple solution to it. The issue is how best to ensure that burdens are equally shared. Third, the efforts of both government and business have intensified the gasoline shortage. A series of mistaken decisions has caused a manageable problem to get out of hand. Fourth, and finally, we have to act now if we want to prevent more trouble later. We must produce more oil at home, conserve it more carefully, and develop alternative sources of energy, such as gasohol and synthetic fuels.

THE HOSTAGE CRISIS WORSENS

The Iranian hostage crisis was among the most important events of the Carter presidency. In the meetings I attended during this time, it seemed that the hostage situation dominated any conversation with the president. What we could do to get the hostages out of Iran became an obsession with Carter and with the country. The hostages ended up being held for 444 days, and Carter's inability to resolve the crisis, along with a failed rescue attempt in April 1980, basically meant the end of his presidency.

Members of Congress were upset not only with the utter failure of the rescue attempt, but also with the fact that they weren't consulted beforehand. At that time I was chairman of the Europe and Middle East Subcommittee, and I wasn't advised about the plan. But I also didn't think I should have been. This was an operational, tactical matter, and it seemed to me that the utmost secrecy was appropriate. I am more concerned that members of Congress should be consulted on broad decisions about American foreign policy.

In this commentary I mentioned the wide range of economic and political steps the president was taking to put pressure on Iran, and I indicated my support for these steps. I should have stated a caveat more clearly. While I supported almost all of the tough steps the president took, I did not favor breaking off diplomatic relations with Iran. That's always the natural response in a crisis, but I don't think it is productive. We need to retain contact with our enemies, not just our friends. We can't make peace just by talking to our friends. Cutting off channels of communication shuts off our ability to negotiate and try to work things out. Over the years I have often returned to this theme, with limited success.

April 30, 1980: "The Hostage Crisis Worsens"
Washington Report
Vol. XV, No. 18

The United States faces a worsening crisis in Iran, where fifty Americans have been held hostage since last November. The full effects of our aborted rescue mission are still unfolding, and they may not become evident for several days yet. The resignation of Secretary of State Cyrus Vance appears to be just one. Hoosiers share my concern about the situation. They deeply regret the loss of life, and they deplore the continued imprisonment of our diplomatic personnel in violation of every principle of international law and human decency.

Since the beginning of the crisis, President Carter has taken many economic and political steps to secure the hostages' safe release. He has ceased the sale of all military equipment and spare parts to Iran, canceled deliveries of some $300 million in military equipment bound for Iran, stopped all our purchases of Iranian oil, frozen all Iranian assets in this country, set in motion procedures to deport Iranian students not studying in accordance with the terms of their visas, and broken diplomatic relations with Iran, expelling all its diplomats. In addition, Mr. Carter has initiated official economic sanctions prohibiting exports, except for food and medicine, from the United States to Iran, blocked all Iranian imports into the United States, inventoried claims against Iran and Iranian assets with an eye to paying reparations to the hostages and their families, invalidated almost all visas issued to Iranians for future entry into this country, halted all but a few financial transactions between Americans and Iranians, outlawed the use of American passports for travel to Iran, and closed American offices of Iranian airlines and oil and gas companies.

I approve of these steps, and I believe that they are beginning to have a serious impact on Iran. That nation has been hurt economically, and it has been isolated within the international community. I also approve of Mr. Carter's efforts to free the hostages through diplomatic and private channels. In my view, no effort should be spared in this regard. I welcome and support the decision of our allies to impose their own economic and political sanctions on Iran. The sanctions will be implemented in mid-May, and their effects will be felt shortly thereafter. If all the measures I have mentioned fail to secure the hostages' safe release, however, we must consider all remaining economic, political, and military options open to us. Included are the embargo of exports of food and medicine, the interruption of communications, further commando raids, and the mining of Iranian ports.

It has been evident since the beginning of the crisis that military measures might become necessary. We have known that the risks of taking such measures include extreme jeopardy to the hostages' lives, further disruption of the oil supplies of our allies, the generation of anti-American hostility in other Muslim nations, and the possibility that the Soviet Union will gain influence in Iran and ultimately the entire Persian Gulf. But there are also risks inherent in the failure to use military force. That Iran might escape punishment for its misdeeds would humiliate the United States and reduce its power abroad. It would make the United States seem helpless in the face of provocation. The United States would pay a heavy price if it did not preserve its reputation for protecting its citizens and interests. If another military move is called for, the mining of Iranian ports appears to be the least dangerous but most immediately rewarding option for us.

I understand the pressures on the president to engage in military action, and I fervently wish that our rescue effort had succeeded. The mission's failure exacted a heavy cost: the lives of eight brave American soldiers. Continuation of the mission in the circumstances could have resulted in a catastrophe for everyone, however.

I remain deeply worried about the well-being of the hostages, especially since the failed rescue mission. While the conditions of their captivity could be much better, recent visits to them indicate that they appear unharmed and are adequately fed. We should do everything we can to assure their safety and continued well-being, and we should be as helpful as possible to their families. We should be planning now for ways to ease their return to normal life at home. With my support, a bill has been introduced in Congress to give the hostages and their families a broad range of financial benefits.

It is clear that the hostages have become embroiled in the domestic politics of a country rapidly approaching chaos. The hostages have in fact become pawns in a struggle for political control of Iran. Throughout the crisis there has been, in effect, no legally constituted authority in Iran that has been both able and willing to resolve differences by peaceful negotiation. At times it seemed to us that such an authority was emerging, and during those times we held back in order to see what would result. Nothing has resulted, so more action against Iran is in order. In the process of trying to deal with Iran's bickering religious and civilian leaders, we have exhausted many avenues of relief. We must continue to press ahead insistently, not allowing the failure of our rescue mission and the sorrow we feel to paralyze our resolve to act.

Too much is at stake to give up.

DEREGULATION

President Carter did have significant success with his deregulation effort. He wanted to reduce or eliminate detailed federal regulations for a wide variety of industries that controlled everything from who could provide phone service to what prices airlines could charge. Government regulation began for good reasons and it often provided important protections for Americans, such as ensuring that the medicine we take is tested for safety, the water we drink is not contaminated, and the money we deposit is protected in case of bank failures. Yet by the late 1970s it was increasingly recognized that federal regulation had gone too far, and it was even a topic brought up frequently by constituents in my public meetings back home. Carter's deregulation effort made a difference by spurring the competitiveness of our industries and reducing costs for consumers. In the airline industry, for example, deregulation changed air travel from something that was mainly for the elites to something that most Americans could afford.

Deregulation is largely a question of balancing the need to protect the American people from harm against the need to allow flexibility in the private sector. Some of the deregulation efforts of recent years went too far, such as further deregulation of the financial sector, which contributed to the economic meltdown toward the end of the George W. Bush presidency. Yet most of the regulatory changes made during the Carter years have generally been considered beneficial and they went a long way toward fueling our nation's economic growth in the decades that followed.

August 20, 1980: "Deregulation"
Washington Report
Vol. XV, No. 34

There is a recurring theme in my contacts with residents of southern Indiana: Hoosiers want less government interference in their lives and less government regulation of the economy. Major steps have been taken in the past few years to do just those things. I consider this trend toward deregulation one of the most significant developments in government today. Several important sectors of the economy are undergoing gradual deregulation. The record shows some modest success even though the deregulation effort itself is complex and the opposition of the groups who benefit from regulation is strong.

The drive to reduce the economic regulation of various industries is supported by those who prefer the efficiency of competition and reliance on the forces of the marketplace to the mandates of the government. The premise behind deregulation is simple: a naturally competitive industry will perform better than a government-controlled one.

Economic reality has spurred the effort to deregulate, in three basic ways. First, the large cost of compliance with regulation has undoubtedly added to the rate of inflation. Second, it is likely that opening an industry to all newcomers will increase overall pressures for higher productivity and lower prices. Third, deregulation is an appropriate response to specific changes in economic conditions. Some regulatory structures are obsolete because the problems they were formed to address have been eliminated. Others have been left behind by technological advances in such industries as communications.

Today people are discussing the quality of regulation, as well as the quantity of it. New approaches are being applied to regulations to evaluate their effectiveness: if the costs of regulation are excessive when compared to the benefits, avoid imposing regulation; if the marketplace is working reasonably well, cut back on existing regulation.

Congress has recently taken up landmark initiatives to deregulate several industries to various degrees. The common threads linking these initiatives are more replacement of government control with competition, easier entry into the market for newcomers,

---

and greater flexibility in rate setting so that prices fluctuate with demand. The following are noteworthy:

Airline Deregulation: With a lifting of many government restrictions in 1978, the airlines were the first of the transportation industries to be deregulated. This action, completed by 1985, takes the government out of the business of regulating the routes airlines could fly and the rates they could charge. There are signs that the deregulation is effective. Average fares have remained well below the increase in the cost of living, and the airlines have realized higher profits and improved productivity.

Trucking Deregulation: Last month Congress enacted a trucking deregulation bill. Regulated by the Interstate Commerce Commission (ICC) since the 1930s, the trucking industry will be freed of many of the regulations that inhibit fuel-saving and efficient operation. The new law also makes it easier for new trucking companies to enter the business, and gives companies more freedom to raise or lower freight rates. It is estimated that substantial reductions in shipping costs will result.

Financial Institution Deregulation: Under a new law passed just this year, consumers will earn more on their passbook accounts as the ceilings on interest rates are gradually lifted, and then eliminated entirely over the next six years. Consumers may benefit as well from the continuation of services currently offered by financial institutions including automatic fund transfers and NOW accounts.

Railroad Deregulation: Under almost total ICC regulation since 1887 and faltering financially with a collective rate of return on activities of less than 1 percent during the last few years, the railroad industry is the focus of a major deregulation move. Under consideration are provisions to exempt many rate increases from ICC supervision, except where there is no effective competition, and to allow railroads to make rate, route, and service decisions based on market conditions without long regulatory delays.

Communications Deregulation: The communications industry has been swept by technological change, but regulation of the industry has served to curb innovation and efficiency. Both the House and Senate are considering bills which would open up long-distance telephone services to competition and eliminate arrangements that discourage innovation.

> The success of deregulation is not guaranteed, particularly not in today's rapidly changing world. However, in my view, deregulation is often worthwhile precisely because of the inability of government agencies to predict tomorrow's technology and to control change. A decentralized marketplace, freed of excessive regulation, is the most powerful, resilient, and flexible system available to produce and allocate the goods and services we all need.

I liked President Carter. He was a good man, and I admired him in many respects. He had good intentions and solid judgment, and he was able to analyze complex issues well. Where he fell short was in implementation and the ability to bring the country along with him. He was a highly principled person, frequently tackling issues and proposing solutions according to what he thought was important and right, regardless of the political consequences. And he was strong willed: if he thought something was the right thing to do, Congress should just do it. His approach was more successful in his postpresidency activities, where his independent style worked better. Carter's ex-presidency has been longer than anyone else's, and he set the standard for conduct of a former president, with remarkable achievements in disease prevention, conflict resolution, and promotion of democracy after leaving office.

Although Carter is generally considered by historians to have been only a moderately successful president, his was by no means a failed presidency. He had solid accomplishments—the Panama Canal Treaty, a new national energy policy, a focus on human rights, the Camp David Accords, and the deregulation of key industries. There were no wars during his presidency, and not a single American soldier died in combat during his four years in office.

Yet the benefits of some of his successes as president, such as his energy policy and the Panama Canal Treaty, were not seen by the voters immediately. And while other efforts like emphasizing human rights or deregulation or reforming the federal bureaucracy are important, they are not the kinds of issues people will cast their vote on when there are overriding pocketbook issues like high inflation and high gasoline prices, or when there is a major blow to national prestige like the Iranian hostage crisis and the failed rescue attempt. Carter was hit with complex, knotty problems, and he had more than his share of bad luck. Despite his good intentions and his considerable efforts, Americans were losing faith in the future, and President Carter was unable to achieve the goal he stated in his inaugural address of enabling "our people to be proud of our government once again."

For its part, the more assertive and more independent post-Watergate Congress was never able to work well enough with President Carter to produce a notable legislative record. Despite being of the same party, they had different priorities. On economic policy, for example, Carter wanted to fight inflation while Congress was more interested in going after high unemployment. While Carter wanted to balance the budget, congressional leaders wanted new programs. There were different approaches to issues and frequent squabbles between the Democratic president and the Democratic-controlled Congress.

The voters were not pleased with the modest accomplishments of Congress, and its public approval rating fell from 40 percent early in the Carter presidency to around 20 percent later in his term. They showed their displeasure in the November 1980 election by shifting control of the Senate back to the Republicans, the first time since the mid-1950s that the Republicans controlled either the House or the Senate. That significantly changed the political landscape, and, combined with a new Republican president, meant that major changes would lie ahead.

FIVE

THE REAGAN YEARS
(1981–88)
Letting the Democratic Process Work

WHEN RONALD REAGAN BECAME PRESIDENT THERE WAS SOME skepticism among Washington insiders about how well the administration of this actor and two-term governor would do. But historians looking back over the years give his presidency fairly high marks.

Reagan had strongly held conservative beliefs, but it always seemed to me that he was more pragmatic than is generally recognized. In his first inaugural address, he talked about government being the problem rather than the solution, but he signed every appropriations bill funding the government and he didn't try to abolish any federal departments. Earlier in his career he had denounced Medicare as socialism, but as president he did not try to repeal it and instead tried to protect it. He called the Soviet Union "the evil empire," but he did not aggressively challenge it and shifted to a "trust, but verify" approach. He wanted steep reductions in income taxes, but realized that he went too far with his first tax bill and corrected course by supporting a large tax hike.

Reagan certainly was not as deeply involved in policy matters as Carter was. He seemed uncomfortable discussing policy with members of Congress without the help of note cards, and he relied heavily on cabinet members to lay out the administration's positions. But he was generally more engaged politically than Carter, recognizing the importance of contacts—including informal meetings—with members of Congress.

Reagan's management style was to delegate many matters to staff, which sometimes got him into trouble. It was his staff who came up with the plan for Iran-Contra, which became the biggest threat to his presidency. And during his first campaign, his staff apparently was involved in making contact with the Iranians to make sure that the American hostages wouldn't be released just before the November election, so Carter would not get a major election-eve boost. I was involved in both the Iran-Contra investigation and the "October Surprise" investigation, and I found the extensive powers delegated to Reagan's staff disturbing.

The key Democratic leader during most of the Reagan years was House Speaker Tip O'Neill. He was a genuine FDR liberal, with strong views about the positive role of government—that it can make a major difference in people's lives. That was, of course, quite different from Reagan's view, so there was a large gulf to be bridged. Tip's affable personality helped. Once when I was upset with some decision he had made, I went down to his office to see him. He was meeting with some of his Massachusetts constituents at the time, and he introduced me to the group and then started to talk to them about what an outstanding member of Congress I was, giving me all kinds of compliments. By the time he was finished, I had completely forgotten why I was so upset. It was difficult to get mad at Tip. He certainly was a strong Democratic partisan, but he had a personality that could click with Reagan's, and personalities make a big difference in politics. When two experienced politicians work together, they can usually resolve an issue.

Reagan was also fortunate in coming along at a time when the Republicans were looking for a hero, much as the Democrats had FDR and JFK. The Republicans had Lincoln, but he was from the distant past. So the Republican establishment rallied behind Reagan and defended him intensely right from the beginning, which benefited him greatly.

The Reagan years were a time of political realignment in Congress, a shift to the right, and Reagan had a solid block of southern Democrats to vote with him on key issues. Reagan's electoral count margins were very high: he beat Carter in 1980 by 489 to 49, and Walter Mondale in 1984 by 525 to 13. Although the Democratic leaders in Congress strongly opposed many of the president's proposals, and fought hard against them, they also recognized that the voters had spoken, and they did not block the process if the president was able to round up a majority of votes. There was nothing like the level of obstructionism we have seen in recent Congresses.

From the meetings I was in at the White House, my overall sense was that Reagan was more interested in communication than in policymaking. In the policy meetings I attended he seemed detached, generally saying very little beyond opening courtesies and then turning the discussion over to his National Security Advisor or one of his cabinet secretaries. What did interest him was communicating themes, positions, and even feelings to the American people. Even in Congress, when I was with him before he spoke to a group in the Capitol, he wanted to know where the cameras were. So I've tended to see him more as a communicator than a policymaker. I often wondered how he could be so detached from the process and yet have the impact he did.

I once met with a group of older women in southern Indiana and I asked them what they liked about President Reagan. One of the women responded, "I like the way he treats Nancy." She was right; the president always treated his wife with great courtesy. I learned then that American presidents don't gain favor with the American people solely by passing legislation or getting treaties ratified. There are other values in life beyond that.

Reagan came across as a likable person and he had an extraordinary ability to connect with the American people—both of which proved to be major assets during the ups and downs of the eight years of his presidency.

The 97th Congress: Key Facts
- January 5, 1981, through December 23, 1982, during the first two years of the first Reagan administration
- House of Representatives controlled by the Democrats, 243 to 192
- Senate controlled by the Republicans, 53 to 46 (1 other)
- 473 bills enacted
- Major accomplishments included passing the Economic Recovery Tax Act, the Omnibus Budget Reconciliation Act of 1981, the Education Consolidation and Improvement Act, the Voting

Rights Act Amendments of 1982, the Small Business Innovation Development Act, the Tax Equity and Fiscal Responsibility Act, the Job Training Partnership Act, the Boland Amendment restricting aid to the Contras, the Garn–St. Germain Depository Institutions Act, the Surface Transportation Assistance Act, and the Nuclear Waste Policy Act

· Support for President Reagan's position in the House: Democrats 45 percent, Republicans 71 percent; in the Senate: Republicans 81 percent, Democrats 49 percent

The 98th Congress: Key Facts

· January 3, 1983, through October 12, 1984, during the last two years of the first Reagan administration
· House of Representatives controlled by the Democrats, 269 to 166
· Senate controlled by the Republicans, 54 to 46
· 623 bills enacted
· Major accomplishments included passing the Social Security Amendments of 1983, the Martin Luther King Jr. holiday, the Child Support Enforcement Amendments of 1984, the Retirement Equity Act of 1984, the Voting Accessibility for the Elderly and Handicapped Act, the Comprehensive Crime Control Act, the Veterans Health Care Act, the Cable Communications Policy Act, and the Semiconductor Chip Protection Act
· Support for President Reagan's position in the House: Democrats 34 percent, Republicans 69 percent; in the Senate: Republicans 79 percent, Democrats 52 percent

The 99th Congress: Key Facts

· January 3, 1985, through October 18, 1986, during the first two years of the second Reagan administration
· House of Representatives controlled by the Democrats, 252 to 182 (1 other)
· Senate controlled by the Republicans, 53 to 47
· 664 bills enacted

· Major accomplishments included passing the Gramm-Rudman-Hollings Balanced Budget Act, the Food Security Act, the Consolidated Omnibus Budget Reconciliation Act (COBRA), the Firearms Owners' Protection Act, the Federal Employees' Retirement System Act, the Department of Defense Reorganization Act, the Safe Drinking Water Act Amendments of 1986, the Superfund Amendments and Reauthorization Act of 1986, the Tax Reform Act, the Anti-Drug Abuse Act, the Age Discrimination in Employment Act, and the Immigration Reform and Control Act
· Support for President Reagan's position in the House: Democrats 29 percent, Republicans 69 percent; in the Senate: Republicans 85 percent, Democrats 38 percent

The 100th Congress: Key Facts

· January 6, 1987, through October 22, 1988, during the last two years of the second Reagan administration
· House of Representatives controlled by the Democrats, 258 to 177
· Senate controlled by the Democrats, 55 to 45
· 713 bills enacted
· Major accomplishments included passing the Water Quality Act, the Stewart B. McKinney Homeless Assistance Act, the Balanced Budget and Emergency Deficit Control Reaffirmation Act, the Malcolm Baldrige National Quality Improvement Act, the Civil Rights Restoration Act, the Worker Adjustment and Retraining Notification Act, the Japanese Americans Reparations Act, the Omnibus Trade and Competitiveness Act, the Family Support Act, and the AIDS Amendments of 1988; setting up the Department of Veterans Affairs; and Senate ratification of the Intermediate-Range Nuclear Forces Treaty
· Support for President Reagan's position in the House: Democrats 27 percent, Republicans 63 percent; in the Senate: Democrats 45 percent, Republicans 70 percent

PRESIDENT REAGAN LOOKS AT SOCIAL SECURITY

President Reagan's first year in office got off to a strong start as he success-fully pushed through Congress his key proposals for domestic spending cuts, increases for defense, and income tax reductions. But that momentum was halted midyear by his decision to try to cut back Social Security. The Democrats, led by Tip O'Neill, hit him hard for cutting back retirement benefits for ordinary working people after he had just gotten through Con-gress large tax breaks for the wealthiest Americans.

The public response to his proposal was overwhelmingly negative, and it was a big factor in turning the tide back to the Democrats in the 1982 congressional elections. After the elections were over, Reagan and O'Neill in early 1983 were able to work out a balanced package of Social Security benefit cuts and tax increases which rescued the system and improved its financial outlook for many years to come. The rescue package passed Congress with broad bipartisan support. It was one of the most significant accomplishments during the Reagan years.

At the time of this newsletter I was keenly aware of how difficult it would be politically to change or reform Social Security. And in the years since it has become even harder, as Social Security has become known as the "third rail" of American politics—too controversial to touch. This pres-ents policymakers today with a formidable challenge, and it also makes the passage of the 1983 rescue package all the more remarkable. That package showed that the third rail of American politics could be touched without devastating political consequences if done in a thoughtful and balanced way—a lesson worth remembering as the soaring cost of entitlements will need to be addressed in the future.

May 27, 1981: "President Reagan Looks at Social Security"
Washington Report
Vol. XVI, No. 21

President Reagan has proposed the first significant cut in Social Security benefits since the system was set up forty-six years ago. His proposal has unleashed a wide storm of protest. My impression is that the proposal seems unlikely to win approval, at least in its present form. These are the things the president would do:

Calculation of Benefits: Mr. Reagan would alter the formula under which initial benefits are calculated for those who retire at sixty-five years of age or later. The change would mean that the average worker retiring at age sixty-five would receive about 9 percent less each month than he would get if the law were not altered. Instead of getting a pension equal to 41 percent of prior earnings, the average worker would get 38 percent of prior earnings.

Early Retirement: Workers can now retire at the age of sixty-two and receive 80 percent of the benefits they would have been entitled to had they retired at sixty-five years of age. The president would reduce that proportion to 55 percent, so that workers who retired at age sixty-two would receive an average of $126 less per month than they would get under current law. About 70 percent of all workers begin drawing their benefits before they reach sixty-five years of age.

Earnings in Retirement: Until they are seventy-two years old, workers who remain employed after age sixty-five have their benefits reduced by $1 for each $2 they earn in excess of $5,500 per year. Mr. Reagan would lift the ceiling on earnings in stages and then eliminate it altogether after 1983.

Employees of Government: Federal and state workers are not covered by Social Security, but have their own systems of retirement. Under current law they can retire from government employment, begin drawing a pension, work for a few years in a job covered by Social Security, and then draw Social Security benefits in addition to the other pension. The president would ease the financial impact of this practice by taking the other pension into account when calculating Social Security benefits for former employees of government.

Tax Rate: The Social Security tax is 6.65 percent of the first $29,700 of earned income. The rate is scheduled to increase gradually until it reaches 7.65 percent in 1990. Mr. Reagan would lower the rate if and when the money in the Social Security trust funds amounted to 50 percent of that which would have to be paid out in the following year.

Disability: At the present time, disability is defined not just in terms of the applicant's medical condition, but also on the basis of his prospects for a new job in view of his age and experience. The president would consider medical condition alone. Also, he would lengthen from five to six months the period during which the applicant must wait to get benefits.

Cost-of-Living Increases: Although Mr. Reagan would not change the manner in which cost-of-living increases are paid, he would shift the date of payment from July 1 to October 1, beginning in 1982. This is the only part of his proposal that would affect the thirty-six million Americans who are now retired and are drawing benefits.

My first comment on the president's plan is that some reform of Social Security is inevitable. The question is not whether the system will be reformed, but how. The "senior boom" has put the Social Security trust funds at risk, and there may well be a problem of "cash flow" as early as next year. It seems to me that Mr. Reagan must be given credit for tackling the problem. He has created the opportunity for a change that all of us know must come.

My second comment, however, is that the president has engaged in "overkill." He has overreacted with a proposal that may not be necessary to solve the problems of Social Security. Mr. Reagan has moved not only to eliminate the near-term deficit in the system, but also to produce a surplus large enough to permit a cut in the payroll tax. In fact, he wishes to reduce benefits by $70 billion over the next five years, a total amount far in excess of the $11 billion deficit expected for that period. Moreover, he has recommended that those who choose to retire early be very stiffly penalized. It seems to me that we break faith with these people if we act without warning to cut them off by suddenly changing what they can hope for when they stop work. Finally, it must be noted that disability benefits were tightened up just last year. It is not at all obvious that there is any need for the changes the president suggests.

The importance of Social Security in this country is becoming clear to everyone. The system is not unassailable, but any change in it must be approached with great care. One reform that appears worthwhile to me is a correction of the cost-of-living index so it reflects the real rate of inflation. A proposal pending in Congress would limit cost-of-living adjustments to wage increases or price increases, whichever were smaller. As I see it, basic fairness demands that sacrifices be spread more or less evenly across all beneficiaries and not be concentrated on a few.

I believe that Social Security reform is a bipartisan issue. Without much bipartisan effort, I suspect not much will be done. In response to criticism of his plan, Mr. Reagan has shown that he may compromise. An agreement may now be possible.

IMPROVING INTELLIGENCE ANALYSIS

I became a member of the House Intelligence Committee in 1981 and began to give considerable attention to the question of how to oversee and strengthen our nation's intelligence system. The committee work was difficult and time consuming, and it took me a few years even to learn all of the acronyms. But I thought it was important work to do—providing independent and robust oversight that can't be provided by the public or the media because of the highly secretive nature of the system. My interest in improving intelligence continued for years after I left Congress, with my work on the president's Foreign Intelligence Advisory Board.

The system is impressive, and I developed a deep appreciation for the people involved in intelligence collection and analysis. As discussed in this newsletter, two of my biggest concerns have long been the politicization of intelligence and inadequate congressional oversight. Those factors would contribute to the intelligence failures we would see in subsequent years, with Iran-Contra, 9/11, and George W. Bush's Iraq war.

I've been disappointed by changes in the selection of Intelligence Committee members over the years. When I served on it, we were mainly senior members who could be counted on not to talk to the press about our work. Indeed, the first and longtime chairman of the House Intelligence Committee, Eddie Boland of Massachusetts, refused to speak to the press about intelligence. Today members fight to get on the committee because it opens the door to the media for them and it increases their prestige.

October 14, 1981: "Improving Intelligence Analysis"
Washington Report
Vol. XVI, No. 41
When asked to think about the nation's intelligence system, many of us envision a thrill-a-minute TV spy episode set in the picturesque capitals of Europe and featuring a James Bond–type hero.

There is some truth to that idea, but most intelligence operations are much less dramatic.

The main tasks of the intelligence system are to provide assessments of the present actions and intentions of other governments and to give timely warning of future ones. Good intelligence is vital to the very survival of our country because it supplies policymakers with information and analysis on topics ranging from the world's oil reserves to the Soviet Union's economic plans.

Although analysis of intelligence takes place in several agencies, the Central Intelligence Agency (CIA) has primary responsibility for gathering and producing estimates for policymakers. The analytical branch of the CIA was set up partly because in 1941 data to indicate that Japan was about to attack Pearl Harbor were not assembled in time. Each year, hundreds of intelligence documents are written, ranging from extensive national intelligence surveys to daily summaries resembling newspapers. The primary intelligence documents are probably the National Intelligence Estimates, reports which attempt to reflect a consensus on a specific topic.

Our technical ability to collect information has improved. We must also improve our ability to analyze the information. We spend a staggering amount on intelligence each year, but lately the quality of the final product has not been uniformly good. Lapses of analysis include the prediction that the shah of Iran was in no danger, the failure to predict the 1975 coup in Cyprus, and the failure to describe the impressive growth of Soviet military power for a decade. The record is one not of constant failure, but of occasional yet significant failure. We must approach intelligence gathering and analysis in a modern way, blending all relevant political, economic, and social skills.

There is much room for improvement in our analysis of the intelligence information. Major suggestions are these:

Give intelligence a higher priority. Countries which emphasize intelligence because they believe their existence depends on it have good intelligence systems. Likewise, when we put a high premium on intelligence, as we did during World War II, it was generally excellent. Quality declined when our overwhelming preeminence in the world, the remoteness of nuclear war, and other factors made intelligence seem less important. Now we realize that we were wrong.

Depoliticize the process. Intelligence estimates too often seem to be made to justify the views of political leaders. For example, after the Reagan administration took a different line on Soviet involvement in international terrorism, the CIA retroactively identified more than a thousand terrorist incidents in the previous year which it had not counted earlier. Suggestions for depoliticizing the process include making analysts feel that politically discordant estimates are welcome, and separating top responsibilities so that the politically appointed director of intelligence does not also head the analytical CIA. Besides trying to minimize political interference, we should be aware of the biases it introduces into the process.

Reform internal policies. There should be more dialogue between policymakers and analysts: intelligence estimates should be tailored to meet the particular needs, but not the views, of policymakers so that the most useful products possible are prepared. We should conduct regular evaluation of estimates to see why they succeeded or failed. Also, we should upgrade personnel policies by recruiting analysts from both academic and practical backgrounds, and dropping the uniquely American notion that good analysts should be rewarded primarily with positions in management.

Increase competition among analysts. In some of our recent intelligence failures, key factual information may have been available and some analysts may have reached correct conclusions. However, dissenting views are sometimes smothered in a process which seeks consensus. Melding divergent views into a consensus can lead to a blandness of prediction, a lack of accountability, and reliance on the "lowest common denominator." More competition among analysts is desirable. The analyst must be free to speak his mind, to disagree, to challenge. We should allow competing estimates from different agencies, improve channels of dissent, and set up a board to play "devil's advocate" with conclusions. Competition can also be provided by experts outside the intelligence community.

Broaden external oversight. In Congress, the Intelligence Committees have given much time and effort to the evaluation of intelligence estimates. This activity should continue. The committees have issued comprehensive reports, and improvements in intelligence agencies have resulted. At present, there is no independent group which performs a similar task in the executive branch. This omission should be corrected by establishing a presidential board of overseers like the one which existed from 1955 to 1977.

Good intelligence is essential to the future of our nation. A great power like the United States cannot survive without a great intelligence service. All of us in government must cast aside our romantic ideas about the spy thrillers and get down to the hard, detailed business of improving our intelligence system. It is no exaggeration to say that the fate of our country depends on it.

THE WEEK THE GOVERNMENT STOPPED

President Reagan had firmly held views on government spending, but Congress soon got the sense that it would be able to work out compromises with him on funding bills to avoid lengthy government shutdowns. There were brief partial government shutdowns during the Reagan years while final negotiations on the budget were wrapped up, but both the president and Congress could be confident that compromises would eventually be found to move the nation forward. Unfortunately, Congress in recent years has been much more willing to employ the tactic of shutting down the government to advance its policy goals.

December 2, 1981: "The Week the Government Stopped"
Washington Report
Vol. XVI, No. 48

With increasing regularity, Congress and the president have failed to enact spending bills by the beginning of the new fiscal year. Time and time again, they have failed to meet the deadlines which govern spending for federal activities. This past week, for the first time in history, all agencies ran out of money when a stopgap financing law expired at midnight on November 20. President Reagan moved immediately to shut the government down. It was the week the government stopped.

It is instructive to review the background of the impasse which led to the shutdown. Congress failed to complete action on the regular appropriations bills (the House has passed twelve of thirteen, the Senate six of thirteen) to keep the government in business. Six months after submitting his budget request and two months after Congress approved his spending and tax proposals, the president insisted that Congress trim another $8.5 billion in spending from the continuing resolution. Later, he said he would accept half this amount. When Congress passed a continuing resolution which the president said did not cut enough, he vetoed it. Most agencies began to furlough "nonessential" employees under an 1870 statute which tells government managers, in effect, that if Congress has not provided the money then they cannot spend it. The impasse was temporarily broken a few days later when Congress approved, and the president signed, a continuing resolution extending current levels of spending to December 15. Since the underlying budgetary problems have not been resolved, another impasse could come in three weeks.

The blame for the impasse must be shared by all concerned. The president believes the free-spending Congress caused it, and he complains that Congress's inaction left the country without a budget for fourteen months. Every member of Congress would agree that the late-night, last-ditch legislating of the past week is a poor way to operate, but other reasons are offered to explain the delay in enacting regular appropriations bills. The House has done almost all its work, but the Senate has kept more than half the regular appropriations bills off the floor because it has been unable to agree with the president on his request for a new round of spending cuts. In fact, the Senate leadership told the president that he should not seek a new round of cuts so soon after the bruising battles of last summer. So the president blames Congress, and Congress blames the president.

By shutting down the government, the president demonstrated his determination to control federal spending. My guess is that his action was good politics—that it played well in the country—and that he wanted to show he would be tough in negotiating spending cuts next year. After a run of bad economic news, the president almost certainly concluded that he had to "take command" of the budget process. The cuts he won with his veto of the continuing resolution were surely not as important as the symbol of a resolute stance against spending. In addition, they were not large enough to have much effect on the 1982 deficit, which is now likely to exceed $80 billion because of the recession and the huge tax cuts. It is hard to see why a continuing resolution which came down to a difference of one-half of 1 percent caused such a fuss.

Throughout the debate on the continuing resolution, there was much confusion about the underlying budgetary figures. The president contended that the continuing resolution was far over his budget. Congress argued that it was under both the president's budget of March and the budget resolutions which he had supported. The dispute was eventually narrowed to a single issue: whether the continuing resolution was over the president's modified budget of September. Congress thought it was very close, but the president believed the difference was larger. The sources of disagreement were many. The president may have misread the continuing resolution, anticipated the passage of bills which Congress did not, and used different economic assumptions. Moreover, errors in calculation were easy to make because there were so many separate programs in the continuing resolution, and separate calculations had to be made for each one. Finally, no accord was reached on the programs to be classified as discretionary, and thus subject to cuts, and the programs to be classified as entitlements, which go up automatically with inflation and increases in the population.

Having just gone through this divisive struggle, I have the strong impression that we must avoid legislating budgets with the threat of a shutdown of government hanging over us. Good legislation cannot be passed in such conditions. Unfortunately, stopgap financing has become the focus of too many disputes because Congress has fallen behind in its consideration of regular appropriations bills. We are using continuing resolutions for long periods of time, yet they should be used only when emergencies arise. We are using them to fund almost all government activities, yet they should be used only in isolated instances. The danger is that the continuing resolution will take the place of the regular appropriations process, yet it has none of the legislative safeguards the latter has.

The deadlocks which have plagued the budget process in recent years reflect structural weaknesses in the process. With four money committees and two budget committees, several stages of consideration, and dozens of votes, the process has become unwieldy. These weaknesses must be corrected. An issue of policy makes matters worse. At the root of the impasse which shut down the government is disagreement between Congress and the president on the segments of American society which should bear the burden of the spending cuts. Until a broader consensus on this issue is reached, Congress's budgetary troubles are likely to continue despite all efforts to reform the budget process.

REFLECTIONS ON THE 97TH CONGRESS

The 97th Congress was the first of four Congresses during the Reagan years, but it was probably the most important legislatively and politically. The Democratic-controlled House fought hard for its views, but in the end Speaker O'Neill let the democratic process prevail and let a majority of votes in Congress carry the day, even if they were largely Republican votes. The House leaders recognized that election results matter and that Reagan clearly had the American people behind him, so his legislative agenda shouldn't simply be blocked.

But the leadership also recognized that by letting Reagan get his basic economic plan passed, from a political perspective it was now the Reagan economy, the Reagan deficits, the Reagan unemployment rate. And indeed, when the economy worsened once the Reagan economic plan was in place, the voters didn't like what was happening. In the next congressional election the Democrats reversed the beating they took in 1980 and actually picked up twenty-six House seats.

Although it sounds simple, a key lesson from the Reagan years is that we resolve disputes in Congress by letting the House and Senate work their will and vote on the issues. Remarkably, that is increasingly not being done nowadays in Congress.

> **October 20, 1982: "Reflections on the 97th Congress"**
> **Washington Report**
> **Vol. XVII, No. 42**
> Now that the gavel has fallen on the final day of regular business of the 97th Congress, a quick review of congressional achievements and failures is in order.
>
> The recently recessed 97th Congress has been a significant legislative achievement for President Reagan. The Congress gave him most of what he wanted, including virtually all of his economic program, when it approved his massive increase in military expenditures, his tax reductions, and his domestic-spending cutbacks. Only at the end of the session did the Congress balk at further enactment of the program. When the president vetoed a supplemental spending bill which complied with the budgetary targets, the Congress

overrode his veto. The president pushed controversial social issues, such as school prayer and abortion, and he demanded a constitutional amendment to balance the federal budget just as he was producing deficits far greater than $100 billion per year. On some of these latter issues, however, the Congress rebuffed the president in the last days of the session.

So, for nineteen of the twenty months of the session, the Congress marched in lockstep with the president. It broke ranks with him only in the last days of the final month.

The federal budget has dominated the 97th Congress. The budget has pushed almost everything else to the side, filling the whole time, causing delays, and forcing the Congress to toss everything into catch-all legislative packages. The Congress failed to meet its appropriations deadlines. It enacted only one of its thirteen regular appropriations bills by the start of the new fiscal year on October 1.

The breakdown of the congressional budget process is not desirable, but neither is it unprecedented. As the Congress adjourned until November 29 for the general election, a groundswell of opinion favored changes in the budget and appropriation processes. Many members are demanding that the budget process be junked, but I am not among them. Undoubtedly, it needs improvement. It does tend to delay appropriations bills, and it has often been based on unrealistic and excessively optimistic assumptions about the growth of the economy. However, the process is still evolving and, with modifications, it will help the Congress move toward greater precision and restraint in budgeting. Generally, it is making members focus on the hard choices. They must look at taxing and spending as a whole and decide on priorities. What should be kept in mind is that severe budget problems must be expected when the federal government is in a period of retrenchment. The Congress is cutting back sharply on spending for many programs and agencies, and it is much harder to give less than it is to give more.

Few legislators have expressed satisfaction with the record of the 97th Congress. One said, "We haven't done a thing." Another said, "Money, money, money, that's all we've talked about." A third said, "We've done a lot of flip-flopping this year." The preoccupation with the budget, brought on mainly by the ailing economy, has all but shut off action on new initiatives. The complexity of our economic problems has frustrated members. When Congress returns for its postelection session, it will sit for about three weeks and will concentrate its attention once again on budgetary and economic matters.

The 97th Congress has also been marked by partisanship, perhaps accentuated because the Senate is controlled by the Republicans and the House of Representatives by the Democrats. The partisanship was in part to blame for the fact that Congress moved at such a slow pace. The Senate sat for 126 days, the House for 121 days. Through September, only 275 public laws were enacted, half of which were not controversial. In contrast, 613 public laws were enacted in the 96th Congress. The slow pace was also attributable to the difficulty of the budgetary and economic issues, the unwillingness of members to tackle them, and the shift of power in the Senate, where the Republican leadership took some time to adjust to the responsibilities and prerogatives of the majority party.

One of the surprises of the 97th Congress has to be the defeat of social issues which were expected to have smooth going early in 1981, but which encountered strong opposition as soon as they were brought up. Such a defeat reflects, I suppose, the lack of a broad consensus to change social policy.

My major concern about the 97th Congress was its use of "omnibus" legislation—the device of packaging many provisions and amendments (sometimes hundreds) into a single bill. Omnibus legislation now accounts for a large share of the work product of the Congress, but it seems to me that the approach is simply not the best way to legislate. The problem is that members are asked to vote on mammoth legislative packages, often running hundreds of pages in length and containing significant changes in law in a wide variety of areas, with little or no time to understand the ramifications of what they are doing. Three legislative devices are being used to excess: budget resolutions, which set taxing and spending priorities for the government; reconciliation bills, which transform those priorities into actual cuts or increases in taxing or spending; and continuing resolutions, which are temporary bills to fund government departments whose regular appropriations bills have not been enacted. There is some merit in the argument that the only way to make these legislative changes is to package them up together. However, the omnibus approach just does not provide the Congress with sufficient time for committee hearings, legislative markups, and detailed floor consideration with the opportunity for amendment.

One of my hopes for the 98th Congress is that it will govern much less by omnibus legislation. Perhaps after the period of economic retrenchment, the regular congressional procedures can be resurrected and restored.

THE MILITARY BALANCE: QUESTIONS AND ANSWERS

In his November 1982 speech to the nation, President Reagan was making his case for a major military buildup, but some of his statements struck me as inaccurate or misleading. A certain amount of overstatement can be expected from politicians, but I think we need to be particularly careful when describing our national-security capabilities. I thought it important to write a commentary that responded to several of his statements. Many of us in Congress of both parties agreed with the president's overall view that our military could be strengthened, but the discussion of that needed to proceed on the basis of agreed-upon facts.

Discussions of military spending also need to be based on our policy needs—what the threats ahead to our nation are, and what is needed to address them. Too often debates on defense become numbers games, as is pointed out here.

During this period the major argument for the US military buildup made before my committee by the Reagan administration was that the Russians were coming and they were developing an overwhelming military capability. We later learned, with the collapse of the Soviet Union, that this was false.

December 22, 1982: "The Military Balance: Questions and Answers"
Washington Report
Vol. XVII, No. 51
Q: Is the United States inferior to the Soviet Union in military strength?

A: President Reagan believes so. He has said that "in virtually every measure of military power the Soviet Union enjoys a decided advantage." I am perplexed by his statement. It runs counter to the position of all of Mr. Reagan's predecessors—that the most basic measure of military strength shows the two powers roughly in balance. I cannot find a single high-ranking military officer who would exchange our armed forces in total for the armed forces of the Soviet Union. Moreover, even if Mr. Reagan is correct, it seems to me unwise for a commander in chief to denigrate our armed forces and to declare them inferior. Such talk can only encourage Soviet aggression.

My summary of how the military forces look would go like this: In strategic forces, we are far ahead in manned bombers and the warheads they carry. We are also ahead in the number of warheads on submarine-launched missiles, but the Soviet Union is ahead in submarines and submarine-launched missiles themselves. They have more land-based missiles. In ballistic-missile defenses, the Soviets are better off, but capabilities on both sides are low. In tactical aircraft, we are behind quantitatively, but our best interceptors are qualitatively better than the best the Soviets have. We are substantially in front in carrier-based airpower and aerial reconnaissance. In naval surface combatants, we are doing better in carriers, both quantitatively and qualitatively. They have more attack submarines, but we lead in capacity to wage antisubmarine warfare. In men under arms, the Soviet Union is ahead.

The comparative figures are important, though they do not tell the whole story. Assessing the balance is never a matter simply of totaling up the figures. However, the figures do show trends in relative strength. By all accounts, Moscow is continuing to outdistance us in numbers of weapons produced, and it is closing the gap in the quality of weapons. One reason for this is that the Soviets have devoted a larger share of their military budget to force modernization.

Q: Do the Soviets invest two or three times more than we do in defense?

A: The Soviet Union spends between 12 percent and 14 percent of its gross national product on defense; we spend between 5 percent and 6 percent. However, our gross national product is nearly twice theirs. If we add the defense spending of the Western allies, we see $300 billion more on our side between 1971 and 1980. Moreover, the dollar-by-dollar comparison is misleading because the forces of the two countries are not really comparable item by item. Comparing figures without looking at mission, geography, the cohesion of the Western allies, and the quality of forces distorts the result.

Q: Do the Soviets have more tanks, artillery pieces, aircraft, and ships than we do?

A: Yes, but the significance of this fact should not be overblown. We should not overlook the Western allies or ignore the quality of our weapons. When the forces of the allies on both sides are totaled up, the numbers on each side are much closer. For example, American ships, though fewer than Soviet ships, are generally larger. Just as important, the total number of ships in the Atlantic Alliance exceeds the total number of ships in the Warsaw Pact.

Q: Is it true that the Soviet Union has two hundred new Backfire Bombers, and is building thirty more each year, while many of our B-52s are old?

A: Yes, but again the view of the experts is that our old B-52s are better than their Soviet counterparts. Our total force of 316 active B-52s (with more than 30 in reserve) and 60 newer FB-111s is rated superior. Also, we are building two new bombers, the B-1 and the Stealth. The Soviet Backfire's reduced effectiveness at long range is another relevant factor.

Q: Has the Soviet Union put to sea sixty missile-bearing submarines in the past fifteen years, while we have only recently put to sea our first missile-bearing submarine in fifteen years?

A: Yes, but we are still far ahead in the number of warheads on submarine-launched missiles, and submarines remain the part of our triad least vulnerable to attack. Our submarines are on patrol 55 percent of the time; the newer Soviet ships do not do better than 15 percent. Ours are more immune to detection, and there is no serious danger to them in the current Soviet antisubmarine arsenal.

Q: Did we freeze the number of long-range, land-based missiles in our triad in 1965?

A: Yes, but we have replaced and upgraded the missiles several times, with the result that they are far more capable than ever before. We have developed the technology to put more warheads on each missile, and in any case qualitative improvements are more important than sheer numbers. Because hardened missile silos can now be effectively attacked, the large proportion of land-based missiles in the Soviet strategic forces will make the Soviet Union especially vulnerable.

In general, the figures do not show that the Soviets have the advantage in military power. The picture is complex and mixed. It is perhaps best described as a "balance of imbalances."

RELIGION IN POLITICS

Bringing the religious Right into politics was a priority of Reagan's, both as a candidate and then as president. That broadened citizen participation, which is certainly good, but it also brought with it the risk of increasing intolerance. Not all intolerance to opposing views comes from religion, but much of it does. In this commentary I'm struggling to find the proper role of religion in the political process, and at the end I appeal to the wisdom of one of my favorite quotes, from Isaiah.

October 3, 1984: "Religion in Politics"
Washington Report
Vol. XIX, No. 40

As participation of religious groups in the political process has broadened, my view is that they do not necessarily overstep their limits when they get involved. Although one may disagree at times with what they say, they have a right to bring up specific religious issues, to try to promote their moral values through the legislative process, and to endorse particular candidates for public office. However, that does not mean that their involvement raises no significant worries. In fact, the involvement of some religious groups in the political process may be quite harmful. Like anyone else, they cross over the line when they bring intolerance into that process. Intolerance, no matter what its source, is the enemy of democracy.

The danger signs are usually obvious enough. When we say that God is on our side on a particular bill, when we say that a political position is based upon divine or revealed truth, when we say that our opponent is godless, or when we say that someone who disagrees with us is sinful or immoral, we raise real threats to the democratic process. People will often disagree on political issues, but we can erode the democratic process when we see the disagreement as a struggle between the forces of light and the forces of darkness.

Such views shut off all debate. They really do undermine the give and take of the democratic process. There is no room for doubt, dialogue, or compromise. Lost under this approach is the requirement that democracy places upon us to accord mutual respect to our political adversaries and to refrain from ascribing evil motives to them. We must be wary of the view that there is always a simple division of the solutions to complex political issues into good and evil, with no middle ground. It reflects a certainty, a feeling that we are so sure we are right, that can undermine the proper functioning of a democracy. A democracy with leaders from several different religious traditions, each of whom proclaimed his own divine inspiration and dismissed his colleagues as ungodly sinners, would soon be paralyzed.

Those of us who would bring our religious views into the political process should recall the clear Biblical theme that each of us is fallible and finite, and that no one knows God's will but God. The New Testament reminds us to look first for the log in our own eye, and only then to the speck in our brother's eye. We must recall that religion in America has been invoked to justify witch hunting, refusal to help the poor, slavery, and racial segregation. Elsewhere in the world, individuals have been persecuted and put to death by church leaders for doubting that the earth was a sphere in orbit around the sun. We should actively resist this kind of error. During the Civil War, President Abraham Lincoln was struck by the extent to which both the North and South claimed to have God on their side. Yet his concern was to be on God's side; he did not presume that God was on his side. Mr. Lincoln's attitude is one that ought to be ours.

People are often strong and sincere in their religious conviction, but I get uneasy when someone says that his position is religious and virtuous, and, by implication at least, that all others are irreligious and sinful. When we are engaged in public discourse on such difficult issues, there is a special need for us to behave with added civility and restraint. While I am aware that there are Christians and Jews who take positions on many issues, I wonder whether we can identify the Christian or Jewish position on most issues.

This is not to single out religious groups for special criticism. Intolerance is unhealthy in the political arena, no matter what the source, be it a religious person, a member of an extremist political organization, or a college student who shouts down speakers on campus. Religious intolerance has no more place or future in our democracy than did political intolerance in the 1950s.

There are special problems with intolerance in a democracy. First, it cuts off all debate at the beginning, as we attempt to make governing prior to the participatory process rather than through that process. Second, it is often counterproductive for the intolerant person himself. It may prompt others to respond in kind, it may lead to smoldering anger and discontent, and it may result in retribution and persecution. Third, causes are more likely to be successful, and solutions more likely to be lasting, if, instead of dogmatically insisting on having our way at every turn, we move forward by accommodating various points of view and developing consensus. With time, education, good will, and the continued freedom to criticize and discuss, we may see our principles accepted. That does not mean that we have to sacrifice our basic principles in doing so. We can still retain them, while at the same time accepting temporarily a proposal that does not satisfy all of our demands. Tolerance and accommodation are essential to a well-functioning democracy. As the American jurist Learned Hand once noted, the spirit of liberty is the spirit that is not too sure it is right.

Let me stress that I do not think that we should try to exclude someone from the political process because of his intolerance. We must not become intolerant of the intolerant. On the contrary, we should welcome them (but not their intolerance) into the political process. This involvement is especially important for religious individuals. For example, those in the Judeo-Christian tradition have been taught a concern for their fellow man and for peace among nations, important assets in the political arena. When those of us from different backgrounds leave our intolerance behind and freely debate the merits of an issue, the democratic process is invigorated by the broadened participation. The prophet Isaiah pointed to the appropriate standard of conduct when he said, "Come now, and let us reason together."

HOW A MEMBER DECIDES

Most votes in Congress are fairly easy for members, but some are not and these can cause a lot of stress. The process for deciding how to vote involves sorting out reasons put forward by a very wide variety of sources, as is explained in this newsletter. One factor that has changed since this was written is the vastly increased importance of campaign contributions for members of Congress, and the much greater weight members now give to the opinions of their donors.

December 11, 1985: "How a Member Decides"
Washington Report
Vol. XX, No. 50

A question that has intrigued me is how various members of Congress decide how to vote. Members cast about four hundred votes a year on the most difficult and controversial issues on the national agenda. My impression is that in deciding how to vote, members weigh three goals: they want to make good policy, gain respect inside Congress, and get reelected. It is impossible to name all the factors that influence the vote of individual members. They must balance many changing pressures, expectations, and demands every day. In the end, of course, they must rely on their own judgment about the merits of a particular bill or amendment, but that judgment is influenced by many factors. Among the most important are these:

Constituents: Constituents are the most important influence on a member's voting decision. Whether members are agents of their constituents' wishes or free to exercise their own judgment is a classic question in a representative democracy. Members have a duty to listen carefully to their constituents and to consider their views. After all, members are not representatives if their actions bear little or no relationship to the views of constituents. Members may not always vote with the views of a majority of their constituents because in the absence of a referendum they cannot be certain what they think. But all members ask themselves on each vote where their constituents stand on the issue. On those issues where the constituency expresses strong preferences, the member is almost certain to favor them. Representatives who fail to reflect generally the views of their constituents will soon need other work. If they vote in a way their constituents may not approve of, they will explain their votes in terms their constituents will respect, even if they do not agree.

Colleagues: Members learn to identify certain colleagues whose judgment they respect on particular issues. Other members are important sources of information because, as professional politicians, they will tailor their advice to a member's needs; they are often well informed on the issue; and they are available at the time of the vote. Members do not seek advice from just any colleague. Instead they seek out those who over time have earned the respect and attention of their colleagues. Members also pay special attention to the other members of their state delegations—as well as to state and local officials—because they share common interests and problems.

Lobbies: Interest groups are neither the most nor least important influence on Congress. Lobbyists can help or hinder a member's work. They can provide members with easily digested information and innovative proposals. They can identify allies, help round up votes, and aid election campaigns. They can provide or withhold campaign contributions, support or oppose a member's reelection. Members ignore lobbyists at their peril.

The Executive: The president is, in many respects, the chief legislator. He and his vice president are the only officials elected by all the people. Although the president's lobbying activities do not differ significantly from those of other groups, the president's prestige, or standing in the polls, is often persuasive to members. At the same time, partisan distrust may create opposition to the president's position. With his excellent sources of information, his ability to initiate legislation, to appeal to all Americans, and to set the legislative agenda, the president has formidable power in the legislative process. But that power no longer yields the unique advantage it once did, as other sources of information—the Congressional Budget Office, the Congressional Research Service, the Office of Technology Assessment, for example—have grown in respect and influence.

Party Leadership: Political party leadership has much less effect on members' decisions. Members of Congress do not hear often from their national party leaders about specific votes on legislation. They do hear often from the leadership of their party in the Congress, i.e., the Speaker and the Majority and Minority Leaders. The leadership does have resources besides gentle persuasion. It controls the scheduling of bills, parliamentary rulings, choice committee assignments, and prerogatives, and it can choose, within limits, who is recognized to speak on the floor. The effects of these tools are not unimportant, and on close votes are often decisive.

Media: News media may have their greatest effect on Congress as agenda setters. By focusing attention on a particular issue, they can get the American people and the Congress to deal with it. The stories the media emphasize, and how those stories are treated, have a real effect on which issues Congress considers and which it puts off. In considering a vote, members must anticipate how that vote will be played by the media.

Staff: It is a mistake to underestimate the importance of congressional staff in the legislative process. Because of members' hectic schedules, they rely on staff to help them evaluate legislation. Today's staffers usually have a good appreciation of political processes, but their main strength is substantive technical knowledge. As a result, staffers have become important actors in the legislative arena. The greater their expertise, the more members rely on them, and the more they shape the legislative product.

Members of Congress vote several times every legislative day on diverse and complex issues. Usually they have more information than they can assimilate, so they need and seek help. They cannot be experts on every bill that comes before the Congress. If all of the factors on which a member ordinarily relies agree, the decision is easy. If these factors point to opposite conclusions, the decision becomes difficult. It is then that decision making becomes a very personal matter. When the voting clock is running down the member must make a decision. The member knows that in our democracy he or she alone will be held accountable for it.

THE APPEAL OF CONGRESS

This is one of the commentaries I would write from time to time on the work of a member of Congress—here analyzing the good and bad points of my job. I particularly liked that being a member allowed you to be a generalist, dealing with and learning about an incredible array of interesting issues. One of the biggest downsides, as mentioned here, was the enormous stress the job places on your family life. Among my friends who were in my entering class, only a handful of the marriages survived because of the pressures of the job.

The newsletter mentions that I liked working with my colleagues in Congress. That included Speaker Tip O'Neill. He once came out to my district in the mid-1970s when forced desegregation in the schools was a hot issue nationwide. Feelings were particularly intense in Louisville, Kentucky, just across the river from my district, because its schools were under a federal court order to integrate. Tip had assumed a national role in defending desegregation, and he became a lightning rod for critics. He accompanied me to one of my public meetings, but when we walked in, a chorus of loud boos started up. I noticed a much-larger-than-expected turnout, from Louisville people who drove in to get to Tip. But he seemed to take it all good-naturedly. After the meeting I asked him what he thought about the reception. He said, smiling, "At first I thought they were booing you. But I knew that wasn't the case. Then by God I finally figured out they were booing me!"

July 2, 1986: "The Appeal of Congress"
Washington Report
Vol. XXI, No. 27

Hoosiers often ask me why I find the US House of Representatives such an enjoyable and fascinating place to work.

A main reason is the people I work with. In many respects, the House is a truly representative body. Its members are personally as well as geographically diverse. They have different personalities, derived from widely disparate backgrounds. Taken as a group, they are remarkably appealing. Generally, my colleagues in the House are well informed, resourceful, and hardworking. Most are motivated by a patriotic sense of the national interest, and not by a particular interest or group. A member is witness to every American characteristic, almost. There are still very few women in Congress, and in certain other areas Congress is not as accurately a reflection of the country as it might be. But the variety and versatility of the members always amazes me. We have in the House a former professional football player, former FBI agents, several ministers, self-made millionaires, a former heavyweight boxer, basketball coaches, professors, farmers, funeral home directors, and sheriffs. Some have long lists of educational credentials, and others are high school graduates.

Persuasion is the name of the game in the House. Members use many means to persuade one another. Majorities constantly shift with the issues, and a member must be able to work with and reach out to those with whom he often disagrees. Some rely on stirring oratory. Others quietly impress with their thoughtfulness or a comprehensive knowledge of the subject. Still others are persuasive only in one-on-one conversation. Force of personality, as in any enterprise, plays a strong role in convincing members.

In one sense, it is remarkable that the caliber of members is as high as it is. I think that the attributes required to win public office have little to do with the qualities needed to govern responsibly. Endurance, agility of mind, ambition, and a telegenic personality are needed to win office. These attributes can be helpful in office, but the qualities needed to govern well—character, wisdom, and above all good judgment—often don't count for much in modern campaigns.

Besides contact with colleagues, the job of a congressman is itself stimulating and exciting. Congress is an unusual learning experience. Its members learn not only about the topics that come before them, but the House is one of the best testing grounds of human relations. The sheer number of people a member deals with daily is staggering. His business forces him to make swift judgments about people: who can be trusted, help solve problems, build a consensus, or make a compromise. There is enormous variety to the work. Nearly every issue has a complexity and fascination of its own. One day the foremost issue may be acid rain, the next day, terrorism.

A member of Congress is in a position to really help other people every day. For many people, he is the only person they can turn to. He will disappoint some and earn the gratitude of others. After speaking recently to a high school class, I was approached by a graduating senior who asked me to recall an incident years earlier when her American parents had difficulty processing papers allowing them to adopt her, an orphaned Korean baby. She thanked me for the help I had given them. Seeing her, grown into a fine young woman, was a great thrill for me.

Nonetheless, the job has frustrations. With the press of the work goes the feeling that the congressman can never learn enough about the issues before him. A member must live with the feeling of never being entirely "caught up." The diversity and number of legislative proposals severely tax one's industry, knowledge, and self-confidence. A member is required to vote on issues he simply does not fully understand. The hectic schedule leaves little time for the contemplation and study the issues deserve. Members must rely on the judgment of colleagues and staff. It is also easy to get stuck in the minutiae of legislation, and occasionally a member must step back from what he is doing to think about where the nation ought to be headed.

The House is itself a complex institution, at times exasperating in its inaction and delay. Many members come to the Congress to change the world, or at least a part of it, and they bring with them their ideals, values, and priorities for this nation. As one-435th of the House, a member must learn the art of compromise in order to get anything accomplished. Everyone in the Congress has ideas about what is good for the country. These ideas are tested against fine minds, great funds of information, and political power. To stand up to this assault, ideas cannot be frail or delicate. In Congress, one quickly learns that governing is tougher than campaigning, that the issues are complicated, and that there are persuasive arguments on both sides of a question. The issues are not as clear-cut as they might appear from afar. The good and the bad are frequently intertwined, and often the only way to get something good is to accept something bad. Members who work to build consensus and compromise are the ones who get things done in the House.

A member's personal life nearly disappears. The long hours and frequent travel take a toll in ruined marriages and lost friendships. Doctors tell us the stress is high, and the loss of privacy is unavoidable. One of my friends who retired from Congress said that he knew it was time to quit when he found that he had no friends, no interests, no energy, nothing except his job.

In spite of all this, I have come to have the greatest affection for the Congress, my colleagues, and the job. I don't know of another place I would rather be working. Most members believe that service in the House is a job worth having and worth working hard to keep. They really do not become rich or take many vacations. They certainly do not have lifetime tenure. But they agree that there is great satisfaction in participating in the federal government and contributing, however marginally, to the direction and success of a free society.

OUR CONSTITUTIONAL HERITAGE

The longer I worked in Congress, the more respect I had for the Founding Fathers. In 1789 the entire population of our country was less than four million, and only twelve cities had more than five thousand inhabitants. As a nation we were incredibly fortunate that from such a small population emerged several leaders of political genius who devised our remarkable system of government. This is a commentary that was widely used in classrooms.

April 15, 1987: "Our Constitutional Heritage"
Washington Report
Vol. XXII, No. 15

Sometime during this celebration of the two hundredth anniversary of our Constitution, we need to get deep into our bones an understanding of the kind of men and women who preceded us in this country, and the marvelous document of representative government which they produced.

The writing of the Constitution was an act of genius. Fifty-five fairly ordinary American citizens met and argued for 127 days during a ferociously hot Philadelphia summer, and produced one of the preeminent documents of world history. They drew up a document which, with only twenty-six subsequent amendments, has provided the framework of government for a nation that has become the most successful democracy on earth. I am astonished even today at its utility and its capacity to adapt to a changing world.

Virtually all other nations which were in existence in 1787 have had to alter their form of government significantly in the intervening years. The United States, adhering to its original written Constitution, has continued with its form of government essentially unchanged. Ours is the oldest nation in the world, with the possible exception of Great Britain, to have found precisely the government which suits it best.

Strangely, the men who had the most influence in Philadelphia were not the household names. Benjamin Franklin was there, but he was old and frail. George Washington was the convention's chairman, but he maintained an air of detachment. Alexander Hamilton made just one speech of note in Philadelphia, but failed to convince his audience. Thomas Jefferson was in Paris. John Adams was in London.

The hard work of the convention was done by a handful of less-known but talented men: James Madison, Edmund Randolph, and George Mason of Virginia; Roger Sherman of Connecticut; James Wilson and Gouverneur Morris of Pennsylvania. Only one of them, the thirty-six-year-old James Madison, was well known outside of America.

James Madison deserves special attention. He was a small man. In his youth he was too sickly to achieve very much. He was timid, and self-conscious as a public speaker. He was often thought to be antisocial, without humor, bookish. I often think that he could

never get elected to office today, and he certainly could not ascend
to political leadership in the country. But his work, more than the
work of any one person, contributed to the success of the Constitution. James Madison is a national hero.

He dreamed up and saw through to completion the creation
of an entirely new political system and a new political culture. An
intellectual genius, he had the remarkable ability to see opportunity
in a crisis, rather than letting the crisis and the problems weigh
him down and paralyze him. Although the Constitutional Convention altered many of his ideas, his plan was the cornerstone. He, of
course, did not produce the Constitution alone, but I think it is fair
to say that the Constitution would have been significantly different
without James Madison.

Madison and his colleagues produced a Constitution that became the instrument for carrying out the ideals set forth earlier
in the Declaration of Independence. This extraordinary document
masterfully addresses and resolves such difficult questions as the
kind of government we should have, the limits of political power,
how to make democracy work and our freedom secure, and how to
balance freedom and responsibility within our system. And it was
all done at a time in history when the establishment of a democratic
government, based upon liberty and equality, was at odds with a
world which cherished order and authority.

Americans still celebrate this Constitution, but not very many
of us read it. We praise it, debate it, and quote it, but not enough of
us know what is in it. Many—far too many—are simply ignorant of
the content and meaning of our Constitution. Only a bare majority
knows that the purpose of the two-hundred-year-old document was
to create a federal government and define its powers.

A Gallup poll some years back found that 60 percent of Americans were unaware that the Bill of Rights is the first ten amendments to the Constitution; 75 percent believed that the Constitution
guarantees the right to free public education through high school;
less than 40 percent knew that the Constitution permits citizens to
preach revolution; and nearly half believed that the Constitution
contains the Marxist declaration "From each according to his ability, to each according his need."

The Constitution should be appreciated as a living instrument.
Each new generation of Americans must protect the Constitution.

There is a danger in a democratic society when so few of us really understand the institutions that protect our freedoms. When asked what the delegates had created, Franklin responded, "A republic, if you can keep it."

Easily one of the most remarkable documents in the annals of history, the Constitution is unsurpassed for substance and durability. In it, power is balanced by counterpower, and authority is checked by counterauthority. A three-part federal government was set up to prevent any one arm of government from dominating the others, and the federal government is balanced by the power of the states. Under the Constitution, the United States has survived wars, waves of immigration, the Great Depression, and sweeping economic, social, and technological change.

The Constitution should not be dismissed as a product of its time and place. If you look at the major themes of American government today—due process, advice and consent, separation of powers, checks and balances, full faith and credit, equal opportunity, equal treatment under the law, the presumption of innocence, freedom of speech and religion—you will find that the basis for each of them is in the Constitution. It remains a splendid vision of justice and fairness, a document that reflects a government system which is strong enough to withstand crisis and flexible enough to permit change.

ISSUES OF THE FUTURE

One of the major challenges facing Congress is to move past its short-term perspective and think fifteen or twenty years down the road. Too often Congress waits until a crisis is about to occur, rather than take up problems at an earlier stage when they are less complicated and less costly to address. The vast majority of votes taken in Congress deal with the pressure of immediate issues.

This commentary, written almost thirty years ago, looked at some of the key future issues. Most of them would still be listed today as continuing challenges facing the country.

April 22, 1987: "Issues of the Future"
Washington Report
Vol. XXII, No. 16

Every now and then in the crush of congressional business demanding immediate attention, I gaze out my office window for a few moments and ask myself what are the great issues of the world the legislators should be thinking about for the twenty-first century. I try to look ahead further than usual, not just to the next hour or the next day, but to the start of the next century that begins in a little more than a decade.

The question is not an idle one. Government, a major instrument for realizing the basic goals of society, is often criticized for its failure to take the long view. Increasingly our perspective should rise above our daily preoccupations to ask, where is our country headed? What are the long-term needs? What kind of world will we leave our children? Inattention to key future issues can lead to shortsighted policies unintentionally thwarting more important long-term goals.

There is no shortage of issues to think about. Some center on technological advances—the robots, the genetic engineering, the advances in health care which will reshape our daily lives. Other issues focus on social, economic, and political trends—increased leisure, US competitiveness, how to encourage better arts and sounder government, how to develop greater compassion. I ask myself what are the key items that we should be giving the highest priority to.

At the top of the list, of course, is peace. The consequences of not doing something about the possibility of nuclear annihilation are beyond imagination. If we do not have peace in a nuclear age, it is not worth talking about anything else. Progress toward world peace has to begin with arms agreements between the United States and the Soviet Union. The arts of diplomacy and conflict resolution have to address regional struggles across the world, and we must work toward a positive condition in which people can solve their problems by law and by talk rather than by force.

I think about poverty, too. The world has far too many hungry, sick, and homeless. Sometimes I think people can be divided into the overfed and the underfed: one group worrying about dieting and the other group worrying about their next meal. Developed nations should be doing more to help their neighbors, not only for altruistic reasons but also because the problems of the poor could well spill over into the lives of the well-to-do.

I think about the environment. The degradation of the environment is second only to the nuclear holocaust in its potential for destroying humanity. We have to be concerned about the destruction of the rain forest, the erosion of topsoil, the pollution of groundwater, the safe handling of hazardous waste, and a wide range of other problems. The responsibility for leaving a vital natural legacy to future generations must be accepted, and major precautionary steps taken now.

I also think about population. The world's population, four billion in 1975, will be six billion by the turn of the century. Overpopulation is a major factor in many of the world's problems, including hunger, disease, poverty, energy insufficiency, and environmental damage. While technology offers some promise in being able to cope, the challenge remains enormous. If population growth is left unchecked, it will cause dissension, huge numbers of refugees, and increased tendencies toward revolution.

I think about our economic future and our growing global economic interdependence. Nations increasingly compete for jobs; markets for goods and services are increasingly intertwined. At home, we must upgrade our education systems and make the necessary long-term investments in scientific research, alternate energy sources, and infrastructure. International cooperation must be improved for addressing global challenges. When major problems develop in one country, such as debt repayment problems, energy shortages, or government instability, the effects can be global.

I am also concerned about children. Children represent our future, yet they are the most vulnerable members of society. Their protection must be pursued vigilantly. We have to strengthen families, improve our schools to meet the purposes of democracy, and make the necessary long-term investments in the future. Although we cannot ignore other groups, such as the growing ranks of older persons or the young men who must fight our wars, surely at the top of our list of concerns must be the children.

I also think about scientific advances. Science and technology have a potential to produce a cure for cancer, new sources of energy, space colonies, and vastly expanded food production. Yet they also have the potential to allow us to tamper with human genetic makeup, render many of today's workers obsolete, and create a new generation of weapons far more accurate and deadly than atomic arms. Ethical and social considerations must play a stronger role in technology assessment.

I also worry about freedom. Individual rights of conscience, movement, and employment must be better protected all over the world. I want to see the rule of law extended and governments improved so that people will get better legislation and better justice. Democracy needs to be expanded; accurate, uncensored information needs to be promoted.

I am also concerned about public morality. The sale of political influence, the failure to tell the truth, and the corruption of the process make morality and virtue a central issue for the twenty-first century. Trust, a vital ingredient in negotiations, is often absent. Political virtue—seeking the common good—is the essence of representative government. Such virtue is not for someone else to attain, but is required of us all.

Of course, a brief list cannot include all the crucial problems that need attention in the twenty-first century. But making even a partial list helps me to get my priorities in line and to separate the inconsequential and the trivial from the important and the urgent. Listing these challenges should not overwhelm us. Most of them already have workable solutions if we give them the priority and the attention they deserve.

COVERT OPERATIONS IN A DEMOCRATIC SOCIETY

The most damaging mark on the Reagan presidency was the Iran-Contra affair. In 1984 the Reagan administration secretly sold arms to Iran, which was then, and is still, considered by our government to be a sponsor of terrorism, in order to raise cash for Nicaraguan Contra rebels, at a time when support for the Contras was specifically banned by law.

I chaired the 1987 House panel investigating Iran-Contra, and for a matter of days during our investigations the continuation of the Reagan presidency was in doubt. Managing the committee was a formidable assignment for me: a rare joint House-Senate committee, large staff, intense public interest on a daily basis. While the committee concluded that the president failed to meet his constitutional mandate to faithfully execute the laws of the land, it did not recommend impeachment, and the president weathered the storm. I appreciated the personal note I received afterward from President Reagan thanking me for the manner in which the investigations were conducted.

I got to know Dick Cheney well because he was a lead House Republican on the committee. He was civil and polite throughout, but deeply suspicious of the committee's investigation and—having served in the White House under Nixon and Ford—he supported the president strongly. He led the House Republican members to file a dissenting minority report, although the committee's main report was approved by a vote of seventeen to eight, with a majority of Senate Republicans signing on.

I was heavily criticized by liberals for not urging the impeachment of Reagan, but we just couldn't get solid evidence that he was personally involved, and all his team testified under oath that he wasn't. They aggressively defended his lack of knowledge on the covert actions and took upon themselves the responsibility for the mistakes. I was somewhat skeptical of their claims, but we had to decide on the basis of the facts and evidence before us. To this day, almost thirty years later, I still hear from people telling me that I was mistaken and Reagan should have been impeached.

November 1987: "Covert Operations in a Democratic Society"
Foreign Affairs Newsletter
Vol. VII, No. 11

The Iran-Contra affair raises again the issue of whether the US can conduct covert operations within the constitutional framework of government. Covert operations can be a useful tool of foreign policy. But can they be conducted both effectively and lawfully, consistent with the accountability required in a democratic society?

Specially appointed select committees of the House and Senate addressed this question once before in the mid-1970s, after revelations of controversial CIA activities. These inquiries led to the adoption of laws and procedures to control intelligence activities, including covert operations. Congress and three successive administrations, working together, created an interlocking system of statutes, executive orders, and national-security directives to provide for accountability. The two branches sought to ensure that covert operations would be conducted only with the prior authorization of the president, and with prior notice to congressional Intelligence Committees. Those committees were specially constituted by Congress in 1976–77 both for the purpose of legislative review and to protect the secrecy of covert operations.

The experience of the past decade has shown that the system governing covert operations can both protect secrets and provide accountability—if procedures are respected. In the Iran-Contra affair, they were not. Presidential flexibility was distorted beyond reasonable bounds. Officials, including the late director of Central Intelligence, withheld information, misled Congress, and skewed intelligence to support the policies they were advocating. Laws intended to reflect a spirit of trust were abused. The commitment to consultation with Congress was abandoned. The process broke down.

The House and Senate Iran-Contra Committees believe that extensive new legislation is not the remedy for the abuse of covert operations in this affair. Rather, the basic answer lies in better attitudes by those who serve in public office. The committees make several recommendations:

First, covert operations are necessary in certain circumstances, but they should not be the preferred tool of foreign policy. They can supplement—but cannot replace—diplomacy and the normal instruments of foreign policy. Particularly close scrutiny should be given to paramilitary or military covert actions, because it is hard to keep them secret or to sustain public support for them. As former national security advisor Robert McFarlane testified, "It is clearly unwise to rely on covert action as the core of our policy." Our government can gain and sustain support for its foreign policy only through open and public debate. Covert operations should not be used to change policy in secret and circumvent that debate.

Second, covert operations should be of the kind that the public would support if they knew of them. They should be consistent with public policies. When they run contrary to public policies, they damage American credibility, risk a major battle between Congress and the president, and lead to policy failure.

Third, the US should not rely on private individuals and funding to carry out its most sensitive business. All government operations, including covert operations, must be funded from appropriated monies or funds subject to the control of Congress. This is a principle at the heart of our system of checks and balances—and the best protection against future abuse.

Fourth, the intelligence and policy functions must remain separate if covert operations are to be successful. In the gathering, analysis, and reporting of intelligence, conclusions should be based on the facts, as objectively as they can be discerned. Conclusions should not be based on what policy advocates hope the facts to be.

Finally, the agencies carrying out covert operations must deal in a spirit of good faith with Congress. New and ongoing covert operations must be reported fully, not cloaked by broad findings. Answers to the Intelligence Committees that are technically true, but misleading, frustrate the process of legislative review. A dialogue that requires Congress to ask precisely the right question if it is to get the right answer is no dialogue at all, and is not a relationship based on trust and mutual respect.

Congress, in turn, has responsibilities. The Intelligence Committees are unable to benefit from a public airing of covert operations. Because their oversight is exclusive, the committees must be thorough. They cannot stop the president from initiating a covert action; the president is required by law only to inform the committees. But they are an important sounding board, and can point out potential policy pitfalls to the president. Had the administration felt obliged to inform the committees, many of the mistakes in the Iran-Contra affair could have been avoided. Strengthening current laws requiring notification to the Intelligence Committees will help Congress perform its tasks better.

Congress also has a responsibility to ensure that sensitive information shared by the executive branch remains secure. Contrary to how its views are sometimes portrayed, the intelligence community has generally been pleased with security on the Intelligence Committees. Nonetheless, a need exists for greater consensus between the branches on the sharing and protection of information.

As a great power with worldwide interests, the United States must deal with nations that have different hopes, values, and ambitions. To provide for its defense, the United States needs not just a strong military, but effective intelligence and the ability to influence developments abroad. A capable intelligence service, no less than a capable military, is fully compatible with democratic government when its actions are conducted in an accountable manner and in accordance with the rule of law.

THE REAGAN-GORBACHEV SUMMIT

One of Reagan's main contributions was that he put pressure on a crumbling Soviet Union system, believing—as many at the time did not—that the USSR was not a permanent unpleasant fact of life but a country that could be transformed.

The big question of the Reagan presidency is how much credit he should get for the fall of Communism. My sense is that it is less than is sometimes claimed. The Soviet Union was rotting from within and the seeds of decay were spreading. And within the Soviet Union there was a serious debate on the sustainability of large military expenditures. Gorbachev recognized all of this. Americans tend to overstate the role of the United States in foreign affairs, and saying simply that we brought about the collapse of the Soviet Union is an example of that. Certainly President Reagan played a role, but the final judgment on how much credit he deserves is still being sorted out by historians. In my various conversations with Gorbachev after I had left Congress, he was always emphatic that US policy had little effect, saying instead that the collapse of the Soviet Union was due primarily to the internal inconsistencies and contradictions of the Communist system.

December 23, 1987: "The Reagan-Gorbachev Summit"
Washington Report
Vol. XXII, No. 51

Washington has rarely seen a week like the one when General Secretary Mikhail Gorbachev came to call on President Reagan. It did not mark a great breakthrough in the difficult relationship between the two nations or resolve all the major issues, but it did achieve pragmatic advances and incremental steps that were important. By any standard it was a momentous week.

The summit was undoubtedly a diplomatic success for both leaders. Mr. Gorbachev impressed Washington and all the world. He probably enhanced his standing within the Communist Party at a time when he is trying to mobilize its vast apparatus behind him. Mr. Reagan revived sagging public support for his presidency and confounded his critics by delivering one arms control agreement and achieving progress toward another. For the first time the two nations signed a treaty to eliminate a whole class of nuclear weapons—intermediate-range missiles—and they opened the way for more sweeping and ambitious bargaining on strategic missiles. My view is that the mood at the summit was quite good, although the boundaries of what the leaders could get done were limited.

Little progress was made on human rights issues or the settlement of regional conflicts. No agreement could be reached on the withdrawal of Soviet troops from Afghanistan, and Gorbachev would not agree to a UN arms embargo against Iran. There were differing accounts of Soviet offers to suspend, under certain conditions, military aid to the Sandinista government in Nicaragua. On human rights, when the Americans talked about Soviet political prisoners and Jewish "refuseniks," the Soviets countered with talk about the plight of the homeless in America and US immigration restrictions. Although there were few concrete results, the Americans elevated human rights and regional issues, and Gorbachev was prepared to discuss subjects previously ignored by Kremlin leaders.

The central focus at the Washington summit was working toward additional reductions in the vast arsenals of nuclear weapons. The two leaders agreed to disagree, for now, over the future of the president's Strategic Defense Initiative (SDI). Gorbachev had insisted on linking strategic arms reductions to a US agreement to forgo SDI tests in space. But in Washington he accepted a vaguely worded paragraph about observance of the 1972 Anti-Ballistic Missile (ABM) Treaty, permitting each side to interpret the treaty as it wished. The whole confrontation over SDI was put off for another day.

Some progress was made on the outlines of a strategic arms treaty aimed at cutting long-range nuclear weapons in half. The leaders reaffirmed the guidelines they agreed upon in Reykjavik, including the overall ceiling of 6,000 warheads carried by 1,600 missiles or bombers. Some issues were resolved, and on others negotiators were directed to work out details. The two sides agreed to set a sublimit of 4,900 on the number of warheads permitted on land-based and sea-based ballistic missiles, and agreed on rules for counting the number of warheads carried on missiles and bombers. They agreed that long-range, sea-launched cruise missiles will be limited, which previously the US had refused to do. The Soviets agreed that they would not encode electronic signals during missile tests, because of US objections that it interfered with monitoring of Soviet treaty compliance. But the two sides failed to resolve some key differences, such as whether further limits should be placed on the number of land-based missile warheads. The leaders instructed their negotiators in Geneva to work out a system for verifying the destruction of weapons, and to clarify differing interpretations of the ABM Treaty, in hopes of clearing the way for a strategic arms reduction agreement to be signed in Moscow this spring.

We should not have any illusions about a strategic arms treaty. It will be much harder to negotiate than the intermediate-range missile treaty just signed because it will require resolving the SDI issue. It will also require far more complicated verification and the painful destruction of major weapons systems. The joint summit statement called for "a process intended to improve strategic stability and reduce the risk of conflict." Thus the leaders expect an evolving dialogue rather than immediate breakthroughs. The success of this summit will be judged by what happens over the next year or two.

I think the view that prevails in Washington is that Gorbachev's approach to world affairs offers a potential turning point in East-West relations, and that we must vigorously test how far he is willing to go in reversing the arms race and the superpower rivalry. All of us who met Gorbachev found him intelligent, direct, and forceful. In conversation he is flexible and skillful, but shows himself absolutely committed to the revolution, socialism, and a one-party state. He is very much a product of the system he is trying to change. What drives him is the imperative of modernizing the Soviet economy and the fear that Moscow's superpower status will be eroded by inefficiency and lagging technology.

After nearly three years in power, Gorbachev has reached a pivotal point. He must begin to provide some payoffs for his countrymen to justify the hardships produced by his initiatives. It is not clear to me that the summit will offer him any immediate, concrete payoffs. His central problem has been the need to free up Soviet resources for economic and social restructuring within the Soviet Union. The arms agreement just signed is not going to save any great amount of money, and large infusions of Western business capital or technology are not yet in the cards.

To sum up, the two leaders finished the immediate-range missile treaty. No date was fixed for a Soviet pullout from Afghanistan, and there was no resolution of human rights issues. No major breakthrough occurred on strategic arms, but progress was made. There was clearly a deepening of the political dialogue. The summit placed relations on a far more candid and realistic basis. Issues were clarified and new impetus was given to search for ways to ease the real differences between the two countries. These may not be the flashiest of results, but they are sound.

THE BUDGET LEGACY OF THE REAGAN YEARS

Although President Reagan's rhetoric was highly critical of government and federal spending, he fundamentally accepted government as it was, and not one of the eight budgets he submitted to Congress was balanced. Indeed, during his presidency the federal budget deficit widened considerably, which then had to be tackled by Presidents Bush and Clinton. The worsening of the budget deficit was one of the most unfortunate legacies of his presidency, and Reagan himself described the new debt as the "greatest disappointment" of his time in office.

March 2, 1988: "The Budget Legacy of the Reagan Years"
Washington Report
Vol. XXIII, No. 9

With the submission of President Reagan's final effective budget, it is an appropriate time to review the president's federal budget legacy.

Under President Reagan, annual federal spending has increased by $377 billion, to more than $1 trillion. Federal outlays, which were 22.7 percent of the gross national product (GNP) in 1981, rose to 24 percent in 1985 before dropping back to 22.5 percent of the GNP in 1988. At the same time federal revenues have not kept up, increasing $298 billion over the same period.

The result is that President Reagan has overseen the creation of more new debt than the combined deficits of all previous presidents. President Carter's largest deficit was $73.8 billion in 1980, but under President Reagan the deficit reached $220.7 billion in 1986. The last few years have shown us that there is no way to cut taxes sharply, increase defense spending strongly, promise not to touch various entitlement programs, and still pay interest on the debt without creating enormous deficits. Reflecting the large increase in public debt, federal interest payments have risen from $69 billion in 1981 to $148 billion this year. Interest payments now eat up 14 percent of all federal spending, and exceed the combined budgets of the Departments of Agriculture, Commerce, Education, Energy, Interior, Justice, Labor, State, and Transportation.

The most enduring legacy of the Reagan period will be the heavily indebted government. To finance the changes brought about during the Reagan presidency, the government has added $500 million a day to its debt. So far, this deficit-spending policy has not caused dramatic economic problems. During the president's watch, inflation and interest rates have come down, the civilian unemployment rate has fallen to 5.8 percent, and we are in the midst of the longest peacetime economic expansion in US history. The concern about the deficits is more long-term. The deficits entail massive government borrowing that mortgages the nation's economic future. They have also weakened the government's ability to undertake important initiatives. The large deficits will make it more difficult for the government to increase spending if the economy falls into a recession and the unemployed and others hurt by such a downturn need government aid.

President Reagan has not dismantled many government programs. Basically his approach has been to consolidate federal programs, and to pare programs rather than eliminate them. Eligibility has been tightened and benefits reduced. The president killed eighteen programs in his initial 1981 budget but many of them were later restored. Revenue sharing—federal funds provided directly to the states and cities—was the only major domestic program repealed in the Reagan years that stayed repealed. At the same time, various new programs have been added, including the Strategic Defense Initiative, AIDS research, and aid to the homeless.

While total government expenditures have reached historic highs during the Reagan years, the portion of the budget going for domestic discretionary spending has shrunk. Overall, the poor have been harder hit than others under the Reagan budgets.

Education and training, community development, welfare, nutrition, housing, and other antipoverty programs were reduced the most. The young have been hit harder than the old. Today we spend four times as much per capita for the aged than for children, and the gap is growing. State and local governments have also received less help under the Reagan budgets. The president has shifted many responsibilities to the states while reducing federal aid to state and local governments by 30 percent in constant dollars. Some middle-class benefits were reduced, but large federal funds continue to flow to programs that benefit Americans of all incomes, such as Social Security, Medicare, and farm price supports. Outlays for these programs have far outstripped inflation during the president's tenure, while federal outlays for poor families with children and for food stamps have declined in real terms. This represents a sharp change from the past when spending on poverty programs rose more rapidly than spending on middle-class entitlements.

Although the president has failed to stop the growth of government spending, he has significantly changed the composition of the federal budget. Measured in dollars adjusted for inflation, what has happened in the federal budget from 1981 to 1987 is as follows: interest on the national debt has risen 59 percent; defense spending has risen 46 percent; Social Security, Medicare, and other retirement programs have gone up 26 percent; while other domestic spending, such as for energy, transportation, and economic development, has declined 21 percent. The programs receiving the greatest increases during President Reagan's years have had some successes. Our defense capabilities have been strengthened, Social Security has been rescued from the threat of insolvency, the Medicare payment system has been restructured, and there has been a turnaround in the farm sector.

The president's rhetoric about government spending as the source of the ills of the economy masks the results of his presidency. In many respects the federal establishment that he leaves behind is remarkably similar to the establishment he found when he came to office in 1981. The basic programs of the New Deal and the Great Society endure even at the end of his administration, and several, including Social Security, Medicare, and Medicaid, have been significantly expanded. So clearly, the legacy of the Reagan budgets is that many of the federal programs created in previous decades will continue in the post-Reagan period. Huge budget deficits will also survive, and the next president will have very little room to maneuver to address pressing problems. Public opinion polls show that the public wants to spend more on poverty, homelessness, child care, and long-term health care, but it is hard to see where the money will come from.

The next president faces a bleak fiscal outlook with defense and domestic discretionary spending squeezed. The leaders and the taxpayers in the post-Reagan period will inherit the burden of paying for the debt if not paying it off.

THE QUIET CRISIS

I would often be amazed at the complexity of legislation passed by Congress—such as environmental bills that looked like my college chemistry textbook—and wonder how it could possibly be implemented by federal agencies. Government has increasingly needed skilled people to carry out programs to address our ever-more-complex national problems. Yet the task of attracting good people to work in the federal government becomes all the more difficult when the leaders of our nation denigrate and devalue public service. We might smile at the Reagan quip that the nine most terrifying words in the English language are "I'm from the government and I'm here to help," but after a while it takes a toll.

> **July 6, 1988: "The Quiet Crisis"**
> **Washington Report**
> **Vol. XXIII No. 27**
> We have heard a lot recently about the urgent need to do something about several crises: the budget and trade deficits, education, drug abuse, AIDS, and others. Let me add another crisis to the list—one which has been dubbed the "quiet crisis." Although not in the headlines, it is getting increasing attention from policymakers. The worry is that the federal government may no longer be able to attract the kinds of quality people it will need to do the essential work of our country in the years ahead. Future presidents could be hampered in carrying out their policies because of a weakened civil service.

While the federal government continues to have many remarkably dedicated and competent employees, my impression is that
talent is getting harder to attract and retain. Over the past decade,
more than half of the federal government's top managers have left.
In a recent survey of civilian and military government managers,
57 percent would not recommend government service to young
people, and 59 percent believed that the quality of hires is declining. Very few of our top students today express an interest in a civil
service career. The Internal Revenue Service, for example, now
hires accountants scoring in the fifty-fourth percentile on the CPA
exam. Recent law school graduates, often in debt, are reluctant to
work for the federal government when they can get double or triple
the pay in the private sector.

Even as it has become more difficult to attract good people into
public service, the need for quality workers has increased. Today we
need top-flight people to negotiate treaties, ensure airplane safety,
oversee the banking and securities system, inspect our food and water, build reliable weapons, monitor nuclear power plants, conduct
AIDS and cancer research, clean up toxic wastes, and fight drug
abuse. Our country needs the most competent people available to
carry out the programs which address our most difficult problems.

The importance of attracting good people was recognized by
our Founding Fathers. Our earliest presidents made sure they
brought with them the best and brightest of their day. As Alexander
Hamilton stated, "A government ill-executed, whatever might be the
theory, is in practice poor government." All Americans, including
those opposed to large governments, have a stake in seeing that
government programs are efficiently run and do not overreach
their bounds.

Several factors have contributed to the difficulty in attracting good people to public service in recent years. Low pay is often
blamed. By some estimates, federal pay and benefits trail those
in the private sector by 7–24 percent. Many are put off by limited room for advancement to positions of responsibility, and by
cumbersome federal hiring practices. The hiring freeze and layoffs
early in the 1980s and the frequent efforts to cut back civil-service
retirement benefits have indicated to many the limits of a federal
career. The public perception of civil service has suffered from the
past two presidents running against Washington and criticizing

its "bureaucrats." Various recent scandals, like the Pentagon procurement mess, have led many to wonder whether working for the federal government is an honorable profession. The excitement that some felt working for a federal government which was attacking our most difficult social problems has dissipated. Young people often express their interest in making money rather than in trying to contribute to society through public service.

In addition, there are several misconceptions about the federal workforce. It is not the bloated, ever-expanding bureaucracy often portrayed. Three agencies, the Department of Defense, the Postal Service, and the Veterans Administration, account for more than two-thirds of all federal workers. While these three have grown in recent years—because of the defense buildup, expanded demand for postal services, and the growing health needs of the aging veterans population—federal employment elsewhere has generally declined. For example, the Departments of Agriculture and Health and Human Services both have seen their workforce drop 17 percent over the past decade. In 1977, each federal worker served seventy-six citizens; in 1987, each served seventy-nine. A recent congressional study found that federal workers are better educated than their counterparts in the private sector, and are increasing their productivity faster.

Yet the civil service is entering a new era when attracting qualified workers will be increasingly difficult. Several reforms have been suggested. They include increasing pay levels, especially to provide bonuses and merit increases for high-quality work; decreasing the number of political appointees in order to open more top positions to career civil servants; giving managers more discretion in hiring and firing decisions; and setting up tailor-made personnel systems for particular agencies. Another proposal is to "decouple" federal salaries from congressional salaries, since Congress's reluctance to raise its own pay has held down salaries for top civil servants. A National Commission on the Public Service headed by ex–Federal Reserve chairman Paul Volcker is expected to have specific recommendations early next year.

My sense is that we must do more than improve particular job benefits. We must correct public misconceptions about government career service, develop a cooperative spirit between political appointees and the career workers in government, and strengthen the educational base for potential government service. We have to be careful that our feelings in opposition to particular government policies do not become an attitude against government and civil servants in general. Finally, we must strengthen our national commitment to public service, returning to the idea stated by Thomas Jefferson that "there is a debt of service due from every man to his country, proportioned to the bounties which nature and fortune have measured to him." The obligation of improving perceptions of public responsibilities rests most heavily on our future leadership—especially the next president.

The federal government is not going to go away. What it does is getting more complicated and challenging each year. Its work will only be done well if there are good people available to do it.

Reagan's admirers have worked aggressively over the years to promote a conservative and successful image of his presidency, and they have succeeded in naming airports, highways, schools, and buildings across the country in his honor—making it difficult to get a balanced picture of his legacy.

Reagan didn't have a detailed policy agenda when he came into office but rather a few key, firmly held beliefs: reduce taxes, cut domestic spending, build up the military, weaken Soviet power and influence, and balance the budget. He had his core convictions, but he also compromised along the way. There were no lengthy government shutdowns during Reagan's time. He did not veto major appropriations bills. Differences were worked out.

We hear a lot today about the need for greater civility, the need to ratchet down the heated—sometimes hateful—political rhetoric. President Reagan deserves good marks for that too. He was involved in some tough battles and fought hard for what he believed in, but he always treated the other side as the opponent, not the hated enemy.

The same was true for Speaker O'Neill. He developed a satisfactory working relationship with President Reagan. Even though they had major differences on what they thought was best for the country, he and the president said the battles stopped at six o'clock, and they would sometimes call each other up and get together for a drink after that. And after President

Reagan was shot, and was in far worse shape than was publicly known, it was Tip O'Neill who was one of his first visitors—holding both of his hands, offering a prayer for his recovery, and reciting with him the Twenty-Third Psalm. That's not something we can easily imagine happening in today's political world.

Reagan and O'Neill exemplified how government should work. They were skillful politicians and they were dealmakers. Each understood that he could not get everything he wanted; rather, they always recognized that the other needed to get something out of the deal. Despite quite different backgrounds, personalities, and perspectives, they found a way to work with each other, and they would often use Irish stories to alleviate tension. It was a civil, workable relationship, as I was able to observe on several occasions, and each had respect for the other. Each thought the other was sincere in his beliefs, just wrong.

To me the chief characteristic of Reagan was his optimism. He was upbeat and had a gift for making people feel good. He believed America worked, and he didn't like to see—and often ignored—instances of trouble. He drew a sharp line between America, which he lauded and praised, and government, which he often criticized—not fully recognizing the extent to which a government contributes to the strength of a nation.

President Reagan came into office when the country was in a state of gloom, and he made America feel big again. And, despite the ups and downs of his presidency, by the time he left office the economy was improving, the Soviet Union was crumbling, and Americans' optimism and confidence were on the rise. Nancy Reagan reported that when the president left the White House for the last time, walking toward the helicopter he said to her, "It's been a wonderful eight years, all in all. Not bad at all." Most Americans shared that sentiment.

Yet while there were major accomplishments during the eight years of the Reagan presidency, there were also some significant mistakes and excesses, and the task of trying to clean those up fell to his successor—George H. W. Bush.

SIX

THE GEORGE H. W. BUSH YEARS
(1989–92)
A New World Order

I KNEW GEORGE H. W. BUSH WELL FOR SEVERAL YEARS, GOING BACK to the time when we both served in the House of Representatives in the late 1960s. He was a decent, honorable, positive person.

And, I might add, enjoyable to be around. I remember a relaxing Christmas Day I was spending at home with my family. We had just finished our holiday dinner when a phone call from the president came through. He wished me and Nancy happy holidays and then asked whether I could meet him in a few minutes in the House of Representatives gym for some games of paddleball, which is not something you look forward to after a large meal. I hesitated, pointing out that the House gym would be locked on Christmas. But he said that would be no problem, he'd take care of it— and as leader of the free world that was something he was able to handle.

Bush excelled at making and maintaining friendships. When he first came to Congress in 1967, he was elected president of the House freshman class. Throughout all his years of public service he was known for writing personal notes, staying in touch. His engaging personality made him popular among members of Congress.

He was well motivated, with a deep commitment to public service. He had come from the Eastern aristocracy and had an Ivy League background, but he was not at all elitist or condescending in his approach to people. He came across as simply a nice person. His concern for the nation's civic life was evident in his inaugural address, when he talked about the need to give something back to the country "that has given us so much."

He was also a modest man, which was a product of his upbringing. And he was always amazed—as well as quite humbled—by the fact that he was president. I remember one time being at the White House with a few other members of Congress for a meeting with him. We were out on the White House balcony overlooking the expanse of the south lawn and then beyond that the magnificent view of the Washington Monument and the Jefferson Memorial. He turned to chairman Dan Rostenkowski, who was standing next to him, and said in a quiet tone, "Can you believe it, Dan? I'm president of the United States."

Congress and President Bush generally had good relations during the four years of his presidency. He faced a Congress that was under Democratic control by significant margins in both the House and the Senate, so of course there were differences and tensions. But in general the relationship was marked by civility and fairly good communication. The House Speaker at the beginning of Bush's term was Jim Wright of Texas, and then for most of the Bush years it was Tom Foley of Washington. The House Minority Leader was Bob Michel of Illinois, but an increasingly aggressive Republican stance was being pushed by Minority Whip Newt Gingrich from Georgia.

As Bush's presidency began there was clearly some resentment among congressional Democrats over the tough 1988 political campaign, which included the "Willie Horton" ads, a barrage of negativity, and personal attacks on Governor Michael Dukakis and his wife, all of which seemed out of character for the George Bush I knew. In his inaugural address he tried to heal the wounds. He set the right tone by extending a hand to Democrats and saying that "the old bipartisanship must be made new again."

The task ahead for Congress and the president at that time was a difficult one, with major problems left over from the Reagan years that needed to be cleaned up. One of the biggest problems, the huge federal budget deficit, created a major challenge for Congress and the president over the next four years as they tried to find the funds to address the pressing needs facing the country.

It was also a time of reassessing the Reagan legacy: Did his supply-side tax cuts work? Should we continue to invest heavily in his Strategic Defense

Initiative? Did his targeting of Great Society programs for cutbacks work out all right?

A more personal carryover from the Reagan presidency for Bush was the continuing question of whether he was involved in Iran-Contra while he was vice president. Bush said many times that he was not in the loop on the decision, but notes from people at various key meetings suggested that he was present. Because I had headed up the House Iran-Contra investigation, he one day sent me a personal note saying in an earnest tone that he was not involved in Iran-Contra. I took him at his word.

The 101st Congress: Key Facts
- January 3, 1989, through October 28, 1990, during the first two years of the George H. W. Bush administration
- House of Representatives controlled by the Democrats, 259 to 174 (2 other)
- Senate controlled by the Democrats, 55 to 45
- 650 bills enacted
- Major accomplishments included passing the Whistleblower Protection Act, the Financial Institutions Reform, Recovery, and Enforcement Act, the Ethics Reform Act, the Flag Protection Act, the Americans with Disabilities Act, the Omnibus Budget Reconciliation Act, the Iraq Sanctions Act, the Nutrition Labeling and Education Act, the Clean Air Act Amendments, and the Immigration Act of 1990; and Senate ratification of the Threshold Test Ban Treaty
- Support for President Bush's position in the House: Democrats 32 percent, Republicans 69 percent; in the Senate: Democrats 48 percent, Republicans 76 percent

The 102nd Congress: Key Facts
- January 3, 1991, through October 9, 1992, during the last two years of the George H. W. Bush administration
- House of Representatives controlled by the Democrats, 267 to 167 (1 other)

- Senate controlled by the Democrats, 56 to 44
- 590 bills enacted
- Major accomplishments included passing the Persian Gulf War Resolution, the Resolution Trust Corporation Refinancing, Restructuring, and Improvement Act, the Intermodal Surface Transportation Efficiency Act, the High Performance Computing Act (internet), the US Nuclear Test Explosions Ban, the Energy Policy Act, the Former Soviet Union Demilitarization Act, the Freedom Support Act, and the Housing and Community Development Act; and Senate ratification of the Strategic Arms Reduction Treaty
- Support for President Bush's position in the House: Democrats 31 percent, Republicans 75 percent; in the Senate: Democrats 38 percent, Republicans 79 percent

SDI REASSESSMENT

The Strategic Defense Initiative was a major new policy initiative of President Reagan's, and early on in Bush's presidency it fell upon him to decide whether it should be continued and in what form.

Reagan's idea of SDI was to develop and deploy an absolutely perfect, impenetrable shield to protect us from any incoming missiles—an enormously difficult undertaking. But as the Great Communicator, Reagan oversold it to the American people, as well as to the Soviets, whose concern about our development of SDI was a significant factor in their decision to curb the arms race with America.

Even in scaled-down versions, SDI basically meant trying to hit a bullet with a bullet without knowing when it was fired. So its development was a major challenge for national-security scientists, and progress was slow. But funding for the program was continued during the Bush years, at around $3–$4 billion annually. Some thirty years after President Reagan initially proposed SDI and after spending many billions of dollars, we have been able to put in place only a partial missile defense system, one that is not impenetrable by any means and which is nothing close to the shield Reagan had sought.

March 1, 1989: "SDI Reassessment"
Washington Report
Vol. XXIV, No. 9

In the early weeks of the Bush presidency, one of Ronald Reagan's most controversial programs is quietly approaching an important turning point. As President Bush begins to define his defense and foreign-policy priorities, important choices will have to be made about the future of the Strategic Defense Initiative (SDI)—the program for defenses against enemy missile attack. These choices will have significant implications for the federal budget, the security of the nation, and the future of arms control.

Since President Reagan proposed SDI in March of 1983, there has been constant debate about its objectives. Should SDI be a research program exploring scientific principles and basic technologies which may have military applications in the twenty-first century? Should it be a program to build massive defensive systems to fully protect the American people from missile attack? Or should we develop more modest defenses with less all-embracing objectives? President Reagan's goals for SDI were always clear. He wanted nationwide defenses that would render nuclear weapons "impotent and obsolete." But that objective may no longer be central in SDI planning. President Bush's nominee for secretary of defense, John Tower, recently testified that any expectation of providing umbrella population defenses was "unrealistic." Most defense experts agree with Tower's assessment.

With nationwide defenses ruled out, there are now two widely talked-about SDI alternatives. One is a modest defensive deployment called the Accidental Launch Protection System (ALPS), which would defend large parts of the country against a few missiles that might be fired by mistake or by a small country with limited capabilities. The other is the so-called Phase I of SDI. This first phase would involve the use of existing technologies to destroy some of the warheads aimed at the United States during a nuclear war. Any decision to deploy limited missile defenses can only be made after we have answered three basic questions:

How well will it work? Judging the utility of any missile defense proposal is difficult unless we know how the Soviet Union will respond to it. If we build defenses, they could build more offensive systems and overwhelm our defensive capabilities. Both sides would then have increased military spending without achieving any measurable gain in security. A Phase I SDI, as currently envisioned, could probably be countered by the Soviet Union unless both sides agreed to limit their offensive weapons; and the Soviets are unlikely to accept new arms control limitations at a time when we are deploying missile defenses.

Modest defensive systems would offer some protection against accidental launches and against attacks from smaller nations that may someday acquire both nuclear weapons and long-range missiles. The chances of an accidental missile attack are hard to estimate, but they have certainly decreased in recent years as both the United States and the Soviet Union have worked to reduce the danger of technical failures in missile control. Limited defenses would not protect us against all kinds of small-scale or terrorist nuclear attacks, such as a nuclear weapon smuggled across our borders. Small defensive systems would give us some added protection, but at a significant price.

How much will it cost? Funding for SDI has risen steadily in the last few years. The final Reagan budget request for 1990 includes $5.9 billion for missile defenses, a 50 percent increase over this year's expenditures. From 1985 through 1989, SDI has consumed nearly $15 billion. This level of spending is modest compared to the costs we would incur in a full-scale Phase I program. Last October the Defense Department estimated that the testing, development, and deployment of Phase I would be $69 billion. ALPS would probably cost less but no official estimates have been made. A commitment to either of these alternatives would affect spending on other defense priorities. In an era of budget constraints, SDI must compete for limited Pentagon funds.

What effect will it have on arms control and the ABM Treaty? Any decision to deploy missile defenses would have an impact on past and future arms control agreements with the Soviet Union. By most accounts, it will be impossible to build the first phase of SDI without violating the Anti-Ballistic Missile (ABM) Treaty of 1972, one of the most important international agreements in the post-war era. A decision to build missile defenses would also threaten the successful negotiation of a Strategic Arms Reduction Treaty (START) to reduce superpower nuclear warheads by 50 percent. Because ALPS would involve fewer interceptors and no space-based weapons, it might be possible to construct without violating our ABM Treaty commitments, but there are serious verification problems in building any limited defensive system without making it appear to be a precursor to a prohibited nationwide system.

The purpose of partial missile defenses is to increase the security of the United States by adding defensive capabilities to our existing offensive weapons. Increasing our security in the nuclear age is an important objective, but there are many ways to achieve it. For example, mobile missiles, which are now under consideration, would improve the ability of our land-based forces to survive a nuclear attack. Alternately, signing a carefully negotiated START agreement could reduce the threat of nuclear war and the need for missile defenses. Taking one of these steps, or both of them, might be cheaper and safer than a decision to proceed with Phase I deployments.

SDI is at a crossroads. Since it was introduced in 1983, the idea of building missile defenses has received serious national debate. There is now wide agreement that we need a basic research program to explore the prospects for future missile defense systems. We have done this research for many years, and so have the Soviets. The harder question for SDI is whether we should go beyond research and begin building actual defensive systems with limited capabilities. As SDI approaches its sixth anniversary, difficult decisions must be made about the immediate future of missile defenses. The Bush administration, the Congress, and the American public will have to make those decisions with great care.

HOUSE ETHICS REFORM

Serving on the House ethics committee—officially known then as the Standards of Official Conduct Committee—is an unpleasant assignment for members because you are asked to sit in judgment of your colleagues, which no one likes to do, and they are always suspicious of you, knowing that you are evaluating their conduct. Tip O'Neill once caught me in a weak moment—after rescuing me from standing out in the pouring rain one night trying fruitlessly to hail a cab in Washington, DC—and asked me to serve on the Standards Committee, which I did, reluctantly. But in the end I felt it was one of the more important things I did: trying to maintain high standards of congressional conduct.

For years I had an interest in strengthening congressional ethics because of the public's demand for integrity as well as my concern that the misconduct of any member taints the institution as a whole in the people's eyes and undermines its effectiveness. Given the difficulty of the task the results have not been impressive so far, but Congress needs to keep trying.

Starting in the late 1980s, congressional ethics took an unfortunate turn, as some members of Congress were using the "ethics weapon" to go after members of the other party. House Republicans were upset over the way Speaker Jim Wright, who had followed Tip O'Neill, was reducing their involvement in House business. So in 1987 Newt Gingrich filed ethics charges against Speaker Wright for questionable financial moves, and the 101st Congress began with a bitter fight that led to Wright's resignation. It was the start of a period in which several leaders of both parties were toppled because of ethics charges by the other side, including Newt Gingrich himself, who was forced to resign a decade later. It was a particularly dark period in congressional ethics.

May 24, 1989: "House Ethics Reform"
Washington Report
Vol. XXIV, No. 21

One of the priorities in the House this session is improving congressional standards of conduct. Members are concerned about repairing the tarnished image of the Congress and a House task force has been set up to make recommendations. Some of the effort will be to revise specific provisions in the House ethics rules, such as tightening up vagueness in the gift rules and cutting back on honoraria accepted by members. Important as such rule changes will be, I believe that several other kinds of efforts would be as important—or even more important—in improving overall congressional ethics.

First, we need to restructure the House Code of Official Conduct to make clear what is at the heart of it. House enforcement of the ethics rules seems to have gotten off track somewhat in recent years. We often get bogged down in "legalese" and technical discussions of narrow provisions in the rules and guidelines. For example, last session one of the Standards Committee's conclusions about a member was that he violated House ethics standards both by arranging questionable personal trips and by using a telephone to do it. Perhaps in the legal world the use of a telephone in interstate trafficking makes a difference, but to say that phone use indicates a violation of basic House ethics norms shows how far we have strayed from the essence of the Code of Conduct. Our major focus should be on broad standards of good conduct—whether or not a particular action by a member reflects credit or discredit on the House, as Rule 1 of the code says.

We should restructure the code—emphasizing first a few broad ethical precepts that form the heart of the code, followed by examples of more specific rules of misconduct (such as gift and honoraria rules) which are not claimed to be an exhaustive list of every kind of conduct that would violate the basic precepts. The basic structure of the code should make it clear to members that their actions should conform to broad standards of good conduct, whether or not they may technically avoid some of the legalistic nuances of a specific rule.

Second, we should broaden our conception in the code of what is involved in ethical conduct or public morality. Basically our focus has been on financial matters. Clearly this is important, but one gets the impression from looking at the 250-page House ethics manual that if you file your financial disclosure forms on time, don't convert campaign funds to personal use, and don't misuse the frank, then you are behaving in an ethically acceptable and moral way as a member of Congress.

Yet such rules capture only a part of what is involved in legislative ethics. Many other kinds of actions by members of Congress can undermine the basic perception of Americans in the integrity of government, such as when a member greatly distorts his opponent's record, misleads constituents about his role in getting some legislation passed or case resolved, or denigrates the competence or value of government. Several basic ethical values and principles apply to those in public services, including honesty, integrity, promise keeping, fairness, respect, excellence, accountability, and protection of public trust. Some of these could be worked into our Code of Official Conduct. The code should contain not just various prohibitions but also some positive ideals that members should be striving to attain.

Third, we need to greatly expand the efforts of the Standards Committee to try to head off possible cases of misconduct before they occur. That means intensifying the committee's preventative ethics role. Possibilities include having Standards Committee staffers visit each member and congressional office every session to let them know of the committee's advisory role; holding more committee briefings for members and staff on key provisions of the code and on the rationale behind the rules; and bringing to the Hill outside speakers on various ethics topics.

Fourth, we must improve the way members of the Standards Committee are treated. It is difficult to get members of Congress to serve on this rather thankless committee, and once they are on it we pillory them for not acting as we would like in particular cases. A frequent defense by members of Congress accused by the committee is to charge the committee with racism or political motives or incompetence. Often a member will defend himself by attacking the committee or the process which he himself approved when the committee was set up at the beginning of the session. It is extremely important to be able to attract good and capable members to serve on the Standards Committee, but that is getting increasingly more difficult to do.

Fifth, clear ethics signals need to come from the top. Reconstructing the House ethics rules and trying to close all the loopholes is important, but the overall tone set by our leadership is more important. Thus I strongly support President Bush's effort to send the right ethics signal to government workers from the very start of his administration—announcing that the highest standards would be required and that even the perception of wrongdoing should be avoided. Speaker Wright and House Minority Leader Michel made strong statements in favor of House ethics earlier this year when they set up the task force on ethics reform. Restating that message frequently will make it clear to members that they will be held to the highest standards of conduct.

Finally, we need to broaden bipartisan cooperation on House ethics. There is little doubt that much of the recent interest in ethics reform has been a thinly veiled desire to use the "ethics issue" to make partisan political attacks. Ethics should not be used as a tool for badgering our political opponents. My concern is that the cynical, partisan basis for some efforts to push ethics reform may in itself be bringing down the public's conception of government integrity. To be truly effective, government ethics must be approached in as nonpartisan a way as possible.

The vast majority of members of Congress are honest, hardworking, dedicated individuals. Yet the misconduct of some can bring down the institution as a whole and undermine its ability to function. Reinforcing our standards of conduct is an effort worth undertaking.

SUPPLY-SIDE ECONOMICS

One of the core Reagan beliefs was his commitment to "supply-side" economics: the view that reducing income taxes provides incentives for people to work harder because they can keep more of their paycheck, which in turn should bring in more federal revenues. The Reagan years could be viewed as a major experiment in supply-side economics. How well did it work?

When I started in Congress, Republicans were deeply concerned about balancing the federal budget and they attacked federal spending all the time. But the downside for them was that they couldn't fund many new initiatives if they were always trying to cut spending. So Reagan's supply-side approach became immensely popular with Republicans, who thought they had found the magic formula that allowed them to reduce taxes for Americans as a way to actually help reduce the deficit. Giving out tax breaks to constituents is certainly more appealing than cutting their programs. And from that time on Republicans were no longer the fervent guardians of the deficit.

With President Bush now proposing additional supply-side tax cuts, I thought it was a good time to pause and assess whether supply-side economics had worked as well as Reagan said it would, and whether you actually could get something for nothing. I never bought into this supply-side approach, even though its political appeal was powerful and seductive.

December 13, 1989: "Supply-Side Economics"
Washington Report
Vol. XXIV, No. 50

The Reagan presidency emphasized a new approach to economics—"supply-side" economics—which favored cutting taxes to boost productivity and reinvigorate the economy. This was our country's guiding economic approach throughout much of the 1980s, and President Reagan credited it with many US economic successes during his term. Because President Bush's call for reducing capital gains taxes is essentially a supply-side tax cut, it is important to determine how well that approach has worked.

Supply-side economics claims that lower tax rates provide powerful incentives for individuals and corporations to work harder and to invest. This higher productivity will result in much stronger economic growth and hence higher revenues to the government. In short, the tax cuts end up paying for themselves. President Reagan used this argument to push through a huge tax cut in 1981, which reduced individual taxes 25 percent over three years and included major tax cuts to encourage new business investment.

Despite the obvious appeal of such an approach—cutting taxes with all gain and no pain—most economists today believe that supply-side economics failed to live up to its promises.

The first major problem is that the 1981 tax cuts did not pay for themselves by producing a surge of new revenue. In 1981, President Reagan estimated that his tax cuts would increase federal revenues from the 1981 level of $600 billion to $710 billion in 1983 and $942 billion in 1986. Of that $170 billion increase since 1981, some $100 billion came from increases in Social Security taxes (due partly to an anti-supply-side increase in tax rates); and the rest is less than would be expected from normal growth in the economy, as revenues did not even keep up with inflation. The promised surge of new revenue never materialized.

The low tax rates generated less of a boom in investment and output than supply-siders had claimed. On any score, the 1980s show no extraordinary burst of work effort. Critics of supply-side economics were predicting that the primary legacy of the 1981 tax cut would be higher, not lower, federal deficits, and that has certainly been the case. While President Reagan in 1981 promised a balanced budget by 1984, the annual deficit in fact increased from $79 billion to $185 billion.

The second major miscalculation of the supply-siders was that there would be a boost in saving, as the lower tax rates would encourage people to save more. Moreover, even if some revenue was lost from the tax cuts, that would not matter because we would get a big increase in savings sufficient to finance both the deficit and an investment boom. Yet savings did not increase. Despite the tax rate cuts and a variety of new tax breaks for saving, personal savings declined sharply—from 7.1 percent of personal income in 1980 to 4.0 percent in 1986. Most Americans spent rather than saved their tax cuts. The personal saving rate has improved only since the passage of the 1986 Tax Reform Act, which did not involve supply-side tax cuts.

Advocates of supply-side economics point to the seven-year record economic expansion as solid proof that their approach works. Yet critics point out that whereas the supply-siders in 1981 were predicting an immediate upturn in economic growth because of the sharpened economic incentives, 1982 instead saw the deepest economic downturn since the Great Depression. Moreover, since the recovery began in December 1982, the growth rate in the economy has been only average, lagging slightly behind the average pace of the pre-supply-side expansions after World War II.

Most economists instead believe that the expansion of the 1980s has been the result of the traditional Keynesian, "demand-side" prescription—pumping up demand in the economy through deficit spending. It is certainly not surprising that the economy would get a boost when the federal government annually spends $150–$200 billion more than it takes in. Another major factor in keeping the recovery going has been the skill of the Federal Reserve in shifting monetary policy to compensate for fluctuations in the economy. The 1980s have been primarily a monetary and demand-side success rather than a supply-side success.

Some of the themes of supply-side economics are not unreasonable; they have just been oversold. Orthodox economists agree with supply-siders that lower tax rates can have beneficial effects on the economy. It is certainly the case that, other things being equal, low tax rates are better than high tax rates. And the Tax Reform Act of 1986, which closed numerous loopholes in exchange for lower tax rates, has had a positive effect on our economy, as personal saving and investment have increased. What was clearly shown wrong about supply-side economics, however, was its something-for-nothing promise—the claim that by cutting taxes we would increase revenues. Not surprisingly, that was mistaken.

Yet we hear similar promises in President Bush's call for reducing capital gains taxes, which he claims will boost savings and investment, and hence increase economic growth and revenues. Our recent experience should have taught us to be wary of claims of enormous benefits from tax cuts. Tax cuts can have positive effects on the economy, but we need to balance those benefits against the damage done to the economy by increasing our already huge federal deficits.

The worst legacy of the supply-side experiment of the 1980s is the run-up in our national debt, which saddles future Americans with enormous debt-service payments. And for all we spent in the 1980s, we did not increase our investment in productive assets, leaving our children no better able to meet these obligations. We did not get the free lunch promised by supply-siders, but instead have billed it to future generations.

NATIONAL SPENDING PRIORITIES

Particularly at a time when we were running large federal budget deficits and it was clear that we couldn't fund everything, I thought it important to get a better "big picture" sense of federal spending to help with setting priorities and making tough decisions. So I was attracted to a "GNP budget" idea being proposed by Herb Stein, who had been the chairman of the Council of Economic Advisors under Presidents Nixon and Ford. The broad accounting of spending from all levels of government as well as the private sector that Stein urged has, unfortunately, still not been widely implemented.

A few years after writing this commentary, I almost got through Congress—with the help of appropriations chairman Dave Obey—a requirement that the president's economic report contain a GNP budget. But the idea died once the Republicans took over the House after the 1994 elections and they had other interests.

April 4, 1990: "National Spending Priorities"
Washington Report
Vol. XXV, No. 14

In recent weeks, the Congress has been working on President Bush's proposed 1991 budget—a 1,500-page document with countless tables and figures outlining $1.23 trillion in spending. The flood of budget figures pouring forth from numerous sources leads to confusion and makes it very difficult to get a sense of direction in the budget. New ways of looking at federal spending could improve our ability to understand national spending priorities.

Each year the federal government funds hundreds of programs spread around scores of departments and agencies. The budget simplifies matters by dividing federal spending into eighteen budget functions, but even these may be too many to illuminate overall trends. For all the budget talk, most of us are not aware of even basic budget facts, such as that the federal government now spends more on older Americans than it spends on anything else, including national defense.

Broader Spending Categories: A clearer sense of basic national spending priorities emerges when the budget is divided into a few broad spending categories: defense, nondefense investment (such as education, research, and infrastructure), programs for the elderly, programs for the non-elderly poor or disabled, economic stability programs (such as unemployment compensation, deposit insurance, and farm programs), general government operations, and interest on the national debt. In 1989, the federal government spent 32 percent of its total outlays on programs for older Americans, including Social Security, Medicare, federal military and civilian retirement, and certain veteran benefits. Federal spending on defense was next, comprising 27 percent of the budget, and interest on the national debt absorbed 15 percent. Some 12 percent of the budget went for assistance to the non-elderly poor or disabled, 9 percent for nondefense investment, 4 percent for economic stabilization programs, and 2 percent for general government operations.

Broader categories give a better overview and help us spot major spending differences (such as our much greater spending on interest on the national debt than on investments in America's economic future). Basic trends also emerge: over the decade of the 1980s, spending on nondefense investment and on government

operations received deep cuts, while spending has increased significantly on interest payments (up 115 percent more than inflation),
defense (up 45 percent), and programs for older Americans (up
35 percent). Together these latter three categories now account for
three-fourths of all federal spending.

Helpful as such a breakdown is in showing basic federal spending priorities, some have argued that an even broader measure is
needed. It is sometimes misleading to look just at a breakdown of
current federal spending when we are trying to set future spending
levels. Some areas of federal spending that look small, such as education, may not be primarily federal responsibilities, so the federal
tally alone does not give a good indication of whether overall needs
are being met. Federal mandates, regulations, and tax incentives
can increase spending by others for a particular need without showing up in the federal spending tally.

"GNP Budget": Thus some economists, including Herbert Stein,
former chairman of Economic Advisors, argue for a "GNP budget."
The idea is to determine what percent of our gross national product—our nation's annual output of new goods and services—goes
for various major uses, such as investment, defense, or private
consumption: this would then be used as a guide for determining
priorities in the federal budget. Large as federal spending is, looking
at total GNP can give us a better perspective on federal spending
priorities.

Cast in broad national terms, defense spending currently
stands at 6 percent of GNP, spending on education (by federal, state,
and local governments and private households) is 7 percent of GNP,
and spending on health care (both public and private) is 11 percent
of GNP. Other consumer spending (for food, fuel, autos, and the like)
totals 56 percent of GNP, while private and public investment (in,
for example, factories, housing, and roads) stands at 16 percent
of GNP. General government (including law enforcement and civil
service) claims 4 percent of GNP.

Although there is some dispute over what the broad categories
should be and what they should include, such a summary helps us
ask whether the way GNP is distributed squares with national objectives. Is 7 percent of GNP for education enough? Is consumer spending too high and public and private investment too low? With US
spending on health care at 11 percent of GNP compared to 7 percent

for the other major industrialized countries, are we spending too much? Ideally, the goal of a "GNP budget" would be to illuminate the national debate on our country's broad priorities.

Such an approach also helps show that if a greater percentage of our GNP goes for one thing on the list, a smaller percentage will go for something else, and stresses that the most important measure is how much of our total GNP, not just federal spending, is devoted to a particular area. For example, if we increase federal spending on health care, but do it in a way that encourages the private sector to sharply cut back its health spending, the net effect could be detrimental. In this sense, policymakers should be budgeting for the GNP—enacting federal spending, tax, and regulatory policies that help to bring about the shares of GNP that the nation wants devoted to particular uses. Of course, the activities of private households and businesses are the major determinants of what we produce in our market economy. But the activities of government have enough direct and indirect influence that we should tally them all and keep track of them in a responsible fashion.

Certainly no accounting tool will resolve all the key budgetary issues facing our nation. But a "GNP budget" can help us recognize and set our broad national priorities in a more informed and rational way.

THE LESSONS OF THE GREAT SOCIETY

A major emphasis of President Reagan's efforts to reduce federal spending was to roll back Great Society programs, which he said "provided jobs for an army of federal bureaucrats" but weren't effective, and, he claimed, even increased the percentage of American families in poverty.

As Congress during the Bush years had to find additional savings in federal spending, we needed to take an honest look at which programs worked and which didn't. I think the assessment here stands up fairly well.

Over the years that followed, the Great Society programs faced tough criticism, but they have been broadly accepted. I supported most of the programs of the Great Society and its effort to help the poor. Our nation's economic system works well for most of us, but a large number of Americans fall through the cracks and they still need our help.

May 30, 1990: "The Lessons of the Great Society"
Washington Report
Vol. XXV, No. 22

The United States is the world's wealthiest nation. Despite
this affluence, many Americans are concerned about poverty: the
growing numbers of poor and homeless, declining opportunities for
disadvantaged youth, the inadequacies of health care for lower-
income people, and the insecurities of old age. In some ways, these
are similar to the challenges that faced the nation in the 1960s. The
federal response was a number of legislative initiatives, generally
known as the Great Society. Twenty-five years later, we can learn
several lessons from this effort.

The Programs: The two major elements of the Great Society
were the War on Poverty and the elimination of discrimination. The
cornerstone of the War on Poverty was the Economic Opportunity
Act, containing programs such as VISTA (Volunteers in Service to
America), the Community Action Program (helping local groups
meet community needs), Jobs Corps (providing job training for
unemployed adults), and Head Start (offering preschool education
to poor children). Other components included broadening Social
Security coverage, creating Medicare and Medicaid for the health
care needs of older persons and the poor, expanding the food stamp
program, increasing support for education, and improving access
to housing. To expand opportunity for minorities, the Congress
also passed the Civil Rights and Voting Rights Acts, prohibiting
discrimination based on race and improving minority political
participation.

The idea behind these efforts was to increase opportunity and
to make the American dream available to everyone—especially
those suffering from disadvantages not of their own making: older
persons, children, the unemployed, minorities, the disabled, and the
handicapped.

Assessment: Over the years, we have been able to assess how
well these programs work—whether each has the desired effect,
is efficient, helps the people it is supposed to, and is fair. Some
programs have had significant success. In this category we should
include the Social Security amendments which reduced the rate
of poverty among older persons from 28 percent in the mid-1960s
to 12 percent today; Head Start, which significantly increased

reading scores of participants; the Voting Rights and Civil Rights Acts, which greatly expanded minority participation in the political system; and the Higher Education Act, which made college more affordable to millions of youth.

In other areas, the results have been much more mixed. The food stamp program has been successful in reducing hunger in America, but only about half of those eligible are enrolled, benefit levels are often too low, and abuses of the program still surface occasionally. Medicare and Medicaid have improved health care for older Americans and the poor, but coverage is incomplete—there is no long-term-care coverage, for example—and the system is very costly. Job training programs have placed people in jobs, but they were often the more talented of the unemployed and were likely to find jobs on their own.

The two most widely criticized efforts were community action and housing programs. The community action program, designed to foster "maximum feasible participation" of poor people in local political and economic institutions, often competed with local government agencies and did not address the sources of poverty. Public housing programs concentrated the poorest families in poor neighborhoods, creating breeding grounds for delinquency and drug abuse.

Changes under Reagan: The election of Ronald Reagan in 1980 brought a new approach to poverty. Although Presidents Nixon, Ford, and Carter reduced the growth of the Great Society programs for budgetary reasons, they supported the federal government's responsibility to address these problems. President Reagan lessened that role, although he did not seek to repeal the programs. The lot of the needy would be improved, in his view, by increasing economic growth, which would benefit all levels of society. To that end, he emphasized tax rate cuts for all and incentives for business and investment.

By the mid-1980s, the results of the Reagan experiment were clear. While the tax cuts expanded the wealth of upper-income people, very few benefits accrued to those at the bottom. Poverty began to increase, especially for children (20 percent now living in poverty). The overall poverty rate, 11.7 percent in 1979, averaged 14 percent during the 1980s. Today there are thirty-two million poor Americans—roughly the same as before the Great Society began.

Lessons for the 1990s: Several lessons can be learned from our efforts over the past twenty-five years. First, federal programs can play a role in reducing poverty. The Great Society programs reduced poverty from over 22 percent in 1960 to 12 percent by 1969, where it generally remained until the programs were cut back in the 1980s. Economic growth alone, as important as it is, cannot eliminate poverty unless at least some of the benefits of that growth are passed through to the poor. Government has a role to play in enhancing opportunities and well-being for the poor. Efforts should be made to fill gaps in today's social safety net, such as the lack of health insurance for thirty-one million Americans; and programs that work, like Head Start, should be fully funded.

Second, we also have learned that government by itself is not the sole solution. The causes of poverty are many, and the government's ability to address them is limited. Federal programs must be multidimensional and should encourage and support state, local, and private actions, while setting and enforcing minimal standards.

Third, well-intentioned programs are not enough; they must be well designed and effectively carried out. Antipoverty programs should encourage self-sufficiency rather than dependency. To maintain the support of taxpayers, programs must be fair, effective, and efficient. Sometimes that might mean using tax incentives—such as expanding the earned income tax credit for the poor—rather than creating new programs.

America is a rich nation, but we have not adequately invested in one of our most precious resources—our people. We need to reaffirm our commitment to ensuring equal opportunity for all persons and to alleviating the burden of poverty.

THE UNITED STATES FLAG AND THE CONSTITUTION

It rightly infuriated Americans to see our flag burned. Yet I opposed the proposed constitutional amendment to prohibit desecration of the flag. That position angered many of my constituents—particularly veterans—and I wrote this commentary to help explain my various reasons for voting the way I did. People will generally give you a fair amount of leeway on your votes in Congress. But they do keep track, and if you cast a vote against the broad sentiment of your constituents you had better be prepared to defend it, with specific, understandable reasons.

July 4, 1990: "The United States Flag and the Constitution"
Washington Report
Vol. XXV, No. 27

Few issues considered by the Congress in recent years have had as much emotional impact as the constitutional amendment to prohibit abuse of the United States flag. Feelings about our flag, a treasured symbol of democracy and freedom, are strong among all Americans, and the proposed amendment to the Constitution has been the subject of intense debate across the country and in the Congress.

The debate about an amendment to prevent flag abuse arose after several recent Supreme Court decisions. The court held that abusing the flag is "expressive conduct" protected by the First Amendment, and that laws barring the abuse of the flag are unconstitutional because of this protection. The ruling of the Supreme Court means the only way to absolutely prohibit flag abuse is through an amendment to the Constitution.

Supporters of a constitutional amendment in the House of Representatives recently failed by a vote of 254 to 177 to attain the two-thirds majority necessary to pass it. The Senate also failed, by a 58 to 42 vote, to obtain a two-thirds majority. These votes end chances of passage this year.

There is no doubt that Americans love their flag. The flag symbolizes our nation, its history, its purpose, and its values. We honor and respect the flag because it symbolizes the United States. I certainly do not want to encourage anyone to abuse the flag, and I share the deep frustration and anger of most Americans when I see people insulting it. Nonetheless, I voted against this amendment for the following reasons.

First, flag burning is not a problem of sufficient magnitude to justify tampering with the Constitution. The acts of a few misguided publicity seekers who set fire to the flag (only four were arrested in 1989) are not worth the potential damage to the Constitution. The original ten amendments to the Constitution that spell out the liberties guaranteed all Americans, the Bill of Rights, have never been altered. The Constitution has served us remarkably well for the last two hundred years, and we should be very careful when considering possible modifications. We have been through a terrible civil war, two world wars, depressions, and riots without finding it necessary to compromise the fundamental principles of the Bill of Rights. We must honor and respect the Constitution perhaps even more than the flag, because the Constitution is not a symbol—it is the essence of freedom, the nation itself.

Second, voting against the flag amendment helps preserve the basic institutions of liberty. The Constitution guarantees that certain individual rights are more important than the government or majority opinion. The First Amendment ensures that the majority cannot suppress a dissident view simply because the view is distasteful.

The Supreme Court recently defined the fundamental protection of the First Amendment: "If there is a bedrock principle underlying the First Amendment, it is that government may not prohibit the expression of an idea simply because society finds the idea itself offensive or disagreeable. We have not recognized an exception to this principle." The flag protects even those who would hold it in contempt. The US flag is a great symbol because it protects everyone, whatever their political views. Government has all the power it needs; the people need all the liberties they can conserve.

The point is often made that there are exceptions today to free speech. But the present restrictions are sanctions against libel, revealing national-security secrets, or crying "fire" in a theater. These examples involve speech that threatens real and specific harm to other people. Burning a flag is offensive but it is an act of political expression. A constitutional amendment to restrict political expression would be entirely new in this country. We should not create an exception to the First Amendment that opens unchartered territory.

Third, a bad precedent would be set by adopting a constitutional amendment to protect the flag against abuse. There are scores of different ways for people to try to insult our country. Deeply offensive acts could be performed, for example, on copies of the Constitution or the Declaration of Independence; on likenesses of the president, the first lady, or the Founding Fathers; or on symbols of the Supreme Court or the White House. The list could go on and on. We do not want to initiate a situation where the Bill of Rights suddenly faces an endless stream of symbol-protection amendments.

Fourth, practical problems abound with the constitutional amendment to protect the flag. It is not yet clear what exactly would constitute a flag under the proposed amendment. Would slight variations in the number of stripes or colors mean that those flags are not covered by the amendment? Furthermore, could people using flag cups, napkins, or other items with the flag on them be prosecuted for potential flag abuse?

Fifth, the constitutional amendment will not end flag abuse. Some will continue to abuse the flag, just as people still commit murder despite laws against it.

Sixth, the extended debate on the flag protection amendment is an example of politics of distraction. It is a symptom of the changes in American politics which increasingly emphasize posturing by political candidates at the expense of substantive approaches to our nation's most pressing problems: deficits over $200 billion, the urgent need to rewrite national defense policy, a health care system in crisis, the savings-and-loan industry in shambles, and inequity of income at an all-time modern high.

Instead of a constitutional amendment, the flag should be protected through statute. The Congress is considering proposals to punish flag abuse in circumstances that promote imminent danger of violence. I support measures that will protect the flag while at the same time protecting the Bill of Rights.

Americans love their flag, and gestures by a handful of people will not change this attitude. We revere the flag because of what it stands for—the Constitution and its guarantees of liberty and justice for all.

THE BALANCED BUDGET AMENDMENT

Earlier in his political career, George H. W. Bush had opposed amending the Constitution to require a balanced federal budget. But once he became president, his first legislative proposal to Congress included a balanced budget amendment. It was an idea that had a lot of public support as an easy way to end the large and ever-increasing federal budget deficits.

My basic view is that the Constitution should be amended only rarely, when the need is compelling. A balanced budget amendment sounds appealing but it's no quick fix, as I explain in this commentary. Congress instead needs to spend the time actually deciding which spending needs to be cut and which taxes need to be raised to bring the budget more into balance. But that's difficult politically, so we spend a lot of time discussing budget procedures and gimmicks. I have always been skeptical of proposals to control spending that rely on changes in process but avoid making the tough, specific decisions on what programs should be cut.

After the balanced budget amendment was defeated in the summer of 1990, Congress did, later that year, work with President Bush to develop a serious deficit-reduction package. Because of the size of the deficit, both spending reductions and tax increases were necessary. But that meant President Bush needed to go back on his oft-repeated 1988 campaign pledge of no new taxes. In my view, his support of the package was a courageous decision for the good of the country. But during the 1992 campaign, rather than play up the courage of the decision and explain carefully why a balanced package of both spending cuts and revenue increases was needed to head off serious problems for the nation, he instead said that his decision to go along with the tax increases was a mistake.

The president's changing views on taxes were a significant factor in his failed reelection bid.

July 25, 1990: "The Balanced Budget Amendment"
Washington Report
Vol. XXV, No. 30

The federal budget deficit is one of the most intractable problems facing the Congress and the president. The deficit must be controlled to sustain our economic vitality and to reduce our dependence on foreign capital. Yet our government has failed to muster the political will necessary for meaningful deficit reduction, and many Americans are now looking at alternative methods to decrease the budget deficit. One popular proposal is an amendment to the Constitution requiring a balanced budget.

The balanced budget amendment under consideration by the Congress would require that total government spending for each year could not exceed estimated revenues unless three-fifths of the Congress provided for a specific excess. The Congress and the president would have to agree in advance on the revenue estimate. The amendment also would require a three-fifths majority to increase the federal debt. The amendment would be waived when a declaration of war is in effect.

Supporters of this proposal in the House of Representatives recently failed by a vote of 279 to 150 to attain the two-thirds majority necessary for passage. The Senate could vote on this issue later this year. The action by the House probably kills the balanced budget amendment for this year.

I agree that the Congress and the president clearly have not done enough to reduce the deficit, and that much tougher steps must be taken to control the growing government debt. Although I voted for a balanced budget amendment in 1982, I do not agree that this proposal will do what its supporters contend. I voted against it for the following reasons.

First, the proposal does not guarantee that a balanced budget will in fact be achieved. It states that total spending shall not exceed <u>estimated</u> receipts. If we have learned anything in the last ten years it is that there is often a dramatic difference between estimates and reality. Recent revenue estimates have been wrong more often than they have been correct, missing the mark by billions of dollars.

Second, evasion would be easy. The president and the Congress have amply demonstrated their skill at manipulating legislative procedures to avoid tough political choices. The Gramm-Rudman budget reduction law, for example, has failed in large part due to the deliberate use of rosy economic forecasts, underestimated costs, bloated savings and revenue estimates, and expenses shifted to other years. The federal government also could follow the lead of many state and local governments of moving programs off budget to balance the budget. State and local units have created over twenty-five thousand off-budget entities to tax and spend outside local and state budget controls.

Third, the proposed amendment is unworkable. It contains no enforcement mechanism for achieving a balanced budget—mandating a result without offering a solution. The proposal is similar to declaring that the United States shall henceforth have clean air or be drug-free. It does not say what happens if the Congress and the president do not agree on the estimated receipts or what happens if the budget is not balanced and the government runs a deficit. If the revenue estimate is wrong, or a crisis emerges, would each program within every agency have to be approved by the Congress, or would each agency be allowed to determine the exact allocation of funding, or would some arbitrary formula be applied? Would the government default on its bills because the increase in the debt had not been approved by a three-fifths majority?

Fourth, the proposal promises to do something about the budget deficit tomorrow, but the problem is today. The measure would not take effect until 1995 at the earliest, sending a signal that hard budget choices can be put off until later. In the meantime, almost $1 trillion could be added to the national debt. The amendment is politics by distraction.

Fifth, the proposal could trigger a recession. The Congress and the president would be required to reduce the budget deficit—however large it might be—to zero the first year the proposed amendment is in effect. The deficit is currently hovering around $200 billion. Pulling large amounts of money out of the economy quickly could cause enormous economic hardship because of jobs lost and benefits cut or eliminated.

Sixth, federal courts would almost certainly be asked to resolve disputes about interpretation of the proposal. If the courts make many of the tough decisions required to balance the budget, that would represent a dramatic shift in authority from elected representatives to the unelected power of judges. And if the courts refuse to become involved in the political dispute over the amendment, the budget process could stalemate. In either case, the proposal ensures an endless stream of lawsuits as various questions are placed before the courts, slowing down the budget process while the Congress and the president await decisions.

Seventh, the proposal would reduce the federal government's flexibility to deal with emergencies and is potentially dangerous. A serious recession or world crisis could produce revenue losses or require spending increases that would result in a deficit. Under the proposed amendment, a minority in one house of the Congress could frustrate the efforts of the Congress and the president to respond quickly in urgent circumstances.

Finally, the proposal would enshrine one kind of fiscal policy in the Constitution. The place to solve the deficit problem is at the budget summit now in progress and not in the Constitution. Meaningful budget reforms are possible without a constitutional amendment. Placing the empty promise of this proposal into the Constitution will only breed deep cynicism about the Constitution as people understand that the measure is unenforceable and cannot deliver what it promised.

The budget deficit represents an absence of political will, not the need to restructure our entire political system. Where there is political leadership, public consensus can be organized around the requirement to pay for what we spend, and a balanced budget amendment is not necessary. In the absence of leadership, an amendment to the Constitution cannot guarantee a balanced budget.

THE PRESIDENT'S ARMS CONTROL SPEECH

By 1991, in the third year of his presidency, George Bush was developing a real touch for foreign affairs, and he generally gets high marks for his arms control efforts. He worked closely with General Brent Scowcroft, and together they set the standard for the relationship between president and national security advisor. Here Bush was proposing that our security would actually be enhanced by unilaterally cutting our nation's nuclear arms, which was counter to what we had been hearing for decades.

Bush's passion was clearly foreign policy, and his presidency occurred at a time of enormously important global developments, with the fall of the Soviet Union and the end of the Cold War. Certainly Bush was not the primary force in bringing all of this about. But he worked well with Gorbachev and there is no doubt he helped move things along skillfully. What was particularly impressive during this period was Bush's lack of triumphalism. He didn't brag and say that we brought about the collapse of the Soviet Union. The president rightly recognized that if we wanted continued good relations with the Soviets in what he called the "new world order," gloating about a victory over them would be counterproductive. It was a solid insight that served the country well.

October 9, 1991: "The President's Arms Control Speech"
Washington Report
Vol. XXVI, No. 41

President Bush's September 27 speech on nuclear arms reductions responds to the remarkable changes in the Soviet Union following the failed coup attempt. The president announced that he will scrap all US ground-based short-range missiles from ships, cancel several nuclear modernization programs, and remove strategic bombers from alert status. He offered to negotiate with the Soviet Union for reductions in the most dangerous missiles, and challenged the Soviets to match US steps. These moves affect one-fifth of the total US arsenal of about nineteen thousand weapons.

The president is seeking to keep pace with world events and to seize the momentum of change. He is also worried that Soviet short-range weapons might fall into the wrong hands. The importance of his speech, however, goes far beyond arms control or nuclear safety. His initiative is a concrete example of American support for Soviet reformers. It sets a new agenda, and marks a dramatic change in the US assessment of the Soviet threat.

Implications for the US: First, the most astonishing aspect of the president's initiative is his call for a unilateral reduction of US armaments. In one stroke, he scrapped much of the now-obsolete nuclear doctrine and Cold War thinking of the past four decades. He has paved the way for a new approach. He is now basing his actions on trust, instead of President Reagan's approach of "trust but verify." In part, the president chose to take unilateral steps and invite reciprocity to avoid long negotiations with a weakened Soviet government.

Second, the steps taken by the president represent a new way of dealing with the Soviet Union. He consulted directly not only with Gorbachev but Russian president Yeltsin, thereby recognizing the shared nature of power in the Soviet Union. His speech implies a level of confidence that did not exist previously between the US and the Soviet Union. He demanded nothing, but he expects a great deal. The initial Soviet reaction to his speech has been positive. Reciprocal unilateral cuts by each side may become a much faster and more efficient method of achieving arms control. It took nine years of strategic arms reduction (START) talks to eliminate the same number of weapons that the president did in one speech.

Third, there is minimal risk to the US. What the president did makes military sense. He is cutting the least controllable and least useful weapons from the US arsenal. For example, aging and inaccurate short-range nuclear weapons in Europe cannot reach targets beyond Poland or Czechoslovakia, which are now friendly, democratic countries. These weapons are obsolete.

Fourth, by eliminating short-range nuclear weapons now, the US wants to push the Soviet Union to do the same. Small, mobile, and hard to monitor, these weapons would require lengthy negotiations to limit. Soviet weapons could fall into the hands of nationalist extremists in republics such as Georgia and Azerbaijan. Getting rid of these weapons now will reduce the threat of nuclear civil war.

Fifth, the president's initiative accepts the view of both European government and opposition leaders that the continent should be free of short-range weapons. The elimination of nuclear weapons from surface ships will also ease political problems with friendly nations such as Japan, New Zealand, and Norway. These nations have long objected to nuclear-armed ships entering their ports.

Sixth, this initiative will increase demands for further cuts in the defense budget. The political momentum in the country is running against defense spending. People are worried about the economy, education, health care, and other domestic issues. They are increasingly concerned about pouring tax dollars into the military budget. It will be hard to defend the B-2 bomber or the Strategic Defense Initiative when the president has decided to cancel other strategic weapons programs.

Seventh, direct savings from the president's plan will be small at the outset. The cost of dismantling weapons and canceling contracts will offset initial savings, but cuts could yield large long-term savings.

Eighth, the initiative maintains the US strategic triad of air-, land-, and sea-based bomber forces. The strategic bomber force will be taken off alert status for the first time since 1957, but will remain intact. Land-based missiles will be reduced on an accelerated schedule, but in accordance with the START Treaty. There will be no change in submarine missile forces. The Soviets will see this as one-sided, because the US has a big advantage in sea-launched ballistic missiles with multiple nuclear warheads.

Finally, the initiative does not mean the end of arms negotiations. There is simply too much at stake, and written agreements will still be necessary. For example, a formal agreement probably will be needed to eliminate land-based multiple-warhead missiles, as the president has proposed. The Soviets will want to include US sea-based missiles and a mutual ban on nuclear testing in those same talks.

Conclusions: It is important to remember that even after this initiative and reductions under the START Treaty are implemented, both the US and the Soviet Union will have more than enough nuclear weapons to wipe out each other. So much work still needs to be done. The president's initiative, nonetheless, offers an opportunity to break with the slow, time-consuming process of arms control talks that have often been overtaken by events. Swifter and deeper arms cuts are possible, and cheating will be more difficult, in part because the Soviet Union is much more open than it used to be. Moreover, its leaders are desperate for Western economic help and eager to cooperate.

Some questions remain. Will the US follow up this step with an equally dramatic challenge to the Soviets to cut long-range strategic nuclear forces? Will the US now concentrate on working with the Soviets to address common threats from the proliferation of nuclear weapons and missile technology? I hope that the president's speech points the way to a new era of rapid progress in arms control, deep cuts in nuclear weapons, and close US-Soviet cooperation. This would make the world a much safer place.

CONGRESSIONAL PERKS

Early in 1992, Republicans in the House were using the House bank and other congressional perks to argue that the Democratic leadership was ineffective, even corrupt. Audits had revealed that more than three hundred House members or former members had overdrawn their accounts at the House bank and paid no penalties. The overdrafts were covered by other members' funds rather than taxpayer funds, with no loss to the US Treasury, so it wasn't the biggest of congressional scandals.

Yet critics, including talk radio hosts, pushed it hard, and it created a public uproar at the time. And in the next election, seventy-seven members of the House who had overdrawn their accounts either lost their reelection bids or retired. Even though I didn't have any overdrafts at the bank, I still faced a lot of angry questions in public meetings about it. The whole episode drove home to me the importance of congressional reform at every turn. The institution needs it, and on a regular basis.

The joint committee on congressional reform proposed in this commentary was approved by Congress, and I became chairman of the House side. As discussed in the next chapter, some of our reform recommendations were adopted, but not nearly enough.

October 16, 1991: "Congressional Perks"
Washington Report
Vol. XXVI, No. 42

In recent weeks Americans have been up in arms over congressional perks. The uproar started over special privileges members of Congress receive at the House bank. A General Accounting Office study reported that during a twelve-month period ending June 1990, more than 8,300 bad checks were written by members. The House bank covered the checks without penalty by temporarily using funds that other members had on deposit. Many members of Congress, including myself, were not aware that this practice was going on.

Next it was revealed that several members had large unpaid bills at House restaurants. Much of the debt involved events of outside groups arranged through members, but under the rules the sponsoring members were liable for the bills. The outstanding funds totaled more than $300,000. Now members are being queried about congressional perks ranging from parking privileges to haircuts to in-house medical care.

How Serious Is the Problem? Some observers dismiss the entire episode as yet another example of the media blowing something out of proportion and our country's preoccupation with less important matters. Members visiting their districts have been pummeled with hundreds of questions about their check writing, while far less attention is given to major national issues such as the president's historic speech on nuclear arms reductions. Many people are amazed that a political turmoil could develop out of what were once considered garden-variety mistakes, such as bouncing a check.

Yet my sense is that such issues resonate with the public because they reinforce their basic suspicion that government is run
by insiders for their own personal convenience and benefit. Americans perceive a double standard—members with perks that no one
else has, living in luxury while many Americans are struggling just
to get by. Members are viewed as corrupt and arrogant about their
power, looking out for themselves while failing to address issues
like health care and crime that Americans really care about.

The result is widespread cynicism and a further decline in public confidence in Congress. The legitimacy of individuals attempting
to make national policy and run the government is undermined.
And that is far from a trivial matter. If Congress does not enjoy public support, it cannot get on with the nation's business.

Solutions: Positive steps have been taken to address specific
abuses. The House voted to close the bank and to instruct the ethics
committee to review its operations. Members can no longer sign
for their meals, and outside groups will have to pay for restaurant
services in advance.

Many congressional perks are relics of bygone days, when traveling across town to a bank or barber through the muddy streets
of Washington was difficult. But times have changed. I believe that
there should be a systematic review of congressional perks to see if
they have outlived their usefulness. My general view is that members of Congress should pay the same as everyone else for meals
and haircuts, and should not enjoy special banking privileges and
the like.

But I also believe a broader look at Congress is needed. In a
word, we in Congress need to try harder. We need to show that we
are able to improve the workings of Congress and deal with the issues that people really care about.

In recent years unwieldy congressional procedures have
often resulted in frustration and institutional gridlock. We have
two-hundred-member conference committees trying to sort out
differences between House and Senate versions of a bill, and two-
thousand-page omnibus bills that must be digested and voted on by
members within a number of hours. An increasing array of issues
before Congress—global warming, terrorism, and drug trafficking—
involve both international and domestic components, and no longer
cut neatly across organizational lines. Almost forty subcommittees

in the House and Senate would be involved in crafting a national energy policy. Congress is swamped by technical information, on everything from the Superconducting Super Collider to arms control verification. Moreover, while the nation faces major long-term challenges such as lagging productivity and declining student achievement, the focus on Congress is primarily short term, driven by budget numbers and concerns about the next election. There is little systematic debate on broad national spending priorities and how they should be gradually shifted to meet future needs and challenges.

I have introduced a measure to set up a temporary House-Senate committee to study and report recommendations on how Congress can improve its effectiveness and efficiency. The committee would be bipartisan and have equal numbers of senators and representatives. Whenever possible, it would draw upon existing staff and unpaid volunteers to minimize costs. The committee would make its recommendations after a few months of study and then go out of existence. It would be composed primarily of sitting members so they can help move the recommendations through Congress.

The committee is modeled upon the 1945 and 1965 temporary joint committees on congressional organization. Their work has been widely recognized as significant and beneficial, resulting in changes such as streamlining the committee structure, developing a legislative budget, and expanding the research capabilities of legislative support agencies.

I believe that it is important for Congress as an institution to step back periodically to see what steps should be taken to make it work better. Yet with the last major House-Senate overhaul along these lines taking place more than two decades ago, another comprehensive look is overdue. The furor of recent weeks only reinforces that now is the time to put our own house in order.

I do not overestimate the importance of structural reform in Congress; we also need the political will to tackle the tough issues. But I do not underestimate it, either. Certainly congressional procedures at times can stymie effective action on national issues as legislation is subjected to numerous obstacles and hurdles. Simply putting all the blame on political will is a prescription to do nothing to try to improve the working of Congress.

The best way for Congress to enjoy public trust is to earn it. A systematic and thorough review of the operations of Congress can demonstrate that we are serious about improving its effectiveness. I do not take the view that Congress is in shambles or is collapsing, but we can do better.

THE CONFIRMATION PROCESS

The confirmation hearings in the fall of 1991 on George Bush's nomination of Clarence Thomas for the Supreme Court showed the need for better consultation beforehand between the president and Congress on possible nominees. Consultation in a variety of areas, though no panacea, goes a long way toward heading off potential problems and gives the president the benefit of a broader range of views than just people in his small group of White House advisors.

In other instances, however, President Bush skillfully engaged Congress in genuine consultation. I'm reminded of his efforts to convince a skeptical Congress to provide large amounts of financial aid to Eastern Europe and the former Soviet Union after the fall of Communism. Rather than try to bludgeon Congress into going along, he involved Congress in designing the aid programs.

My general view on Senate confirmations is that the president is entitled to have an up-or-down vote on his nominees within sixty or ninety days. Today the process has become highly politicized and nominations for important posts can be held up for months as a way to weaken the administration.

November 20, 1991: "The Confirmation Process"
Washington Report
Vol. XXVI, No. 47
The Clarence Thomas hearings raised concerns and questions about the confirmation process for nominees to the Supreme Court. It was an American tragedy on television, marked by tales of pornography, harassment, obscenity, lies, and betrayals. Like other Americans, I wondered throughout the hearings how the confirmation process could be reshaped. I kept thinking that some

great injustice had been done, but did not know what or to whom. I kept wondering whether the committee would ever get to the truth. Was there some way of avoiding this type of spectacle in the future? Surely, no citizen could take satisfaction in this recent confirmation hearing, even if a majority of Americans thought that in the end Thomas received a fair hearing from the Senate.

My constituents were upset by the confirmation process, especially the Senate's handling of the sexual harassment charges against the nominee. One woman said, "Nobody emerges from this looking like a winner." After it was over, I kept asking myself if this was the best way to elevate a person to this nation's highest court.

Process and Problems: The Thomas hearings highlighted several clear problems with the current process, including the public airing of sensitive private issues, the nominee's sidestepping of basic constitutional questions, the politicization of the process, and the lack of consultation between the president and the Senate during the nomination process.

Since the hearings, I have talked to knowledgeable observers of the process who believe that the confirmation process is an inevitable product of divided government and that changing the process will never happen. They feel that an effort to change the system is a pipe dream. They may be right, but I'm not so sure. At least an effort should be made to try to improve the process.

The Constitution gives the president the right to nominate the justices to the Supreme Court. Article II of the Constitution says that the president "shall nominate . . . with the advice and consent of the Senate . . . Justices to the Supreme Court." Politicians and scholars have argued for over two hundred years about how much authority this clause gives the Senate in the confirmation process. Some have suggested that the Senate defer to the president once a nominee shows that he or she meets a minimal set of qualifications. Others say that the Senate should independently investigate and scrutinize the record and constitutional philosophy of a nominee to a lifetime appointment to the Supreme Court.

The hearings also raised concerns about the increased politicization of the confirmation process. Everyone can agree that it has gone too far and that we need to pull back, but it may be unrealistic, and perhaps even unwise, to remove politics completely from the process. I doubt if any procedure can be foolproof against political pressures. Out of the rough and tumble of debate and competing

views comes the consensus that has enabled the United States to
endure for more than two hundred years.

Historical Perspective: The history of the confirmation process
does not provide us with much guidance on possible reform. Only
two nominees testified before the Senate Judiciary Committee
before 1955: Harlan Fiske Stone in 1925, and Felix Frankfurter in
1939. Since John M. Harlan testified before the panel in 1955, it has
become common practice for nominees to testify on judicial philosophy and legal issues. The process has worked reasonably well for
most of our history. Only in recent years has it proved unsatisfac-
tory. The recent practice of nominees sidestepping even the most
basic constitutional questions is disconcerting.

Process Reforms: Today the selection of a justice is considered a
life-and-death confrontation between the president and the Senate.
The whole process has become too confrontational. A way must be
found to encourage agreement between the president and the Senate. The president needs to take the Senate's advice as seriously as
it does its consent. This means the president should consult with
senators about who should be nominated for the next Supreme
Court vacancy. The aim should be to nominate a consensus candidate of true distinction.

I also think that the Senate should scrutinize nominees for the
court both as to their political ideologies and as to their judicial
competence. There is no suggestion in the Constitution that one
branch is superior to the other in this process. It is appropriate for
the nominee to discuss constitutional issues just so long as he or she
says nothing that might be construed as a commitment for a decision in a pending case.

On the narrow issue of how the Senate should treat a credible
and serious allegation of misconduct, it seems to me that the Judiciary Committee should be able to hold a full hearing in executive
session. This would at least spare the country from the simply awful
testimony at the Thomas hearings. This format would also protect
the privacy of the nominee and witnesses.

Another way to encourage agreement between the president
and the Senate would be for the Senate to advise the president by
passing a sense-of-the-Senate resolution setting forth the professional and philosophical criteria it will use in deciding whether to
confirm a future high court nominee. This would put the president

on notice as to what the Senate would accept, and it would advise him that if he did not send a nominee who met the criteria, his nominee could face a confirmation battle.

Conclusion: The president himself has the power to restore a sense of balance and decorum to the choice of Supreme Court justices. Part of the difficulty is that conservative presidents, in office for the past eleven years, have made eight Supreme Court nominations with the sole objective of revamping the judicial ideology of the high court.

In general the presumption exists that, unless there is a clear disqualification of a nominee, the president is entitled to his nominee. The president, of course, has to earn that presumption by the character of his nominations. What has been missing is political moderation, both in the nomination by the president and the reaction by the Senate.

IRAQ AND THE PERSIAN GULF WAR ONE YEAR LATER

The House and Senate debates in 1991 on authorizing the president to carry out the Gulf War against Iraq after it invaded Kuwait were impressive, with Congress living up to its constitutional role in decisions about military intervention. Too often Congress wants to leave the politically tough decisions on going to war to the president, and then praises him if all goes well and criticizes him if it doesn't.

President Bush carried out the Persian Gulf War effectively, and he put together a solid coalition of international partners rather than act unilaterally. Yet I believe this was a good example of a preventable war and it reinforced the need to spell out policy positions clearly.

Although our ambassador to Iraq, April Glaspie, knew that Saddam Hussein had a border dispute with Kuwait and was amassing large numbers of troops in the area, she told Saddam that the United States had no opinion on such Arab-Arab disputes. A few days later, he invaded. Had our ambassador or her superiors given a clear signal that we would attack Iraq if it invaded Kuwait, Saddam would not have gone ahead with the invasion, as I have heard on several occasions from Iraqi diplomats over a period of years.

**March 1992: "Iraq and the Persian Gulf War One Year Later"
Foreign Affairs Newsletter
Vol. XII, No. 3**

One year after the Persian Gulf War, it is time to reassess. The US performed well during the Gulf crisis and war. But in the period prior to Iraq's invasion of Kuwait in August 1990, US policy failed, and since the end of the Gulf War in March 1991, policy has had little success.

Before the War: In the 1980s, the US helped to create the Iraqi military machine it later had to confront. Worried by Iran's success in the Iran-Iraq War, the US shifted policy in the early 1980s and gambled on Saddam Hussein. In 1982, the US took Iraq off the list of countries supporting international terrorism. In 1984, after a seventeen-year break in diplomatic relations, the US renewed ties with Baghdad. To help Iraq, the US shared intelligence, allowed the export of goods with potential military use, encouraged allies to sell arms, provided Iraq up to $1 billion per year in food credits, and provided several hundred million dollars in trade credits. Well into 1990 the US continued to pursue good ties and to help Baghdad, even as evidence mounted that US credits were being misused and diverted.

The Gulf War was avoidable. If we and our allies had acted with restraint, Iraq would not have become the menace it became in 1990. Iraq purchased over $50 billion in military equipment in the 1980s and acquired nuclear, chemical, and biological technologies and weaponry in large part because we and our allies permitted it.

The war might also have been avoided if we had acted differently in the days before the Iraqi invasion of Kuwait. There is no evidence that the US made it crystal clear to Saddam that if he stepped across the border, we would oppose his actions militarily. Only two days before the invasion, US officials stressed publicly that we had no commitment to defend Kuwait.

Crisis and War: Following the Iraqi invasion, the president successfully built an international and domestic consensus to confront Iraq. His strategy—of tough sanctions, tough diplomacy, and ratcheting up pressure on Iraq—had overwhelming public support. The president later abandoned that course and decided to pursue the war option.

Americans disagreed in January 1991 about whether to go to war against Iraq. Before the war, a major issue in the debate concerned who had the power, under our constitutional system of government, to lead the nation into war: the president acting alone, or the president through authorization by the Congress. Americans debated, the Congress voted, and after the start of the war all rallied around our armed forces and the president. We can be proud of what our fighting men and women achieved. The coalition forces won an impressive battlefield victory over Iraq, and the US was the linchpin of that effort.

After the War: The postwar balance sheet is incomplete. No doubt the Gulf War accomplished some objectives: it expelled Saddam's army from Kuwait, knocked his army down several pegs, and exposed, although it did not destroy, his programs to acquire weapons of mass destruction. The war also generated a sense of pride among Americans.

Yet as time passes, the battlefield victory recedes in significance. Many of our postwar objectives remain unfulfilled. Saddam is weaker because of his defeat and continuing sanctions, but he is still in power. We have obtained only grudging and minimal Iraqi compliance with UN Security Council resolutions, including those on weapons destruction. Political reform in Kuwait and Saudi Arabia is unimpressive. Income disparities and the slow pace of economic reform threaten the region's long-term stability. Arms sales to the region are accelerating, insuring that the next conflict will be more lethal. States in the region are failing to build new security structures so five hundred thousand Americans would need not return to defend them.

US Policy: It is unacceptable to win the war but lose the peace. We must stay engaged in the region in order to protect and promote US interests. Several steps are necessary:

First, we must maintain a strong and intrusive UN presence inside Iraq. The UN, with US support, should provide and expand protection for Iraqi civilians, including the Kurds and Shiites; ensure adequate supplies of food and medicine; and give UN weapons inspectors all funding necessary to carry out their work. If Iraq will not sell oil to pay for such programs, as UN resolutions require, then Iraq's frozen assets, including oil in transit, should be tapped until it agrees to sell oil to replenish asset accounts.

Second, tough sanctions must be maintained until Iraq complies fully with UN resolutions and until the Iraqi people remove their repressive leadership.

Third, the US has the means, working through the UN, to ratchet up pressure on Iraq. We should provide armed protection for weapons inspectors and relief workers in Iraq; stop air traffic to and from Iraq; seize frozen Iraqi assets; and work with Jordan and others to tighten sanctions. The threat of force by the US and its co-alition partners remains an option if Iraq does not comply with UN resolutions. It should be a policy of last resort.

Fourth, we need to press the Gulf states harder on political and economic reform as well as more effective regional defense cooperation.

Finally, the Middle East peace process is critical. Face-to-face peace talks are a milestone. The Gulf War had less to do in creating this breakthrough than the end of the Cold War, but progress in the peace process can facilitate progress elsewhere. Conversely, tensions in one area can affect the entire region. Our task now is to try to achieve progress in both the Middle East and the Persian Gulf. Our 1991 battlefield victory will be hollow if we cannot.

The legislative accomplishments of Congress during the four years of the Bush presidency were modest. Although some important domestic measures passed, including the Americans with Disabilities Act and the Clean Air Act amendments requiring cleaner-burning fuels, there were limits to what Congress and the president could do to address national needs given the huge budget deficits they inherited from President Reagan. And those large annual deficits even increased during the Bush years, rising from $152 billion in 1989 to $290 billion in 1992.

A second major factor in the modest legislative output was the changing of the guard in the House, with the rise of Newt Gingrich and other conservative Republicans who were not pleased with the moderate approach of President Bush and what they felt was the too-cooperative approach of established Republican leaders like Bob Michel in the House and Bob Dole in the Senate. An era of heightened political warfare was beginning. By the end of the Bush term, public approval of Congress had dropped to half of what it was at the start.

Although only a modest amount of legislation passed during the Bush years and although the difficulties and tensions within Congress were increasing, it was a remarkable time of change in the world. By the end of the Bush presidency, the Soviet Union no longer existed, most of the Warsaw Pact nations had become democracies, East and West Germany were reunited, and the Cold War was over. It was a truly remarkable time of fundamental change in the world for the good, and President Bush deserves praise for the positive role he played in the transition out of the Cold War.

SEVEN

THE CLINTON YEARS
(1993–2000)
Opportunities Missed

IN MY COMMENTARY AFTER THE 1992 ELECTIONS I LOOKED AHEAD
with considerable anticipation to the Clinton years. For the first time in
more than a decade, we no longer had a divided government at the federal
level, with the Democrats now in control of the presidency as well as both
houses of Congress. In addition, Clinton came across as someone who was
moderate, willing to look for new ways of doing things, willing to rethink
the role of government, and able to work with people of the other party.
That, combined with public demands for change, gave me reason to think
that "highly productive" days lay ahead. Despite my own optimism as well
as the optimism of many others, Clinton's presidency started out badly, the
next eight years were a time of major ups and downs, and the overall results
of the Clinton years were to me disappointing. There were important and
impressive achievements, but much more could have been accomplished
had the president not been distracted by his personal misconduct.

Much was expected of Clinton because of his strong political skills.
He loved politics and the many formal and informal interactions with
members of Congress. He also loved thinking about policy issues and was
highly intelligent. Once I was aboard Air Force One with the president for a
long trip overseas. I was in the back of the plane, reading some article about
the problem of discrimination against black farmers in federal commodity
programs. Clinton came back, knelt down in the aisle next to me, and asked
what I was reading. And then for the next twenty minutes he talked with
a depth of knowledge and conviction about discrimination in agricultural
commodity programs. It was impressive and showed his command of the

substance of the issues—and this on a topic that he could have in no way prepared for in advance.

Clinton also had the benefit of starting his time in office with a good set of well-respected leaders in the House: Tom Foley as Speaker and Bob Michel as Minority Leader. Both were decent, civil, able men. They were both strong advocates for their respective parties, but they were of the school that the legislative process had to work. You would state your case forcefully and push for it as hard as you could and get every available advantage, but at the end of the day you would make the compromises and accommodations necessary to move important legislation through for the good of the country. Yet for both of these leaders, after decades of service, this would be their final Congress: Bob retired because he just didn't like the new, confrontational direction Congress was starting to take, and Tom was defeated for reelection.

I knew Tom Foley particularly well. We came to Congress the same year, 1965, and as Tom rose through the ranks in the Democratic leadership—to Majority Whip, Majority Leader, and then Speaker of the House—he would ask me to place his name in nomination before the Democratic caucus. He made the decision early on to vote the party line on key issues, even though he knew some of his votes would create problems for him back in Spokane. That helped him move up the House leadership ladder quickly, but in the end he was defeated by a challenger who portrayed him as "out of touch" with his district, and one of Congress's most able members was gone, the first sitting Speaker of the House ever to be defeated.

The Clinton years were a time of increasing partisan frictions. Republican members of Congress were wary of Clinton from the start. Many told me that he had lied to them, and they were quite upset about it. But I was often in the same meetings, and my impression was different. Clinton uses highly nuanced language that can give the impression he's on your side when he actually might not be, and he always makes his points with an open and friendly manner. I found that I had to listen carefully to try to discern what Clinton was actually saying.

I remember one of my early meetings with Clinton—in which I did get his point clearly. As president-elect he pulled together in Washington a number of congressional committee chairmen to give him a better sense of what issues he'd be confronting as president. So he heard from House and Senate chairmen about health care, energy, the environment, and several other topics, and he would generally nod, make some comments, and move on. During my time I made the point that I thought his presidency would likely be defined by his handling of foreign-policy issues, as was generally the case for his predecessors. He clearly did not agree. He thought domestic issues would be most prominent, because he'd been all over the country and rarely had a citizen brought up a question of foreign policy.

I'm not sure who turned out to be right on that, whether foreign-policy issues or domestic-policy issues stood out more in the public's eye. Some would say we were both wrong, and that the most prominent issues during his presidency revolved around his personal misconduct. But looking back I think a case could also be made that the most significant, long-lasting development during the Clinton years instead had to do with governance—a basic change not for the better in the workings of Congress and the overall functioning of our system of government.

The 103rd Congress: Key Facts

- January 5, 1993, through December 1, 1994, during the first two years of the first Clinton administration
- House of Representatives controlled by the Democrats, 258 to 176 (1 other)
- Senate controlled by the Democrats, 57 to 43
- 465 bills enacted
- Major accomplishments included passing the Family and Medical Leave Act, the Motor Voter Act, the Omnibus Budget Reconciliation Act, the National and Community Service Trust Act, Assistance for the Newly Independent States of the Former Soviet Union, the Brady Handgun Violence Protection Act, the North American Free Trade Agreement Implementation Act, the Goals 2000: Educate America Act, the Violent Crime Control and Law Enforcement Act, the Bankruptcy Reform Act, and the General Agreement on Tariffs and Trade Implementation Act

- Support for President Clinton's position in the House: Democrats 79 percent, Republicans 44 percent; in the Senate: Democrats 88 percent, Republicans 37 percent

The 104th Congress: Key Facts

- January 4, 1995, through October 4, 1996, during the last two years of the first Clinton administration
- House of Representative controlled by the Republicans, 230 to 204 (1 other)
- Senate controlled by the Republicans, 53 to 47
- 333 bills enacted
- Major accomplishments included passing the Congressional Accountability Act, the Unfunded Mandates Reform Act, the Paperwork Reduction Act, the Lobbying Disclosure Act, the Telecommunications Act, the Freedom to Farm Act, the Antiterrorism and Effective Death Penalty Act, the Line Item Veto Act, the Health Insurance Portability and Accountability Act, the Welfare Reform Act, reduced regulation of the banking industry, the Defense of Marriage Act, and the Illegal Immigration Reform and Immigrant Responsibility Act
- Support for President Clinton's position in the House: Republicans 30 percent, Democrats 75 percent; in the Senate: Republicans 33 percent, Democrats 82 percent

105th Congress: Key Facts

- January 7, 1997, through December 19, 1998, during the first two years of the second Clinton administration
- House of Representatives controlled by the Republicans, 227 to 207 (1 other)
- Senate controlled by the Republicans, 55 to 45
- 394 bills enacted
- Major accomplishments included passing the Balanced Budget Act of 1997, Medicare reforms, the State Children's Health Insurance Program, the Taxpayer Relief Act of 1997, the Taxpayer Bill of

Rights, the Chemical Weapons Convention, the Food and Drug
Administration Modernization Act, the Workforce Investment
Act, the Children's Online Privacy Protection Act, the Copyright
Term Extension Act, and the Foreign Affairs Reform and
Restructuring Act
· Support for President Clinton's position in the House: Republicans
29 percent, Democrats 76 percent; in the Senate: Republicans
52 percent, Democrats 87 percent

106th Congress: Key Facts
· January 6, 1999, through December 15, 2000, during the last two
years of the second Clinton administration
· House of Representatives controlled by the Republicans, 223 to 211
(1 other)
· Senate controlled by the Republicans, 55 to 45
· 580 bills enacted
· Major accomplishments included passing the Gramm-Leach-
Bliley Act (reducing barriers between the banking and securities
industries), the Trade and Development Act, the US-China
Relations Act (trade), the Water Resources Development Act,
the Iran Nonproliferation Act, the Oceans Act, the Victims
of Trafficking Protection Act, the Comprehensive Everglades
Restoration Plan, and the Commodity Futures Modernization Act
· Support for President Clinton's position in the House: Republicans
26 percent, Democrats 76 percent; in the Senate: Republicans
41 percent, Democrats 89 percent

QUESTIONS ABOUT CONGRESS

In the early 1990s there was a major effort by Republicans, particularly under House Minority Whip Newt Gingrich, to portray Congress as corrupt
and poorly run, in the hope that the voters would throw out the Democrats
in the next election.

Certainly Congress had problems, but I was finding that most of my
time back home in public meetings was spent answering questions about

my bodyguards, my free health care, my chauffeur in DC—none of which was true—rather than answering questions about our nation's slow economic growth rate or the unfolding tragedy in Bosnia. So I put together a newsletter to use as a response to the large number of letters complaining about congressional waste or excesses.

Perks for members of Congress were a particularly sensitive topic for voters, but there were also many complaints about the large number of congressional staff. Certainly cuts could be made, but I remember holding committee hearings challenging the State Department on policy. I would have two or three staff members assisting me while they would be able to rely on hundreds, even thousands of experts in their department.

February 3, 1993: "Questions about Congress"
Washington Report
Vol. XXVIII, No. 5

Constituents often tell me of their concerns about the operation and management of Congress. I usually agree with their views—often to their surprise—but find that there is sometimes confusion, and even misinformation, over some basic facts. This newsletter attempts to set the record straight on some of the questions Hoosiers commonly ask about Congress.

How many people work in Congress? Staff in the legislative and executive branches of government has increased since the end of World War II, mainly because of the growing role of government in our society. However, while the executive branch has continued to grow, congressional staffing has remained relatively stable over the last decade—with House staff at around twelve thousand and Senate staff at around seven thousand. There has been some dispute about the precise number of people working in the legislative branch. Congressional critics say that Congress employs about forty thousand people. The facts do not support this claim. Adding together the staff for the House and Senate as well as congressional support agencies, like the Capitol Police and the Library of Congress, the total staff for the legislative branch in 1991 was 30,662. This marks a 2.2 percent decline from the 1979 total. Furthermore, legislative branch staff is tiny when compared to executive branch departments. Excluding the military, there are eighty executive branch employees for every legislative branch employee. Additional cuts are likely in both branches.

How big is the congressional budget? The congressional budget has been cut in recent years after growing since the 1970s. The congressional budget for this fiscal year totals $2.3 billion, a 6.5 percent cut from last year's level. Congress has cut mailing costs and official expenses. I agree with constituents who say that additional cuts can and should be made, but also stress to them that eliminating all spending on Congress, the Library of Congress, and support agencies would save only 0.2 percent of the federal budget. Meaningful deficit reduction will require across-the-board cuts in executive branch budgets and, more importantly, in entitlement spending.

Why does Congress exempt itself from federal laws? Congress does not and should not "exempt" itself from the laws which apply to the private sector and to the executive branch. Certain laws, as applied to Congress, are, and should be, enforced differently for constitutional reasons. Allowing executive branch agencies to enforce federal laws in Congress would violate the separation-of-powers doctrine in the Constitution and could compromise the autonomy of the legislative branch. The House and Senate have taken steps to ensure that their employees have the same rights and protections as employees in the private sector. In 1988 the House approved a resolution which provides House employees and job applicants with protection against discrimination based upon race, color, national origin, religion, sex, handicap, or age. The resolution also gives employees a full range of remedies, including timely hearings, an appeals process, and the right of financial compensation. House employees are also covered by the overtime and minimum wage requirements of the Fair Labor Standards Act and the employment provisions of the Americans with Disabilities Act. Better enforcement of these provisions is still necessary.

What has Congress done to improve its management practices? The House banking scandal of 1991 spurred a flurry of reforms. The House voted to close the House bank, and has adopted a series of reforms to improve Congress's overall operations. The House has hired a nonpartisan administrator, a former army lieutenant general, who is now responsible for managing and coordinating all nonlegislative services and facilities of the House, including management of House accounts, internal mail delivery, and service employees. The administrator is implementing policies that will, ultimately, abolish patronage hiring in offices under his jurisdiction. The House has also established the post of House inspector general, responsible for auditing the financial operations of the administrator and other House activities.

Do I answer my own mail? I am responsible for all letters that leave my offices in Jeffersonville and Washington, DC. Given the volume of contacts—about 550 a week by phone and mail—my staff assists me in responding to them. Following my directions, my staff answers routine mail. I read most of the letters and comments from phone calls asking my position or my view on certain issues, and, working with my staff, respond to them.

What about congressional perks? On the general issue of perks, my view is that members of Congress should be treated the same as any other individual—no better, no worse. I have consistently supported the elimination of perks.

Do members receive free health care? Members participate in the same health plans as other federal employees, and pay the same rates. I pay market rate for health insurance premiums for my wife and me. There is not, as many suggest, a free medical clinic serving Congress. Members do not receive free prescriptions or free hospital care; they purchase prescriptions and are treated in hospitals in the commercial market. There is a physician in attendance at all times at the Capitol. Members are required to pay about $500 a year to use the physician. The physician also assists any of the tens of thousands of visitors who come to the Capitol each year who require emergency aid.

What about retirement benefits? Members of Congress contribute up to 8 percent of their salaries to retirement, including the congressional pension plan and Social Security.

What about other "freebies"? I pay for the gas I use to drive to and from work, just as my staff and other members of Congress do; pay $400 a year to use the House gym; pay $10 for my haircuts, and my meals are not subsidized. I do not enjoy free use of military aircraft or free golf, tennis, and hunting privileges, and do not receive immunity from parking tickets, or have the use of military officers' clubs. I do have free parking.

Why does Congress enjoy franking privileges? The frank refers to the practice by which members of Congress use their signatures, rather than postage, to send mail to constituents. The Founding

Fathers established the frank in 1775 as an aid in communicating with constituents and informing them of important issues facing Congress. Every year Congress receives over 215 million pieces of mail. My offices receive about 29,000 contacts a year. Congress appropriates money every year to reimburse the Postal Service for the use of the frank. In 1990, the House greatly reduced the permissible uses of the frank, and then cut its mailing budget by 57 percent. Further cuts are expected this year.

REINVENTING GOVERNMENT

Clinton's presidency got off track early, as he began to seem more like a traditional liberal than a New Democrat with his push within the first few months for gays in the military, increased taxes, and a 1,342-page health care reform bill. His public support started dropping rapidly.

One of the more positive initiatives during his first year was the "reinventing government" initiative under the leadership of Vice President Al Gore. It was a solid effort, one that tried to make the federal government work better and cost less, and it was one that I strongly supported. The federal workforce was downsized, money was saved, and "customer" service improved overall. Some progress was made, but not enough.

Every administration comes in saying it wants to reform government and make it work better, but the efforts are sporadic and they almost invariably get lost in the crunch of other issues. Any efforts along these lines need to be continued for years, even decades.

September 22, 1993: "Reinventing Government"
Washington Report
Vol. XXVIII, No. 38

The Clinton Administration has embarked on an ambitious effort to "reinvent" government—overhauling the executive branch to make federal programs work better and cost less. Following the efforts of various states and businesses, the aim is to replace a large bureaucracy and its bloated chains of command with a more entrepreneurial, decentralized government with power and accountability shifted more to workers. The goal is to make government leaner and more customer-oriented, and to help restore public confidence in government. Based upon a National Performance Review headed by Vice President Gore, the administration's reform effort proposes hundreds of specific recommendations, ranging from eliminating half of federal management jobs to changing the way the government buys computers. President Clinton has made reinventing government one of his top priorities.

Main Themes: The report, which is very tough on government, criticizes the way government hires people, buys things, centralizes decision making, duplicates programs, and uses outdated procedures. It recommends lengthening the federal budget process from one year to two, minimizing congressional restrictions on federal agencies, cutting federal personnel regulations, giving managers more flexibility in hiring and firing, decentralizing decision making, updating procurement procedures, cutting government regulations in half, adopting measurable performance goals for programs, closing unnecessary field offices, consolidating some agencies, and opening up federal monopolies like the Government Printing Office.

The plan would save an estimated $108 billion over five years, primarily through eliminating some 252,000 federal jobs—12 percent of the civilian, nonpostal workforce—as well as through procurement reform and upgrading government technology. About half of the recommendations can be implemented by the president by executive action. The rest would need the specific approval of Congress.

Positive Factors: Although there have been about a dozen major executive branch reform efforts this century, several factors suggest that this attempt could be more successful. First, the effort to cut back the government bureaucracy is being undertaken by a Democratic president, which means the recommendations are being met with less initial skepticism—and he will be working with a Democratic-controlled Congress. Second, the Gore task force was staffed by those working within government rather than outsiders, and the report has received support from federal employee unions because it aims to free workers to better do their jobs. Third, President Clinton strongly believes in the reinventing-government effort. He undertook similar reforms while governor, and made it an early campaign theme. Fourth, the report—one of the best government reports I have read—has strong bipartisan support. Fifth, there is a widespread recognition that in this era of federal belt-tightening, programs must be shown to operate efficiently if they are to survive. Finally, Americans are clearly upset about overall government performance, and the basic themes of this effort resonate well with the public.

Criticisms: Yet skeptics argue that there are several problems with the overall reinventing-government effort. First, the report focuses on how government agencies can perform their tasks better, rather than asking the more basic question of whether the agencies should still be performing those tasks at all. Second, much of the reinventing-government effort boils down to less oversight of executive branch employees—by reducing management, employee regulations, and congressional oversight. What some see as red tape, others see as political and financial safeguards. A backlash could emerge, for example, if favoritism creeps back into personnel decisions and government purchases, or if newly empowered mid-level employees make decisions costing taxpayers millions of dollars. Third, deep personnel cuts could come from popular departments and agencies. If carried out proportionately, three-fourths of the cuts would come from the Departments of Veterans Affairs, Treasury (which includes federal law enforcement), Health and Human Services (which handles Social Security and Medicare), and Agriculture. Fourth, some say that the executive branch is not grossly overstaffed. The federal civilian workforce of three million (including some eight hundred thousand postal workers) has not grown over the past twenty years. Indeed, it has shrunk from 3.5 percent of all civilian employment in 1970 to 2.6 percent in 1990. The real growth in government employment has been at the state and local levels, where jobs have grown from ten million to fifteen million since 1970. Finally, it is difficult to apply the lessons of businesses and the states to the federal government. Some state experiments have not worked well, and the success of large businesses in "reinventing" themselves has been mixed. Moreover, lessons are not easily transferred to the federal government because of its sheer size and lack of competitors, and because its goals are not easily quantifiable and its "customers" often make quite conflicting demands.

Overall Assessment: The process of reinventing the federal government will certainly not be easy. Many powerful constituencies would be affected by the changes. Neither politicians nor bureau-crats give up turf easily, and government entities tend to grow inexorably. Serious roadblocks to the major recommendations could arise in Congress, not just because members might protect constituents or pet programs, but also because of genuine disagree-ments with the executive branch over program goals and the proper oversight role of Congress.

Yet I believe that the overall direction being recommended by the administration is correct. We need a government that is smaller and smarter. We must follow the example of corporate America which for years has been "downsizing" and becoming "lean." Al-though some of the specific proposals will need careful scrutiny, the broad themes—that government should be more innovative, allow its managers to manage, be more responsive to its customers, and give more attention to results—are right on target.

But for recommendations to become reality, it is crucial that President Clinton demonstrate clearly that he is serious about the effort. He must quickly sign executive orders to implement various recommendations that he can carry out himself. He must show that he will put his power and prestige behind pushing other recom-mendations through Congress. And he must make it clear to all that he is in this for the long haul—frequently updating the American people on what has been accomplished so far and what remains to be done. The reinventing-government effort will take many years, and it will take serious constant presidential leadership. The report is an important first step, but implementation and follow-through will be crucial.

PUBLIC CYNICISM

Public trust in government, which was close to 80 percent during the early years of the Johnson administration, was down to 20 percent at the time of this commentary. As I found on numerous occasions, it was a challenging exercise for a politician to stand in front of a group of people and talk about Congress and what it was doing.

Overall, I don't think Congress gave enough attention during this time to government reform efforts as a way to counter the public cynicism. I was chairman of a bipartisan committee to put together a package of reforms to make Congress more effective and accountable. But our proposal, which included cutting back the number of House committees and subcommittees, upset committee chairmen and they strongly opposed it. I pressed Speaker Foley hard to allow it to come to the floor for a vote. To this day I think it would have passed and would have helped show the public that Congress was being responsive to their complaints about how the institution was being run. But the Speaker would not allow it to be considered, and other reform bills which also were supposed to highlight the efforts of this "reform Congress" likewise didn't pass, including health care reform, welfare reform, and campaign finance reform. Within a few months the Democratic-controlled House was repudiated at the polls and the Speaker was voted out by his constituents.

A major factor in the public cynicism was the failure of the Clinton health care reform package. It was the administration's first major policy initiative and a lot of work went into it, including the months of work by Hillary Clinton. One of the president's top aides came to the House Democratic Caucus to explain the package in great detail, but he couldn't answer a basic question about how much it would cost. That was indicative of how this key initiative was handled, and in the end it failed to get through either the House or the Senate.

My overall sense in 1993–94 was that the upcoming election would be a difficult one for Democrats. So I spent even more time than normal back in Indiana meeting with constituents—returning there most weekends and every recess. That was criticized by my staff and other members who thought I should be taking more trips overseas as Foreign Affairs Committee chairman. But I saw a tough election coming up, and did my best to prepare for it.

January 12, 1994: "Public Cynicism"
Washington Report
Vol. XXIX, No. 2

The headline of a major national newspaper caught my eye: "Mistrust of Washington Spreads across the Country." It is easy to see why people distrust Washington. Most Americans lead very busy lives which permit only limited attention to politics. But they hear and see plenty to worry them. Stories of Washington's stupidity and self-interest are abundant. As one constituent put it to me the other day, "You certainly are a bunch of idiots up there." A large number of people simply believe that politics, particularly as practiced in Washington, is fundamentally corrupt.

Sources of Cynicism: Most surveys today show that large segments of the electorate are deeply angry at government and that the politics of discontent is very much a part of contemporary politics.

Americans certainly have a lot to be cynical about. Government deficits, wasteful spending, the personal lives of many politicians, Watergate, Iran-Contra, and bungled policies give them plenty of ammunition. So the voter is often angry and disillusioned, and it is not difficult for various people to play upon this unhappiness and amplify it.

Politicians contribute to the problem by spending much time attacking each other and each other's motives. Political campaigns use TV and print ads to attack opponents, and the political combat, which used to be restricted to election time, seems to go on all the time now. Members of Congress often run for Congress by running against it.

Many interest groups have developed direct mail techniques to an art form and use heated rhetoric to convince people that they are being endangered by sinister politicians. Millions of pieces of direct mail go out every month soliciting funds and playing upon the hopes and the fears and the checkbooks of Americans. A whole industry is built on portraying government as corrupt. The more these industry groups can persuade people of official deception and bungling in Washington, the more money they can raise to carry on their campaigns for whatever objective they seek.

The national media seem to enjoy nothing more than attacking prominent politicians and criticizing every misstep by the president or the Congress. Political coverage has become much more negative in the past several decades. TV journalism today is filled with programs whose purpose is to show how bad the system is and to highlight outrageous events. It is no wonder that people think there is nothing right with the system at all. Many of the most popular commentators are people who have mastered the sound bite and are able to make hard-hitting observations, but who really do not spend much time talking about the complexity of the problems or the difficulty of the solutions.

Sorting through all of the available information is a tough job for any voter. More information does not always lead to more understanding. Many people would say that it is ultimately the voter's responsibility to pay attention to the process and to decide among the charges and countercharges what is true and important and what is not. For most voters the political combat leaves a blur of evidence that government just does not work very well. They hear bits and pieces from television and read snatches of reports in the print media but it is very hard for them to put it all together. They have very little opportunity to hear about or see much of the hard work and effort that go into the process of government in Washington.

Consequences of Skepticism: Everyone would acknowledge that skepticism about government is healthy. The difficulty arises when the skepticism is so deep that voters end up with no faith or trust in government. Our government's institutions in the end are based on people's faith in them, and without that faith they simply cannot work properly.

The climate of cynicism and skepticism—which politicians themselves have done much to create—makes it very hard to bring about change in the system. It is difficult to launch a new initiative today to meet a pressing need because of the depth of public cynicism about government. Not long ago I asked a group of Hoosiers to name a government program that they thought worked pretty well. No one offered any example, not even older people in the group who cash a Social Security check every month.

It is almost impossible to persuade voters today that there are politicians who are seeking to bring about change for the public good and are not just working for some personal advantage. We live in a time when there has been an increase over three or four decades in the amount of skepticism and cynicism about politicians. All of us engaged in the political process find it difficult to function in the present climate in which our character, values, and motives are always suspect.

The largest danger of this deep-seated cynicism is that it undermines principled and reasoned discussion and democratic deliberation. The cynic takes the words and actions of a politician and, rather than discuss and debate those words and actions, simply attributes them to an effort by the politician to serve his own purposes. The cynic is always looking for something nefarious behind the words and actions of the politician; for example, a politician opposes a certain bill not because he has a principled view in opposition to it but because of his ambition to gain higher office or because he has some financial interest involved or because he has been bought off by special interests. It has become harder and harder for the voter to believe that a politician advocates a certain course of action simply because he believes in it.

This is not to say that politicians do not behave in ways that foster cynicism. Voters would be foolish indeed to take everything they hear at face value. But it is also true that if voters judge everything on the basis of hidden motives, we never get around to discussing the substance of an issue. It is much easier to attack the politician for being unprincipled and having nefarious motives than it is to discuss the merits of the issue.

One of the most difficult tasks of a politician today is to try to bring out the best in the country and the best in people. In the present climate it is not easy to elevate their thoughts and to make them believe that good things are possible.

THE TERM LIMIT MOVEMENT AND CONGRESSIONAL CHANGE

A major idea being pushed by Republicans and conservative talk show hosts at this time was term limits: putting a limit on how long a representative or senator could serve in Congress, typically six years (three terms) in the House and twelve years (two terms) in the Senate. Some states passed term limit bills for members of Congress, but a May 1995 Supreme Court decision held that states could not impose term limits on their federal representatives or senators.

Although some constitutional amendments for term limits are still being introduced in Congress and even though the public still continues to raise the issue—I rarely have a public session when it doesn't come up—term limits are not under serious consideration nowadays in Congress. And that is true no matter which party, Democratic or Republican, is in control.

Someone who served thirty-four years in Congress will certainly have a bias on this issue. But my basic view is that our goal should be expanding choices for the voters, not taking the most prominent person out of the race, and that term limits weaken Congress and, by limiting voter choice, representative democracy. Yet this proposal remains popular to this day, reflecting voter dissatisfaction with Congress.

April 6, 1994: "The Term Limit Movement and Congressional Change"
Washington Report
Vol. XXIX, No. 14

In recent years public confidence in the performance of government has been undermined because of various scandals and a lack of progress on the budget deficit and other pressing national problems. This public frustration has fueled the movement to limit the terms of legislators at the state and national level. Starting with Colorado in 1990, voters began to approve state initiatives to impose term limits on members of the US Congress. The movement picked up steam in 1992 when voters in each of the fourteen states with congressional term limits on the ballot approved them, often by overwhelming margins.

The Constitutional Debate: The 1992 victories spurred on both proponents and opponents of term limits for members of Congress. Opponents immediately launched constitutional challenges in court. They argue that the Constitution specifies only three qualifications (age, citizenship, and state residency) for becoming a member of Congress, thus prohibiting states from imposing other qualifications on candidates. Opponents believe that the only way to impose term limits would be through a constitutional amendment rather than through state law.

Proponents of term limits, on the other hand, believe that states can impose such limits, citing the Constitution's provisions allowing states to regulate the "times, places, and manner" of elections. Many such state regulations, which can have the effect of imposing qualifications on candidates, have been upheld by court rulings.

Thus far, the opponents of term limits have won the major court battles. Term limits in Arkansas and Washington State have been ruled unconstitutional, in separate cases by the Arkansas Supreme

Court and a federal court. It is likely that one of the challenges will be appealed to the Supreme Court. Indeed, the constitutional issues are gray, and a Supreme Court ruling would be helpful. The worst result would be to have a patchwork of state restrictions, with some states limiting terms and others not. Power in Congress, which is tied to seniority, would then be completely skewed.

Arguments against Term Limits: In my view, regardless of the constitutional arguments, the risks of term limits outweigh the possible benefits. Mandatory turnover in congressional membership will do little to resolve the real problems the country faces, and may in fact compound them by undermining democratic choice and the representative process.

Dissatisfaction with a Congress that has not always performed satisfactorily does not justify removing all members of Congress, the good as well as the bad, after a certain number of years. Nor does it justify denying the people their choice of representative. This republic has been well served since its birth by the belief that accountability in elected officials should be enforced by voters through the requirement of frequent elections. Many of our most revered and respected politicians served for many years. Why should voters be denied the right to return those who have maintained their public trust? That is why I have also opposed term limits on presidents. Term limits dilute the fundamental responsibility of citizenship to decide who will govern.

Those favoring term limits seem to believe that experience is a virtue in almost any profession except that of legislator. Moving legislation is a tough, exacting task. It requires not only a knowledge of issues but a keen judgment of individuals and the ability to find areas of compromise on widely varying positions. Experience will likely be needed even more in the future, with the dizzying pace and complexity of the world and the nature of governance in a $6 trillion economy. Even voters in states approving term limits seem to acknowledge the value of experience. The voters in the fourteen states that imposed term limits also returned nearly 90 percent of the members to Congress running for reelection who had served longer than the limits the voters wanted to impose.

One unintended consequence of term limits is that by decreasing the number of experienced legislators they increase the power of legislative staff, lobbyists, and bureaucrats. Power does not simply evaporate; it flows somewhere else. Term limits would also tilt the balance of the constitutional system even more in favor of the executive. It is hard to imagine a greater advantage for a president than to purge Congress of experienced legislators who are specialists in issues, who understand the workings of government, and who remember the problems of the past.

Some argue that a Congress with a continuing flow of fresh ideas would result in better government than that provided by representatives with long tenure. The other argument is that experience is an important characteristic for legislators. Each viewpoint probably has some validity, but the best solution is to allow the voters to determine the proper balance between freshness and experience.

Congressional Change: A misperception about congressional turnover underlies much of the term limits debate. Most Americans believe that Congress has a fixed, long-standing membership, when in fact turnover is quite rapid. 75 percent of House members have been elected since 1980. Four hundred out of 435 House members have been elected since the Watergate break-in.

The 1992 elections produced 110 new representatives, one-quarter of the membership. The 1994 elections are shaping up to be a near repeat of 1992—retirements are close to the 1992 pace and many members are facing competitive races. The odds are that when the 1994 elections are over, more than half of the House will have been elected in the 1990s.

Conclusion: The frustrations with Congress that motivated the term limits movement are understandable. Certainly Congress must do a better job of solving the problems that foster public anger and distrust, and some progress has been made recently in ending legislative gridlock. In addition, competitive elections are more important than arbitrary limits on service. Giving priority to campaign finance reforms and increased voter registration and turnout would benefit the political process far more than a potentially counterproductive change in our Constitution.

I believe we have to protect the fundamental right of the voters to choose those who govern them. I think that term limits, by weakening the power of the legislative branch, injure the republic. The fight for term limitation distracts attention from the search for answers to serious problems facing the country.

THE CONTRACT WITH AMERICA

The results of the November 1994 midterm elections were devastating to the Democrats, as the voters were upset with both Clinton's presidency and the Democratic-controlled Congress. Both the House and Senate went Republican, the first time they both would be under Republican control since the early Eisenhower years. It was one of the biggest losses of seats in the House ever, for either party, even more than the number of seats the Republicans lost after Watergate.

One of the strategies the Republicans used during the campaign was to put together a ten-point "Contract with America" explaining what they would do if they were in control of Congress. I didn't hear many constituents mention the contract during the campaign, but the incoming Republicans considered it their mandate from the voters.

Although the contract started out in the new Congress with much fanfare in the House, as the session progressed the Republican-controlled Senate killed several parts, and only a few items actually became law.

> **April 19, 1995: "The Contract with America"**
> **Washington Report**
> **Vol. XXX, No. 16**
> The House recently completed one hundred days of action on the leadership's ten-point Contract with America, taking up and passing measures ranging from legal and congressional reforms to a balanced budget amendment.
>
> Despite all the attention to the contract in Washington, I have been impressed in a number of public meetings in Indiana that the contract only rarely comes up for discussion. Most people know very little of its provisions. Of those who do, many support the major elements of the contract but also say that the House leadership has tried to do too much too quickly. Still others see Congress as operating under the "politics as usual" rules, criticize the spending cuts, or disagree with cutting taxes before balancing the budget.
>
> Summary: Crafted last fall, the Contract with America was organized into ten major planks, plus a prologue making procedural changes in the House. The promise was to bring all of the items up for a vote within one hundred days. All passed the House except

the constitutional amendment limiting congressional terms. Some
of the measures passed by the House—such as the balanced budget
amendment and welfare reform—differed in significant ways from
the versions outlined in the contract. The Senate has not yet acted
on most of the contract, although it did defeat the balanced budget
amendment. Only two parts of the contract have become law—requiring Congress to comply with the laws it passes for everyone else
and reducing unfunded federal mandates.

As it turned out, the contract is really a starting point for negotiations. It is clear to me that the raw and unrefined bills passed by
the House will be softened by the Senate, or may be even stopped.
Even after surgery by the Senate, some contract initiatives face possible presidential vetoes. Which parts of the contract will eventually
become law is far from clear.

I voted for several parts of the contract and opposed others.
The House first took action, with my support, to cut the number of
committees and congressional staff and to require Congress to live
by the laws it passes. These proposals were similar to legislation
I sponsored last session based on the work of the Joint Committee on the Organization of Congress. I also voted for a balanced
budget amendment, a version of the line-item veto, curbs on federal
mandates on the states, and restrictions on excessive government
regulations, among other measures. I did not support certain other
provisions, including a bill that would restrict individuals' Fourth
Amendment protections against government searches, a term limits proposal that would kick in some nineteen years from now, and
an expensive tax cut—largely for the wealthy—that would make it
enormously difficult, if not impossible, to balance the budget.

Accomplishments: There have been several positive aspects to
the Contract with America. First, the House leadership did what
they said they would do. They took on several major issues and
moved them through the legislative process expeditiously. They
deserve credit for that. They have seized extraordinary control of
the political agenda and the terms of the debate.

Second, several contract items represent significant reforms.
For example, the measures that have been signed into law—congressional compliance and restrictions on unfunded mandates—are
important changes.

Third, the contract has helped bring about a serious reassessment of the role of government. The House leadership has focused greater attention on several very important questions. How big should the federal government be? Should the functions of income maintenance and regulation be permanent features of our government? Can we pay for whatever we decide the government ought to do? Do states have sufficient resources and capabilities to resume their full role under the Constitution?

Drawbacks: There are also several drawbacks to the contract. First, the contract has dealt to a surprising degree with legislative and regulatory procedures rather than substantive legislation. For example, the contract had us vote on sending to the states a constitutional amendment to require Congress to eventually balance the budget rather than have us simply vote on a balanced budget. As the Speaker said, "We cleverly picked popular things to do."

Second, the contract failed to deal with many of the real problems facing our nation. As House consideration of the contract was coming to a close, I kept thinking to myself that it was now time to get about the business of the nation: doing something about jobs, incomes, health care, and education. The real test is not how many bills are passed or the popular ratings score or the checklist on the contract's progress. The real test is whether we improve the lives of Americans and improve our prospects for the future.

Third, several of the contract items went too far. For example, a central part of the contract has been to cut back programs for millions of struggling Americans while at the same time providing tax cuts mainly for the rich—tax cuts the Wall Street Journal called "the biggest tax-saving bonanza in years for upper-income Americans." I do not find broad support for the proposals to cut federal programs that benefit children, the elderly, or the middle class.

Fourth, the tough budget decisions lie ahead. The basic contract promise, of course, is to cut federal spending and balance the budget. If the new leadership fails at that, they will have failed altogether. The contract's tax cuts were a major step in the wrong direction. It will be impossible to both reach a balanced federal budget and provide big House-passed tax cuts without putting the entire budget on the cutting table, including Medicare and Social Security. So far the House leadership has spoken only in generalities about cutting spending. Sooner or later, they will have to detail politically difficult spending cuts.

Conclusion: It is far too early in the process to say that the contract has been a success or a failure. The House has certainly not finished its heavy lifting, and in many respects the tough decisions lie ahead. Still, a good start has been made on certain items, and it is quite possible that with the Senate serving as a filter and a brake, the legislative results will be pretty good.

A SENSIBLE ROLE FOR GOVERNMENT

During this period of strong feelings against the role of government, I felt it was important to balance out that prevailing sentiment a bit so that government was not viewed simply as the enemy. The notion of a sensible and limited role for government has remained a major theme of mine.

By the end of the Clinton presidency, the tide was turning on this issue, as Americans were getting a sense that government was having a positive impact on the economy and in their lives.

June 14, 1995: "A Sensible Role for Government"
Washington Report
Vol. XXX, No. 24

The heart of the political debate today is over what the core responsibility of government is. Some insist that fairness requires federal standards for assistance and help to all who qualify. Others say those federal standards have created a mess and want to shift various social programs to the states. Some see government responsibility to help rebuild neighborhoods and communities and to promote common moral and social principles. Others see an activist government as the problem, not the solution, and insist that government has destroyed people's sense of responsibility.

Most Americans would agree that government cannot solve all our problems but does have a role to play. Government is, after all, nothing more than people coming together to accomplish what they could not do on their own. It's about cooperation and helping each other for our mutual benefit. What Americans want is a government that works better and costs less, that is more responsive to the needs of the average American.

To develop a sensible role of government, I think we need to keep a few basic points in mind:

Government Successes: First, there have been major government successes. In public meetings in Indiana I will often ask whether anyone can name a federal program that works well. Usually not a single hand goes up, even when the audience is filled with people who are getting Social Security checks every month, drove to the meeting on the interstate highway system, or received a first-rate education because of the GI Bill.

There have, of course, been failings of government programs, but we should not let the shortcomings blind us to the very real successes of government programs. Social Security, for example, is the biggest federal program and is also one of the most successful. Without it, the poverty rate of seniors would jump from 14 percent to 50 percent. And Social Security's administrative costs are less than 1 percent of benefit payments.

Many other examples could be given. Programs to feed infants and pregnant women or to teach preschool children in Head Start classes, student loans, safe drinking water, and medical research are all valuable programs. Our agricultural research and extension service has helped make US farmers the world's best. The aerospace and computer industries owe their origins to federal programs. Even the enormously popular internet was set up by the federal government. The FBI is the most respected law enforcement organization in the world. And our armed forces are preeminent in the world.

It may be unpopular to point out some good things about government, but it really ought to be done. We simply will never get a sensible role for government if people think of government as the enemy.

Government Failures: Second, there have been government failures. The "Star Wars" antimissile defense system, burdensome regulations on business, and tax subsidies that lead US companies to move jobs overseas are all wasteful. There is no reason to have 689 federal programs for rural development or more than 150 job training programs.

Every problem does not have a legislative solution, and legislators, who are used to solving problems, must remember that. One particularly bad procedure, often used in recent years, is to try to solve a national megaproblem with one huge megabill, consisting of thousands of pages. Congress must narrow its agenda.

Various federal programs—no matter how well intentioned and no matter how impressive the titles—simply don't work. And we will never be able to develop a sensible role of government if we think otherwise.

Sensible Role of Government: Third, our goal should not be big government, or small government, but effective government. The American public is very skeptical of government, and is demanding a less government-centered approach to national problems. Government still has many valuable roles to play, but only if it can do things more efficiently and more effectively. To get there we must be willing to think about the role of government less ideologically and more pragmatically—what, after all, works. Those government programs that work should be kept or expanded; those that don't should be reformed, terminated, or turned over to someone else.

The private sector has taken this approach in recent years. Government should follow suit. Those companies which have been most successful in reforming themselves did not try simply to downsize—to cut costs or personnel by a certain amount—but to rethink what they had been doing—looking at their various missions and expanding on what they were doing well and abolishing what didn't work.

The same should be true for government. From the president on down to the local level, public officials and citizens need to get engaged. We need to address several questions:

· What should be the appropriate role of the federal government as we approach the twenty-first century?

· If the federal government weren't already carrying out a certain program, would it be created today?

· Can we pay for whatever we decide the government ought to do?

· Do states have sufficient resources and capabilities to resume their full role under the Constitution?

· What should be the balance between the private sector and the public sector?

If we undertake this effort, I think we will be getting at what bothers Americans about government and its performance. And we would be undertaking a comprehensive, objective review of the federal government that is clearly long overdue. We might not only get better government, but also government that is more broadly supported by the American people.

THE BUDGET BATTLE

There was a sense among the public that Speaker Gingrich and the Republicans overreached in the government shutdown over budget differences in the fall of 1995, as explained below, and they were blamed more than the president. Yet the lesson has not been fully learned, and the tactic of trying to shut down the government over policy differences still continues in Congress to this day.

The budget battles in Congress and government shutdowns indicate a basic unwillingness to find common ground. The federal budget is so huge, and involves so many programs and issues, that there is plenty of room to find compromise if people are interested and willing to do so.

November 22, 1995: "The Budget Battle"
Washington Report
Vol. XXX, No. 47
As the federal government shut down on November 14, many Hoosiers found themselves angry about the dispute that precipitated the shutdown, unsure about how long it would last, and concerned about how it might affect them.

The shutdown occurred because Congress has not completed action on all of the measures to provide funding for the government during the current fiscal year, which began on October 1. A short-term funding measure, called a continuing resolution (CR), was passed in September and gave Congress until November 14 to enact spending bills. But by that date only three of the thirteen appropriations bills had been signed into law.

Congress and the president have not been able to agree to extend the CR. The congressional leadership attached a number of provisions to the second continuing resolution, including an increase in Medicare premiums. President Clinton objected to these provisions, and vetoed the measure. With my support, Congress then passed a continuing resolution that would keep the government open until December 5 and called for balancing the budget in seven years. However, President Clinton also vetoed this measure.

On November 14, about eight hundred thousand of the federal government's two million civilian employees were furloughed. Many federal government offices were closed, including national parks and museums. New applications for federal benefits, such as Social Security, could not be processed, though payment of Social Security and Medicare benefits continued. The Agriculture and Energy Departments remained open because their funding had been approved. In addition, employees vital to the safety and health of the public, such as air traffic controllers and guards in federal prisons, were kept on duty, as were those on active duty in the military.

A short-term shutdown of the federal government produces plenty of frustration, inconvenience, and confusion, but probably little enduring harm. Congress has typically ensured that federal workers receive pay for the time they spend on furlough. However, a longer shutdown could create major problems for many people. Companies with federal contracts, individuals receiving veterans' benefits, and federal employees could see their payments delayed.

In addition, shutting down the government is expensive. Pay for furloughed federal employees is estimated to cost about $150 million per day. The shutdown process itself—preparing plans, notifying employees, securing property, and so forth—also carries a price.

But perhaps the greatest cost of the shutdown is that it simply reinforces the cynicism and bitterness so many Americans feel about the federal government, particularly elected officials. They see the shutdown as the result of partisan bickering and political posturing, and they place blame on leaders of both parties for gridlock.

Complicating the situation further is disagreement on raising the federal debt limit. Treasury Secretary Robert Rubin has taken a number of steps to ensure that the federal government remains below the debt limit, since at that point the government could no longer borrow money to meet its obligations. A default by the federal government could have serious, long-term implications for the American economy, though no one really knows how the markets would react. The big unknown is that much of the debt is held in places abroad where the understanding of American politics is

meager. In any event, my view is that we should do everything we
can to avoid default. There is no good reason to push the nation to
the edge of financial catastrophe.

I agree with those who find the current standoff unnecessary
and counterproductive. Both sides are engaging in political theater
at the expense of substance. Congress has had several months to
complete work on the appropriations bills. Voters expect us to work
together to get the government's business done, and we should do so.

The current standoff is essentially not about short-term funding, but about competing views on how to balance the budget.
The congressional leadership is trying to use the spending and
debt-limit legislation, where they have a lot of leverage, to force the
president to sign the reconciliation bill—the bigger fight where they
have little leverage. This is the most difficult struggle over budget
priorities I have ever seen since I have been in Congress. It is a high-
stakes dispute over what the role and the priorities of the federal
government should be over the next several years.

The short-term solution to the shutdown of the government may
appear manageable, but it is extremely difficult to see the solution
to the long-term division between the president and the congressional leadership. The real fight comes when Congress passes the
reconciliation bill and the president vetoes it. What is at stake there
is the future of Medicare, Medicaid, the welfare system, rules governing the environment, and federal efforts in education, employment training, and technology.

We must take several steps to get beyond the current impasse.
I believe that sensible compromises are within reach. First, in my
view, Congress should enact a "clean" continuing resolution and
debt-limit increase, without extraneous policy provisions. Second,
we ought to continue negotiations in an effort to enact the rest of the
appropriations bills for the current fiscal year. Third, we must to
the extent possible seek agreement on policy issues contained in the
reconciliation bill.

I suspect in the end we will not be able to resolve all of these
major policy differences in 1995. The way out will be to keep the
government operating largely under present policies on these unresolved matters and then have a public debate on the budget between
now and the 1996 elections. Both sides would then have an opportunity to clarify exactly what they are for. I think this approach
would make the voters much more comfortable.

The question with respect to the shutdown is, do we want a battle or a bill? I believe that Hoosiers want the government to get the people's business done. They are tired of this game of political chicken and are not going to view either party in this debate favorably. Both the president and Congress must seek reasonable solutions, not political points.

CIVILITY IN CONGRESS

By 1995, the incivility in Congress had gotten so bad that a Republican colleague of mine from Indiana, John Myers, and I sent around to every member of the House a Congressional Research Service report titled "Decorum in House Debate."

Civility isn't just about manners and it doesn't mean that we all agree and become friends. But it does mean that we listen to and respect the opinions of others and recognize that in a divided country like ours, governing means finding solutions with people who have many varying opinions. Civility affects the quality of the work done by Congress by making it possible to reconcile different and opposing views. It is an art that requires continual application.

I got a good lesson on civility early on from Senate Majority Leader Mike Mansfield. As a young member of the House Foreign Affairs Committee I was part of a small delegation he led to meet with top government officials in Mexico. He was an enormously respected national leader with great stature on international issues, and the Mexican officials hung on his every word. But what impressed me was that he treated me as if I were totally his equal—turning to me in meetings to ask my advice, insisting that I be included in all discussions. I'm sure the Mexican officials were puzzled to hear so much from a young junior member of the House, but his gracious, courteous manner made quite an impression on me, and I've never forgotten his lesson in treating colleagues with basic civility.

December 6, 1995: "Civility in Congress"
Washington Report
Vol. XXX, No. 49

In his recent press conference announcing why he would not be a candidate for president, Colin Powell mentioned the "incivility that exists in political life today." He's right. In national politics and in Congress we have seen a clear decline of basic civility. This year in Congress there have been mean personal attacks, shouting across the aisle, shoving matches, hissing and booing, and members going out of their way to antagonize those of the other party. Press accounts have described the situation in Congress as "nasty," "full-scale partisan warfare," and "the politics of poison." Partisan tensions are as bad as I can remember. As one senior member recently noted, "Boy, it's mean out there."

President Clinton recently called for more mutual respect in public discourse, echoing the sentiments of President Bush, who called for an end to the "climate of ugliness" on Capitol Hill. The situation certainly isn't as bad as in other countries where we see brawls and fistfights breaking out among members of parliament, but it does merit some attention.

Hinders Legislation: The bitter, contentious exchanges in Congress certainly do not reflect well on the institution; they lead to public cynicism and make the job of legislating more difficult. As Thomas Jefferson stated, "It is very material that order, decency, and regularity be preserved in a dignified public body." Excessive partisan bickering poisons the ability of members to come together to pass legislation for the good of the country. In a democracy like ours, the willingness of members of Congress to listen and to talk to each other in a civil way is essential to our ability to reach a consensus on the difficult policy issues facing our nation—from balancing the budget to sending troops to Bosnia.

Certainly spirited debate is appropriate for the many important policy questions before Congress. Members have strong feelings on particular issues, and naturally get upset when they believe that programs very important to their constituents are being gutted or when they feel the other side is putting up unnecessary roadblocks to their legislative agenda. But members can carry the legitimate debate too far and argue in ways that undermine serious policy deliberation.

Past History: The problem of a breakdown of civility in Congress is certainly not a new one. In past years, especially during periods of national turmoil such as the Civil War or the civil rights movement, there have been major breakdowns in decorum. Over the years, members have been formally punished by the House for making statements such as describing another member as one "who is the champion of fraud, who is the apologist of thieves, and who is such a prodigy of vice and meanness that to describe him would sicken imagination and exhaust invective." Heated debate at times led to fistfights, pistol duels, and a frequent response in earlier days, hitting another member over the head with a cane.

Enforcement: Congress has two basic ways of disciplining members for inappropriate speech. If the remarks occur during debate on the House floor, another member can object and request that the speaker's "words be taken down." If the words are ruled inappropriate by the chair, the speaker either can withdraw the statement or be prohibited from speaking on the floor for the remainder of the day. Broader enforcement can come from the House Standards of Official Conduct Committee—the House ethics committee—which has been given wide-ranging powers to punish members for any actions which do not "reflect creditably on the House of Representatives." Formal charges could be filed against a member, and the Standards Committee could recommend a range of sanctions. In the past, members have been formally censured by the full House for disorderly words spoken in debate.

Remedies: The vast majority of the contacts between members of Congress are civil and courteous. But there are intemperate exchanges—often getting extensive media coverage—which hurt the ability of the institution to properly function. Several steps would be helpful in minimizing them.

First, the Standards of Official Conduct Committee should issue an advisory opinion to all members of Congress spelling out to them what are the proper limits of discourse and what are the consequences of going beyond the limits. The Standards Committee has a separate Office of Advice and Education which was set up specifically for such an advisory role, to help head off misconduct before it occurs.

Second, we need more consistent enforcement by the chair and by the Standards Committee. Rulings by the chair can be spotty and inconsistent, and the rules requiring penalties for improper remarks have at times been waived. The Standards Committee has failed to act on some fairly egregious cases of improper speech in recent years.

Third, outside groups can be helpful watchdogs in keeping an eye on members' statements. A bipartisan group like the Former Members of Congress, for example, could play a useful role in monitoring and publicizing proper and improper discourse on the floor.

Fourth, we need tougher enforcement by the voters. At times a member of Congress might rise to prominence through a negative, confrontational style. If other members think the nasty approach to politics works, they will emulate it. The voters need to send a clear signal that negative and nasty doesn't work.

Finally, members must take it upon themselves to uphold appropriate standards of debate. In the end, it is up to each of us in Congress to set the proper tone and to work with our colleagues to maintain decorum.

Conclusion: Breakdowns in civility in Congress can reflect the passions of the moment, the polarizing nature of the policy issues, or even a less civil tone in the larger society. But there is no excuse for letting particularly intemperate and inflammatory speech go unchecked. Reining in the excesses can go a long way toward improving the ability of Congress to tackle the tough legislative agenda before us.

(Information was taken from a Congressional Research Service report, "Decorum in House Debate.")

THE BUDGET SURPLUS

The biggest accomplishment of Congress and the president during the Clinton years was finally getting the federal budget deficit under control. The deficit was hurting the economy and threatening our nation's long-term economic future. Yet little progress was made under previous presidents, and the deficits had reached record highs during the Bush years.

To his credit, Clinton was convinced by economists early on in his presidency that something had to be done and soon, with Federal Reserve chairman Alan Greenspan and other prominent economists warning of a catastrophe looming ahead. So even though Clinton's preference was to increase federal spending for investments in infrastructure and education, he put together a tough plan of spending cuts and tax increases and pushed hard with members of Congress to get it passed. In the summer of 1993 a major deficit-reduction package passed Congress by the narrowest of margins, with not a single Republican member in either the House or the Senate voting in favor. Newt Gingrich and others were arguing that it would kill jobs and actually increase the deficit. Neither happened, and the economy got a significant boost.

A second deficit-reduction package was approved by Congress in the summer of 1997, this time with the support of both Democrats and Republicans. And by the summer of 1998, the budget deficit situation had improved so much that we were actually running a budget surplus and were debating what to do with the surpluses, such as using them to pay down the accumulated national debt.

Yet the period of surpluses would be short lived, as large tax cuts and other policies during the George W. Bush presidency ballooned the deficits again and created a lasting imbalance between incoming revenue and outgoing spending. It is hard to imagine the time when we'll be having the sort of discussion again that we were having during the Clinton years—of what to do with budget surpluses.

The tough budget decisions during the Clinton years put the federal debt held by the public on the path toward complete elimination. Instead, our federal debt today exceeds $13 trillion—an enormous burden we pass on to our children and grandchildren.

June 10, 1998: "The Budget Surplus"
Washington Report
Vol. XXXIII, No. 23

One of the most striking economic developments this year has been the return of the federal budget surpluses. For the first time since the Johnson administration the federal government will spend less than it receives in revenue. The deficits reached a record $290 billion in 1992 under President Bush, and for many years they have dominated the policy debate in Washington. Turning this around has been a major accomplishment. Now Congress is faced with the quite different question of what to do with the surpluses.

Latest Projections: The latest projections are that the federal budget will run a surplus of around $50–$60 billion this year. The projections are even better after that, as the combined surpluses over the next ten years could exceed $1.5 trillion. These surpluses reverse the trend of the past three decades in which the federal government built up most of the national debt, which now stands at $3.8 trillion.

Reasons for Surplus: Part of the credit for the surplus goes to Congress, especially for passing the 1993 deficit-reduction package. That helped to slow the growth of government spending and built greater spending restraint into the budget law. Major factors in holding down spending have been the shift toward managed care in Medicare and defense downsizing after the end of the Cold War.

But even more important than the spending restraint has been the growth in revenues coming into the Treasury because of the strong showing of the US economy. More people have been working and hence paying taxes; the stock market has been booming, generating a sharp increase in capital gains taxes; and corporate profits have been high. Tax revenues during the month of April were some 14 percent higher than a year ago, and, because of the strong economy, tax receipts as a share of the economy have risen to 21.5 percent, a postwar record.

Need for Caution: Yet that dependence of the budget surplus on the economy's remarkable performance means we must be particularly cautious. Our economy will at some point slow down. The current economic expansion is the second longest since World War II, and the business cycle hasn't been repealed. When the economy slows, incoming revenues will drop and the surplus could be reduced or eliminated altogether. Even an average-sized recession could mean a $100 billion budgetary shortfall for a year or two.

There's a second reason to be careful with these surpluses. Long-range forecasts can be quite unreliable. The forecast of a surplus five or ten years from now is not much better than an educated guess. Early last year, for example, the administration was forecasting a $121 billion deficit for 1998; now they are forecasting a sizeable surplus. If we cut taxes or increase expenditures now, that will be very hard to reverse if the forecasts are wrong.

A third reason to be cautious is that the surpluses are to some degree an illusion. They occur because the tallying of federal spending and receipts includes the surpluses in Social Security. If the Social Security accounts are removed, the remaining tax payments fall tens of billions of dollars short of covering the full cost of providing government services.

The fourth reason for caution about the surpluses is a longer-term one. When the baby-boom generation begins to retire in about ten years, the whole demographic structure of our population changes. Between now and the year 2030 the number of people aged sixty-five or older will double, but the number of people aged twenty to sixty-four will increase by only about 15 percent. As the baby boomers become eligible for Social Security, Medicare, and Medicaid, that will put an enormous strain on federal spending. The biggest chunk of federal spending, by far, currently goes for programs for older Americans, and that will only increase in the years ahead.

Policy Options: The surpluses put us into an altogether new policy field, and there are many proposals in Washington today to cut taxes or increase spending. Yet I think a very strong case can be made for using the emerging surpluses to pay down the federal debt.

Despite the bright projections for the budget, the short-term uncertainties and the future imbalances due to the baby boomers' retirement are cause for major concern. A key issue before Congress and the president is how to begin to prepare for the budgetary shortfalls that will surely arise. I find it helpful to think about this problem of the immediate surpluses in terms of ourselves and our children and grandchildren. If we cut taxes or increase spending now, we can certainly provide benefits for ourselves. On the other hand, if we keep the surpluses to pay down the country's debt, that will boost the supply of private savings and investment and provide higher incomes for the next generation. Passing on a huge debt burden, which today requires interest payments of almost $250 billion each year, is quite unfair to our children and grandchildren and it is a poor way to prepare for the next century.

We cannot count on the favorable trends continuing; the wise thing to do is to wait and see what happens. We should also wait until Congress takes steps to shore up Social Security. We should not be spending the surpluses until the government's revenue and spending excluding Social Security are in balance and Social Security's long-term fiscal imbalance has been addressed. It is certainly premature to talk about spending a surplus when we have huge entitlement costs looming before us in the near future. We shouldn't spend money we may not have. Moreover, I don't see the American people crying out for government action, either on the spending side or the revenue side. And with the economy performing quite well, I see little reason for changing the government's fiscal approach at the present time. So I think we should resist the proposals calling for new tax cuts or increased government spending. I believe we will get a higher economic return from future surpluses by using them to whittle down the $3.8 trillion in federal debt held by the public.

I understand that it is possible to use the surplus to carefully craft tax cuts or new spending programs that deepen the nation's long-term capital base and encourage economic growth. But I am not at all sure that those sound proposals would emerge from the legislative process. On balance, debt reduction probably makes more sense.

Conclusion: So my preference is to leave the budget surplus alone, and if sizeable surpluses do in fact arrive they should be committed to our future, not to the present. It seems clear to me that those who want to reduce the surpluses, whether by tax cuts or spending increases, will be impairing the incomes of our children and grandchildren. They are making a clear choice, preferring our generation to future generations.

THE STARR REPORT AND THE CONGRESSIONAL RESPONSE

The Monica Lewinsky scandal undermined Clinton's second term and probably had implications beyond that by hurting Al Gore's chances to become president. It also had a broader impact on the public's already low opinion of politicians.

But it was also a case of congressional Republicans overreaching. They could have gotten through Congress, with fairly strong bipartisan support, a resolution censuring the president. Most Americans thought impeachment was too strong, but the Republicans still pursued it, knowing they didn't have the votes for Clinton's removal from office.

My position, after reviewing all the evidence—and that was not a pleasant task—was that the House and Senate should have jointly passed a resolution of censure. The president's misconduct, though serious, never in my opinion rose to the level that would require the termination of a presidency. I've often heard constituents say that this or that president should be impeached and removed from office, but the standards for overturning a popular election and ending a presidency are high—as they should be.

When the revelations came out I questioned whether Clinton would be able to stay in office. But he was helped significantly by the timely support he received from two women in his cabinet: Madeleine Albright and Donna Shalala. Equally important was the strong economic recovery that Americans were enjoying during the Clinton years. Most Americans were now feeling good, and they put Clinton's stewardship of the economy above his personal misconduct.

September 23, 1998: "The Starr Report and the Congressional Response"
Washington Report
Vol. XXXIII, No. 38

On September 9, 1998, independent counsel Kenneth Starr submitted his report to Congress regarding President Clinton's relationship with Monica Lewinsky. The US House of Representatives now begins the process of reviewing the evidence the independent counsel has gathered from his grand jury investigation as well as evidence provided by the president and others. The House, after reviewing the Starr report and other evidence, will decide whether to proceed with formal impeachment hearings. The key judgment will be for the House to determine whether the president's conduct amounts to "high crimes and misdemeanors," the constitutional standard for removing a president from office.

The Starr Report: The 453-page Starr report alleges that President Clinton committed acts that may constitute grounds for impeachment. The report lays out in graphic detail the chronology of events surrounding the president's affair with Ms. Lewinsky, and concludes that the facts may establish eleven possible grounds for impeachment, including lying under oath in the Paula Jones case

and before Starr's grand jury, obstructing justice, witness tampering, and abuse of power.

The president has acknowledged that he had an inappropriate
relationship with Ms. Lewinsky and that his conduct was wrong,
but rejects the view that he committed the offenses catalogued in
the Starr report. Furthermore, the president's attorneys contend
that his conduct, while inappropriate and wrong, does not rise to
the level of "high crimes and misdemeanors," and therefore does not
warrant Congress proceeding with an impeachment inquiry.

Presidential Conduct: I have read the Starr report in full, and
like many Americans, am shocked and dismayed by its contents. I
recognize, of course, that the report represents only the prosecu-
tor's assessment of the facts and that Congress has a duty to examine all the evidence, including evidence which tends to exonerate
the president.

Putting the Starr report to one side, I have nonetheless been
deeply disappointed by the president's conduct. The sexual misconduct was offensive but that really was not the worst of it. He misled
his wife, his staff, and the country. His pattern these last several
months to hide his improper relationship has been to conceal, fab-
ricate, stonewall, and attack Starr. He surely could have saved the
country much agony by making a confession months ago. His legalistic hair-splitting on the issue of lying defies the common sense of
most of us.

Where We Go from Here: Congress now faces the grave responsibility of deciding whether to move ahead with a formal impeachment proceeding against the president. Overturning the results
of a popular election is very serious business. Next to declaring
war, Congress perhaps has no greater duty under our Constitution. Hence, we must proceed in the weeks and months ahead with
deliberate speed, but with caution and fairness, to seek the truth
and make a judgment. This process is not about partisan political
advantage, but about the future of our country.

The key question will be whether the president's conduct,
disgraceful as it is, constitutes "high crimes and misdemeanors."
The framers of the Constitution borrowed the expression from the
English common law to suggest grave offenses against the state—
offenses which undermined the integrity of the presidency or
our constitutional system of government—but did not define what

precisely those offenses might be, aside from treason and bribery.
"High crimes and misdemeanors" has been generally understood
to encompass public misdeeds, such as abuse of official power that
threatens the country, but not private misconduct.

Nature of Process: The impeachment process is a mix of law,
politics, and public opinion. It should not be used to remove a president with whom Congress has political differences, nor should it
be limited to possible violations of criminal law. Rather, it should
primarily ask whether a president's conduct is so bad that he can
no longer be trusted to serve. The president's ability to govern the
country has been damaged. The looming question is whether he
retains enough of the confidence of the American public that he will
be able to govern effectively.

Congress will pay close attention to public opinion as this
process unfolds. In effect two processes are now taking place: one
in Congress and one in the public. Both are necessary. Of the two,
the process in the American public is more important. The public
deliberation taking place over the next several weeks will drive this
process and will eventually drive congressional action.

Thus far, the American public does not support impeaching
the president. The public is of two minds about the president. They
believe he is doing a good job as president and is a strong leader in
touch with their problems. On the other hand, they do not like his
morals and question his integrity and his character. The public today appears to favor some form of censure of the president, short of
impeachment, and wants Congress to get through this process and
back to the people's business as quickly as possible.

My Assessment: The Starr report presents a strong case of presidential misconduct. The evidence that the president lied under oath
about the relationship with Ms. Lewinsky is persuasive. The president does not challenge the basic facts of the report, which paint a
devastating portrait. Starr's charges of obstruction and, particularly, abuse of power are less compelling, and there is considerable conflicting testimony relative to these charges. I have doubts, at this
point, whether the president's misconduct rises to the level of "high
crimes and misdemeanors" to warrant his removal from office.

I am not advocating at this time censure, resignation, or impeachment. Congress has the constitutional obligation to weigh
the evidence presented by the independent counsel very carefully,

as well as evidence presented by the other side. I do not see how we can make a judgment about the president until we have had a chance to evaluate all the evidence. I do not think the Congress should adjourn while these issues about the president's future are unresolved.

The question on my mind is how best to get through the next two years with the least harm to the country. We must be very careful with the institution of the presidency. We must avoid a paralysis of the presidency and the inability of the president to lead effectively. I do think some kind of judgment needs to be given on the president's conduct. What kind of judgment it is will depend on the evidence. But even on the basis of the information we now have, we cannot permit the impression to prevail that the president's behavior is acceptable.

THE WORK OF CONGRESS

In August 1998, I knew that I would be retiring from Congress within a few months, at the end of that session of Congress. I was beginning to look back over my thirty-four years as a member of Congress and think about the main features of the job. This commentary spells out my thoughts and concerns about Congress at that time, including ways I had seen the work of Congress become more difficult over the years.

One change mentioned is the much higher cost of running for Congress. As the costs have skyrocketed over the years, members need to put in an enormous amount of time fundraising, time which could have been spent much more productively. The perpetual money chase was one of the reasons I decided to retire from Congress.

August 19, 1998: "The Work of Congress"
Washington Report
Vol. XXXIII, No. 33
The work of Congress often seems laborious and painfully slow. We hear complaints about legislative stalemate, excessive partisanship, and the "do nothing" Congress. Sometimes it is hard to discern good reasons for the inefficiencies and delays that occur. But often

the difficulty of passing legislation stems from the very nature of our representative democracy and from our changing country and changing political climate. The work of Congress has become much more difficult over the past several years.

The Job of Congress: Although the job of a congressman involves several different roles, the main ones are as representative and legislator. As a representative, a member serves as an agent for his constituents, ensuring that their views are heard in Congress and that they are treated fairly by federal bureaucrats and other public officials. As a legislator, a member participates in the lawmaking process by drafting bills and amendments, engaging in debate, and attempting to build the consensus necessary to address our nation's problems. Fulfilling these roles may sound easy, but it can be enormously difficult.

Some things, it must be said, have helped to make the work more manageable in recent years. Congress has moved into the information age, as computers, faxes, and internet access help members communicate with citizens. Large numbers of congressional staff help members respond to constituent mail and research legislation. The expansion of think tanks and public policy research helps provide lawmakers with detailed analyses of policy options.

Increased Difficulty: However, the elaborate constitutional system of separated powers and checks and balances created by our Founding Fathers still requires that compromise and consensus occur for legislation to pass. This protects people from the tyranny of the majority, but also makes it difficult for Congress to act. Since I have been in Congress the job of a congressman has become increasingly difficult, for several reasons.

First, the country has grown larger and more diverse. The population of the country has more than doubled since I was in high school. Each member of the House now represents almost six hundred thousand constituents, almost 50 percent more than in the 1960s. Americans also vary more now in terms of occupation, race, religion, and national origin. The increasingly diverse background of constituents expands the range of interests and differences that must be reconciled to produce consensus on major issues.

Second, the issues have grown more numerous and more complex. Today's Congress tackles a host of topics that simply were not around a few decades ago, from campaign "soft money" and HMOs to cloning and cyberspace. Also, the issues we consider have become more technical and complicated. A recent environmental bill before Congress reminded me of my college chemistry textbook.

Third, the issues have also become more partisan. The policy agenda always has included divisive items, but in past years these divisions typically were not partisan. An individual you disagreed with on one issue likely would support your view on many other items, making it easier to strike bargains and achieve consensus. With the intensity of American politics today, issues often have a sharper, partisan flavor. Policy debates frequently split constituents and their elected representatives by party, making the two major parties resemble warring camps more than potential partners in compromise.

Fourth, there are more policy players in the legislative process. For instance, in the 1960s just a handful of major groups were actively involved in foreign-policy making. Now there are literally hundreds, including the business and agriculture communities, nonprofits and public interest groups, labor unions, ethnic groups, and international organizations. The cast of important players has similarly expanded in the numerous other policy areas.

Fifth, although the workload of Congress has expanded, the number of hours in session in recent years has actually dropped. The leadership has chosen to have the House work basically only two-and-a-half-day weeks, with many members arriving in Washington on Tuesday afternoon and leaving for their districts on Thursday evening. As a result, members have less time to know each other well and to work out their differences, thus making consensus building even harder.

Sixth, the cost of campaigns has skyrocketed, driven largely by the cost of television advertising. Members today must spend a disproportionate amount of time fundraising, which means less time with constituents discussing the issues and less time with colleagues forging legislation and monitoring federal bureaucrats. Also, special-interest support may drive some members to lock in their views earlier, reducing their flexibility and making compromise harder.

Seventh, the tone in Congress has changed dramatically over the past several years, with more partisan bickering and personal attacks, and less civility. That takes a significant toll. It poisons the atmosphere and complicates the efforts of members to come together and pass legislation for the good of the country. In the end, Congress works through a process of give and take, which is far more difficult with strained relationships across the aisle.

Eighth, the media tend to favor the extreme views on any given issue, emphasizing the differences and downplaying the areas of agreement. That can polarize the issue and make agreement more difficult to reach.

Finally, public suspicion of politicians is greater today than it was in past decades. Americans have always had a healthy skepticism about government, but problems arise when they become cynical and have little trust in what their leaders say or do. It is difficult for members of Congress to even discuss the issues with constituents when their character, values, and motives are always suspect.

Conclusion: It is easy to criticize Congress. As members are clearly aware, many criticisms of the institution are justified. But we need to get beyond that and recognize that certain perceived shortcomings of Congress are actually inherent features of any legislature in a large, diverse, and complicated country. Members of Congress need a certain degree of trust from their constituents if they are to fulfill their roles as representative and legislator—not unconditional trust, but support meshed with constructive skepticism and a reasonable understanding of the difficulties the institution confronts.

THE RECORD OF THE 105TH CONGRESS

This was my last commentary summarizing for constituents the record of a Congress. The contrast with the 89th, my first Congress, is stark. Then, we were brimming with enthusiasm, optimistic about the future, and passing a series of major bills on a bipartisan basis to meet pressing needs—from Medicare to civil rights to aid to education. The 105th was fractious and divisive, and accomplished little. Confrontation rather than cooperation became the norm. Congress had changed in fundamental ways.

And so had the nation. During my initial years in Congress there was considerable turmoil in the country—with Vietnam, assassinations, race riots—and relative calm in Congress. In my final years in Congress, there was turmoil in Congress but relative calm in the country.

October 28, 1998: "The Record of the 105th Congress"
Washington Report
Vol. XXXIII, No. 43

The legislative record of the 105th Congress was meager. Only a
limited number of important measures passed, many key initiatives
died, and the leisurely pace meant fewer legislative days this year
than in any in memory. Most agree that Congress left town with a
lot of America's business unfinished. There were several reasons for
this poor showing, including divided government, slim majorities in
the House and Senate, and the focus of Congress on the president's
personal problems and impeachment hearings.

Accomplishments: During its two years, the 105th Congress
did have some significant accomplishments. In the first session it
passed the historic legislation to balance the federal budget, modest
tax cuts on capital gains and estates and for families with children,
modernization of the process for approving prescription drugs
and medical devices, and major changes in Medicare to offer new
options to older people. The Senate approved the chemical weapons
convention which bans the production and use of chemical weapons,
and the House voted to reprimand and fine Speaker Newt Gingrich
for abusing tax laws and lying to the House ethics committee.

In the second session Congress approved the largest public
works program in the nation's history, more than $200 billion over
the next six years; legislation establishing an outside board to
oversee the Internal Revenue Service and giving rights to taxpayers; lower interest rates on federal college loans for students, and
expanded grants; a reform of public housing giving local housing officials more authority; and $18 billion for the International
Monetary Fund with new limits on its loans to foreign governments.
Congress also passed a $6 billion emergency farm aid package,
added $9 billion to the military budget, and approved a modest tax
cut which basically renewed several expiring business tax credits
and gave limited relief to farmers and self-employed people. The
Senate voted to expand NATO to include Poland, Hungary, and the
Czech Republic. The House began a full-scale, open-ended inquiry
into the possible grounds for impeaching President Clinton, only the
third time in history that such an inquiry has been undertaken.

Unfinished Agenda: What the 105th Congress did not do was
also significant. It failed to pass legislation to regulate tobacco
products and reduce teen smoking. It failed to reform the campaign

finance system, in particular failing to pass House-approved measures addressing "soft" money and issue-advocacy commercials. It failed to pass a bill to define patients' rights and to help contain costs in managed health care. It failed to renew negotiating authority that would allow the president to negotiate trade agreements that Congress could accept or reject but not amend. It failed to provide serious oversight of federal programs in a large number of areas.

At the beginning of this Congress there was bold talk of scrapping the entire tax code and replacing it with a flat tax or a sales tax. At the end there were only modest tax cuts helping a few selected groups. At the beginning of this Congress there was much talk, guided by the polls, of the importance of education. The polls showed the public by an overwhelming margin wanting to spend education funds on building more classrooms and hiring more teachers. In the end only modest progress was made.

The Budget: Congress for the first time in decades dealt with a budget in surplus. The result was not very impressive. First, Congress was never able to agree on a budget resolution, which is meant to provide a framework for all the tax and spending bills. This has not happened since the congressional budget process was established in 1974. Second, the Senate and the House could not pass eight of the thirteen spending bills needed to keep the government running. So at the end of the session Congress lumped all eight bills together into an omnibus bill. Third, in order to get a budget passed a lot of gimmicks were used. The most important was designating $20 billion as "emergency" spending so programs did not have to be cut elsewhere to offset the new spending. That gimmick alone used up one-quarter of the anticipated budget surplus. Fourth, the big debate on the budget began on whether to spend or save the surplus—whether to use it to shore up Social Security or to cut taxes or to pay off the debt. That debate was inconclusive and will go on for several years.

The failure of Congress to adopt a joint budget resolution set the stage for delay in the passage of the regular appropriations bills. Much of the federal budget was deferred until the final few hours of the 105th Congress, when members were given the option of voting up or down on one huge omnibus bill to continue to fund the operations of government. The omnibus bill embraced thousands of subjects having nothing to do with one another except that they were all left for the final days of the session. The $486 billion bill contained scores of controversial provisions and knocked down the strict spending caps that many members hailed as their greatest accomplishment just last summer. This was a poor way to legislate. Leaving so many key matters to one huge bill in the final rush to adjournment enables just a few members to make all the final key decisions. It is a profoundly undemocratic process. In the budget conferences and in the back offices this handful of members hammered out the major policy differences, and were able to include—without any public accountability—items that were not requested by the president and not approved by either the House or the Senate.

The President's Agenda: The president had limited success with his agenda. He did win some notable victories toward the end of the session on education, relief for farmers, and financing for the IMF. But many of his proposals went down, including antismoking legislation, reform of health maintenance organizations, an overhaul of campaign finance laws, subsidies to help middle-class families with child care, and an increase in the minimum wage. And even on education, the president won funds for new teachers but was rebuffed on funding for school construction.

Conclusion: Throughout, this was a difficult, partisan, and acrimonious Congress. I have found that very few constituents can name a single thing that Congress has done, other than the impeachment inquiry into President Clinton's behavior. I left the concluding days of the 105th Congress with the impression that the focus on impeachment had diverted Congress from its important responsibilities, and that this Congress will be known more for what it did not do than for what it did do.

WHY VOTING MATTERS

By late December 1998, my congressional office had largely shut down. I and a few remaining staffers were working out of temporary space shared by several other departing members in the basement of one of the House office buildings. My selecting "why voting matters" as the final topic of my congressional commentaries to constituents indicates the central importance I give to it. Low turnout rates are a significant worry, for a variety of reasons spelled out here. This commentary has been frequently reprinted in various newspapers and journals and is one that I still refer back to from time to time.

After leaving Congress I was on a commission that dealt with federal election reform, headed by former president Carter and Jim Baker. One of our conclusions was on the need to improve our country's voting infrastructure—with its delays, outdated voting machines, and limited access to the polls. That is mainly a state responsibility, but we all have a stake in it. Americans assume that the mechanics of the process will continue, but I have seen over the years how fragile that system is. Breakdowns occur in our system regularly.

Unfortunately, voting rates in presidential and midterm elections are still more or less what they were when I wrote this commentary in 1998. And Indiana, I'm not pleased to say, ranks near the bottom in both registration and voting. So one of my efforts in recent years has been to give particular attention to improving the voting rate in Indiana.

December 29, 1998: "Why Voting Matters"
Washington Report
Vol. XXXIII, No. 51

The right to vote is the central feature of our system of government. A century ago some 80 percent of all eligible voters regularly turned out for American presidential elections. Today the rate has dropped to less than 50 percent. The United States, the great beacon and bulwark of modern democracy, now ranks behind almost every other free country in terms of voter participation. The conventional wisdom is that low voter turnout is troubling primarily because it can affect who wins elections, and thus the content of public policy. But low turnout is also a signal of more fundamental problems in American political life, particularly a citizenry increasingly alienated from politics, and a lack of public awareness about the day-to-day importance of government. I am deeply concerned that politics is becoming increasingly a spectator sport.

Understanding the Decline: Several factors help explain why certain people are more likely to vote than others. Education is strongly related to turnout, with more highly educated citizens substantially more likely to participate in elections. Young people disproportionately abstain from voting, mostly because they are so focused on securing jobs and starting families, and are not yet fully integrated into their communities. People who move from one locality to another are less likely to vote. Electoral laws also affect voter participation. States and localities with more demanding regulations about how and when voting can occur tend to have lower turnout rates. And citizens are more likely to go to the polls when an election is interesting and perceived as important.

While these factors help us to understand variations in turnout among different groups of people, they cannot fully explain why turnout has fallen over time, or why it is so low overall. As an electorate, we are growing older and more educated, which suggests that turnout rates actually should be going up and not down. A number of recent changes in our electoral rules, such as the Motor Voter Act, have actually made voting easier. There also has been no across-the-board decline in electoral competition capable of explaining why turnout has dropped.

So why has turnout fallen in recent years? The decline in electoral participation reflects a growing public distrust toward politicians and government, and a general sense of alienation from the political process. People have a decreased sense of civic responsibility, a loss of faith in government, and a feeling of impotence to bring about change in the system. Many people now perceive that officeholders are unethical and insulated from the concerns of ordinary citizens. Thirty years ago, the vast majority of Americans believed that the national government could be trusted most or all of the time. In the 1990s, most citizens, particularly young people, have felt otherwise. According to a recent survey, only 29 percent of citizens ages eighteen to twenty-nine trust government to do what is right most of the time.

I am also disturbed by how little awareness so many people have about the impact of government on their daily lives. The interstate highway system, medical research, Social Security, and Medicare—these and other federal programs have a profound and immediate effect on millions of Americans. But citizens increasingly believe that the activities of government, especially at the federal level, have little direct consequence for them as individuals. Not surprisingly, these people are unlikely to invest the time and effort necessary to vote.

The Costs: Low voter turnout certainly has the potential to affect electoral outcomes. The partisan balance in Congress has been very tight during the 1990s, and a small shift in seats from one party to the other could change partisan control of the legislative branch. Yet this impact can be overstated. Based on the best evidence from surveys, it seems that low turnout rates do not systematically alter electoral outcomes or public policy. The views that people hold about candidates and issues simply do not vary that much across the different characteristics that distinguish voters from nonvoters. By most estimates, if voter turnout had been 100 percent in recent decades, very few elections would have resulted in a different outcome.

Instead, the decline in voter turnout primarily is troubling for other reasons. Nonvoting reflects public distrust toward government, but it also serves to reinforce and deepen this corrosive cynicism. The intention to vote is one reason why individual citizens pay attention to and learn about public policy. When they withdraw from the electorate, they have fewer incentives to stay informed about the major issues of the day. The act of voting tends to make people feel more connected to their communities and to the political process. Regular abstention drives yet another wedge between individuals and their civic obligations.

Low voter turnout also contributes to the polarization of American politics. Overall voter apathy makes potential candidates more responsive to their party's most loyal, and most partisan, voters. This in turn has certainly contributed to heightened political divisions in the country and to a stark divide on many emotional issues like abortion, school prayer, welfare policy, and tax cutting.

Addressing the Problem: What can be done to increase voter turnout in America? First, we need to simplify the voting process. Millions of people could be brought into the voting process by streamlining registration. Lowering the barriers to registration and extending voting hours could help. On many occasions potential voters have said to me that they are simply too busy to vote and the hours for voting are too short.

Second, serious campaign finance reform would help level the electoral playing field and make campaigns more competitive and interesting, perhaps increasing turnout. Third, the reapportionment process, through which boundaries of House districts are realigned every ten years, should be carefully monitored to ensure that district lines are not drawn to promote the interests of one officeholder or party.

Fourth, we need to strengthen the citizen's sense of civic duty and civic involvement. More attention needs to be given to driving home the basic message of the importance of the act of voting, for our country and for each of us as citizens. A voter needs to understand that by voting he affirms the democratic process, that he cares about a form of government in which he is free to participate. He also needs to understand that the vote dilutes the power of special-interest groups which usually go to the polls in very large numbers, and that voting makes elected officials more responsive and guides their official actions and policies.

Finally, people need to be educated more effectively about how government actually operates and its impact on everyday life. The most significant causes and consequences of low voter turnout relate to public alienation from government. Too many citizens are not aware of the practical difficulties of forging consensus in a nation as diverse as the US, and they have unrealistically high expectations about what government can accomplish. And too many people hold unrealistically low estimates of the ethics and ability of public officials in this country. People need to be educated about the pervasive impact that government has on them. There is simply too much at stake with government and politics for Americans not to exercise their right to vote.

Clinton's presidency was not spectacular, and he had significant legislative failures that included not being able to get his major health care initiative through either the House or the Senate. Yet he had successes on important issues like deficit reduction and welfare reform that were politically very difficult and beyond the reach of previous presidents and Congresses. The American economy also improved considerably during the Clinton years, as the unemployment rate dropped to the lowest level since the late 1960s, inflation was low, economic growth was strong, and consumer confidence hit record levels. And although people will often talk about Reagan's contributions to restoring our nation's confidence, the fact is that in no recent presidency has public trust in government improved as much as it did during the Clinton years. Clinton connected well with the American people, and his resilience in bouncing back from adversity was remarkable. He was one of the rare presidents in recent memory who left office as popular as when his term began.

Yet the Monica Lewinsky scandal and his impeachment took a major toll. It was a time of opportunities missed, as important national issues on his agenda for his final years in office—like shoring up Social Security and Medicare and addressing the nation's racial divide—were put aside and the legislative accomplishments during his second term became thin. My main thought again and again during these trying times was how much more could have been accomplished by this talented man for the good of the nation if he were not distracted by his personal problems.

Certainly not all of the fault for legislative failures lies with Clinton. During the first two years of his presidency, the Democratic-controlled Congress was simply unable to produce a solid legislative record, and they paid the price for that in the November 1994 elections. And for the next six years Clinton faced a Republican-controlled Congress that was not at all disposed to work cooperatively with him.

The most significant long-term development in Congress during the Clinton years was the rise of Newt Gingrich as the Speaker of the House and national leader of the Republican Party, and his confrontational approach to politics. He was the single most important factor in the changing tenor of Congress. From the Republican point of view he was able to accomplish what none of his predecessors had since the 1950s: bringing the Republicans back into control of Congress. But the toll that his aggressive approach to politics took on the institution has been high, and that legacy remains to this day with our polarized and highly partisan Congress. In the years since he left Congress there have been glimpses from time to time of Congress operating as it should, yet overall Congress has continued in the partisan direction he took it.

Hopefully at some point we'll see leaders in Congress who will lead in the other direction, taking the institution back to what the Founders intended it to be: a body that reflects major differences within our diverse country yet in the end works together to find common ground to address the nation's many challenges.

Many Americans were hopeful that Clinton's successor, George W. Bush, would help address the discord in Washington, and live up to his campaign claim that he was a "uniter, not a divider."

EIGHT

THE GEORGE W. BUSH YEARS
(2001–2008)
A Timid Congress

BY THIS TIME I WAS WATCHING CONGRESS MORE FROM A DISTANCE —as head of the Woodrow Wilson Center in Washington, DC, and the Center on Congress at Indiana University—and I was still writing regular columns on Congress, representative democracy, and the importance of civic engagement.

I got to know President Bush primarily through my work on both the 9/11 Commission, which looked into the 9/11 attacks and recommended steps to guard against future attacks, and the Iraq Study Group, which was tasked with assessing the war in Iraq and making policy recommendations. In both cases the president was initially opposed to our work and hesitant to cooperate, feeling that our findings would be critical of his administration's actions. So members of the two groups had to work hard over an extended period of time to establish our credibility with him. I felt he listened respectfully and wasn't just going through the motions with us. In the end, he helped get many of our 9/11 recommendations approved by Congress, and the administration's overly optimistic statements on progress in the war in Iraq became more realistic after our Iraq Study Group report was issued, with the president admitting for the first time that the situation in Iraq was "bad."

His discussions with our groups were almost always in generalities, and he certainly was not a detail man. But he was always courteous, never confrontational, and he made a good personal impression. My sense was that he prided himself in being a strong administrator and decision maker. Vice President Dick Cheney was always present in our meetings with the president. Although he strongly opposed our work on both reports, he remained totally silent in our meetings, as far as I can recall. But it was clear he had significant impact behind the scenes on policy decisions, particularly early on in the administration.

President Bush generally received high marks for his response to the 9/11 attacks. There was a question about whether he had paid enough attention to President Clinton's warnings about terrorism as Clinton was leaving office. But Bush showed strong leadership in response to the attacks. He made changes to improve our nation's intelligence system and reform our military, and he got Congress to set up a new Department of Homeland Security, as the 9/11 Commission had recommended. The months after 9/11 are generally considered some of the strongest of his administration.

Although the fight against terrorism took much of his attention, he had some notable achievements as president that included bringing national attention to excellence in education, expanding prescription drug coverage for seniors under Medicare, and taking a lead in fighting AIDS in Africa, which saved many lives.

But other aspects of his term were viewed as much less successful: taking his eye off Osama bin Laden and instead going after Saddam Hussein, taking us into war against Iraq based on claims of weapons of mass destruction that were never found, pushing through large tax cuts that wiped out the progress on the budget deficits made during the Clinton years, and taking a lax regulatory approach that contributed to the meltdown of the housing and financial sectors.

As a result his standing with the American people plummeted and his job approval rating by Americans, which was as high as 90 percent after 9/11, ended up around 30 percent by the time he left office. An initially promising administration ended with only modest public support.

Yet some of the public criticism of President Bush seems to me to be missing the mark. Certainly the president and his team made mistakes. But I believe there would have been far fewer mistakes had Congress done its job as envisioned by the Founders: as a coequal branch of government, acting as a check on presidential power rather than a rubber stamp, forcing the administration to clearly articulate and defend its policies, and casting a skeptical eye on what was presented as evidence. A share of the blame for the "Bush policy failures" during this time rests with the Congress.

After years of being in the minority, the Republicans had taken control of Congress during the Clinton years, and with George W. Bush they finally had a Republican president to work with and to support. During the first six years of the Bush administration, the Republicans controlled the House and were in control of the Senate most of the time. The approach of the Republican leadership in Congress during this period was basically one of passivity and deference to the president. Their eagerness to support a president of their own party was understandable, but they went too far in following his lead uncritically. Congress did not live up to its constitutional responsibility and in the end failed the country. Not giving the Bush policies more careful scrutiny was a major mistake and cost the country dearly.

The Speaker of the House during the 107th–109th Congresses was Dennis Hastert of Illinois. He had become Republican Minority Leader after both Newt Gingrich and Bob Livingston resigned amid ethics charges. Hastert was an able member of Congress, but his decision as Speaker not to bring forward legislation unless a majority of his caucus approved it—the "Hastert Rule"—was a major departure from traditional practice in the House. It's a mistake not to let the House work its will and instead give control of the legislative agenda to a portion of the majority-party caucus.

In my view, Speaker Hastert did not appreciate the constitutional role of Congress as a separate, independent branch of government. He saw his job instead as supporting the president and getting his plan through Congress. And during his six years as Speaker the House Republicans usually voted in lockstep with President Bush on the key issues. For example, House Republicans supported the president 219 to 0 on his major tax-cut plan in 2001, 218 to 3 on his 2003 tax cuts, and 215 to 6 on the resolution authorizing the president to go to war in Iraq.

107th Congress: Key Facts

· January 3, 2001, through November 22, 2002, during the first two years of the first George W. Bush administration

- House of Representatives controlled by the Republicans, 221 to 211 (3 other)
- Senate initially controlled by the Republicans, 50 to 50, then by the Democrats, 50 to 49 (1 other)
- 377 bills enacted
- Major accomplishments included passing the Economic Growth and Tax Relief Reconciliation Act, the Authorization for Use of Military Force against Perpetrators of the September 11, 2001 Attacks, the USA PATRIOT Act, the Aviation and Transportation Security Act, the No Child Left Behind Act, the Campaign Reform Act, the Trade Act of 2002, the Corporate Fraud Accountability Act, the Help America Vote Act, the Authorization for Use of Military Force against Iraq, the Homeland Security Act, and the E-Government Act of 2002
- Support for President Bush's position in the House: Republicans 89 percent, Democrats 33 percent; in the Senate: Republicans 96 percent, Democrats 70 percent

108th Congress: Key Facts

- January 7, 2003, through December 9, 2004, during the last two years of the first George W. Bush administration
- House of Representatives controlled by the Republicans, 229 to 205 (1 other)
- Senate controlled by the Republicans, 51 to 48 (1 other)
- 498 bills enacted
- Major accomplishments included passing the Jobs and Growth Tax Relief Reconciliation Act, the Partial-Birth Abortion Ban Act, the Medicare Prescription Drug, Improvement, and Modernization Act, the Fair and Accurate Credit Transactions Act, the Flood Insurance Reform Act, the Project Bioshield Act, and the Intelligence Reform and Terrorism Prevention Act
- Support for President Bush's position in the House: Republicans 88 percent, Democrats 29 percent; in the Senate: Republicans 95 percent, Democrats 68 percent

109th Congress: Key Facts

- January 4, 2005, through December 8, 2006, during the first two years of the second George W. Bush administration
- House of Representatives controlled by the Republicans, 232 to 201 (2 other)
- Senate controlled by the Republicans, 55 to 44 (1 other)
- 482 bills enacted
- Major accomplishments included passing the Class Action Fairness Act, the Bankruptcy Abuse Prevention and Consumer Protection Act, the Energy Policy Act of 2005, the Transportation Equity Act, the Deficit Reduction Act of 2005, the Tax Increase Protection and Reconciliation Act, the Federal Funding Accountability and Transparency Act, and the Secure Fence Act
- Support for President Bush's position in the House: Republicans 83 percent, Democrats 28 percent; in the Senate: Republicans 86 percent, Democrats 45 percent

110th Congress: Key Facts

- January 4, 2007, through January 2, 2009, during the last two years of the second George W. Bush administration
- House of Representatives controlled by the Democrats, 233 to 202
- Senate controlled by the Democrats, 49 to 49 (2 other)
- 460 bills enacted
- Major accomplishments included passing the Foreign Investment and National Security Act, the Implementing Recommendations of the 9/11 Commission Act, the Protect America Act of 2007, the Honest Leadership and Open Government Act, the Water Resources Development Act, the Energy Independence and Security Act, the Economic Stimulus Act, the Genetic Information Nondiscrimination Act, the Housing and Economic Recovery Act of 2008, and the Emergency Economic Stabilization Act
- Support for President Bush's position in the House: Democrats 12 percent, Republicans 68 percent; in the Senate: Democrats 36 percent, Republicans 74 percent

WHY THE PRESIDENT NEEDS THE HELP OF CONGRESS TO MAKE FOREIGN POLICY

This commentary was written a few months after 9/11, and expressed the hope that during those difficult times President Bush would reach out to Congress for serious consultation on foreign-policy issues. Such consultation would be especially important for this president, who came into office with almost no foreign-policy experience.

Yet President Bush generally didn't go in this direction. He developed his positions after only modest input from and consultation with Congress. That was unfortunate, since foreign-policy decisions would be among the most important he would make during his presidency. Bush instead was heavily influenced, particularly in the earlier years, by the neoconservatives in his administration and their views about projecting American power around the world.

December 15, 2001: "Why the President Needs the Help of Congress to Make Foreign Policy"
Comments on Congress

Once, when Harry Truman was president, someone asked him who made US foreign policy. His reply was simple: "I do."

No president today could make that claim—indeed, not since John F. Kennedy was president has foreign policy been the preserve of even a few policymakers, let alone just one. As our country engages the world with renewed vigor and interest in the wake of the September 11 attacks and the war in Afghanistan, this is worth keeping in mind. Congress, too, is an important player in foreign affairs, a fact that might seem inconvenient at a time of crisis, but that actually benefits the country in many ways. It is worth remembering that in terms of foreign-policy powers specifically enumerated in the Constitution, Congress was granted more than the president.

The president is the chief foreign-policymaker. There is no question about that. But he regularly works within the framework of policies that exist in the laws passed by Congress. When Congress and the president understand their respective roles in foreign policy and make an effort to work together, better policy will emerge.

True, it can be difficult for a president to work with Congress. For one thing, senators and representatives as a whole tend to focus more on domestic issues, just as their constituents do, and many give limited thought to foreign affairs except when a vote is pending or a crisis breaks. It is also true that power on Capitol Hill is diffuse, and shifts with each issue. In the old days, the president could consult with Congress simply by talking to a few important congressional leaders and committee chairmen. Today, dozens of members of Congress and many congressional committees play major roles in foreign policy. Members are younger, more aggressive, better informed, more diverse, and less respectful of traditional authority. So it no longer works for the president to consult with a handful of people and assume the rest of Congress will go along.

And let's remember that the writers of our Constitution never envisioned an entirely unfettered presidency. The president may be commander in chief, but it's up to Congress to declare war, make the nation's laws, and pay for whatever policies the president pursues. The president has the power to negotiate treaties, but they can't take effect unless the Senate ratifies them. Without cooperation, in other words, some of the most basic tools of foreign policy cannot be used successfully.

And the plain truth is, no wise chief executive would want to try. To begin with, American foreign policy always has more force and punch to it when the president and Congress speak with one voice. Congress is our most representative branch of government. It best articulates the concerns of different segments of the population. When the president takes these views into consideration in formulating foreign policy, the policy that results is more likely to have strong public support.

Though it might seem awkward to have to consult with congressional leaders, presidents can profit from the experience. The president is quite isolated in our system of government—as Lyndon Johnson's press secretary, George Reedy, once put it, in the White House no one tells the president to go soak his head. But members of Congress do not serve at the president's favor, and that independence gives their advice added weight. The president may not like or take their advice, but he'll probably forge better policy if he considers it.

You can see this if you look at some prominent examples of poor consultation: the Vietnam War of the 1960s and '70s, and the Contra War in Nicaragua during the 1980s. These examples stand out not simply because the White House barely consulted with Congress, but because the various presidents and their advisors excluded congressional leaders from their discussions; they wanted to conceal information from Congress and the public. In both cases, policy was controlled by a small group of high-level officials, and few others either inside or outside the executive branch knew the full extent of our government's activities. It would be hard to argue that the country was well served by this approach. On the tough foreign-policy questions the president needs help. The decisions should not be made by just one person.

Others, beyond our shores, know this. It used to be that when prominent foreign visitors came to Washington, they'd meet the president, the secretaries of state and defense, and perhaps the heads of the International Monetary Fund and the World Bank. Then they'd go home. Today, almost invariably, they also pay a visit to Capitol Hill. It's an example no president should ignore.

THE MERITS OF CIVIC ENGAGEMENT

Like his father before him, President Bush had a deep commitment to public service, despite having come from the country's aristocracy. He emphasized citizen engagement in his first inaugural address, and it was one of the key initial themes of his presidency. As he stated, "The most important tasks of a democracy are done by everyone. . . . I ask you to be citizens: citizens, not spectators; citizens, not subjects; responsible citizens building communities of service and a nation of character."

When I was in Congress I was impressed by how important local leadership and local involvement were in communities—why one community went ahead and flourished while others struggled. The kind of citizen engagement President Bush was urging not only builds and strengthens communities, but is the best antidote to public cynicism that I know of, as explained in this commentary.

Yet citizen engagement was a theme that moved down in priority for the president as it was overtaken by events fairly soon into his presidency that shifted his attention to other matters.

October 15, 2003: "The Merits of Civic Engagement"
Comments on Congress

During my thirty-four years in the Congress, I must have talked to hundreds of groups in my district about the importance of civic participation. They expected a big speech—and usually got one—but they were often surprised by what I had to say.

Since I was a federal legislator, they assumed I'd be full of advice about getting involved with national politics: writing letters, meeting with members of Congress, following congressional debates on television, or checking members' voting records. These are certainly worthy pursuits that merit encouragement. But I'd tell my constituents that civic life is best lived in the neighborhood, and that they could perform no better service than finding a problem within their community and doing something about it.

We would all like to engage to resolve the big problem. Fixing health care. Saving Social Security. Changing the tax code. Defending our nation against its enemies. Some of us have those opportunities, but most of us don't.

On the other hand, all of us can work for small, incremental changes. You can work to get a school rebuilt or a road repaired. You can make sure that ramps for the handicapped are carved into street corners. You can convince local officials to put up a safety signal at a dangerous intersection. You can help a worthy, disadvantaged student to enter medical school, or make sure that a young woman who lives in your town steps into the world with more opportunity than her mother.

These are not trivial examples. They save lives and communities, and make them safer and better. The wellspring of American democracy lies in countless small actions like these that make ours a better nation. Indeed, I've always liked the attitude of the carpenter who said, "I cannot solve the world's problems, but I can help build this house."

It's not always easy to become involved. We have other things to worry about—our jobs, our bills, the well-being of our families. No doubt, taking care of these private interests is a civic virtue in its own right, and we are good—in this country—at protecting our individual interests. But all of us benefit from giving at least some of our attention to advancing the public interest, or, as the Founding Fathers called it, the "common good."

Most Americans would like to live in better communities, a better state, and a better nation. But they simply don't know where to go, whom to talk to, what to do. The first step is to look around. Most of us are good at finding things that need improvement. What in your community needs fixing? What needs repair? Who are the key players in the town or city whom you could talk to? How can you best communicate a grievance or articulate a solution?

If you get to know your community well—the problems that need addressing, the various residents and the issues that engage their attention, the people who hold formal power and the informal leaders who have the ability to get a message out or pull a crowd together—you can become involved and you will achieve results. Set goals, craft messages, organize, and share the credit when you're successful. You'll be surprised at what you can accomplish.

When we become involved in our communities, our cynicism dissipates and morale improves. Indeed, civic engagement is the greatest antidote to cynicism I know. Through it, we do more than improve our lives and surroundings—we reach a better understanding of our ability to influence change, and we no longer feel distant from centers of power and decision making. Just as important, we gain an appreciation for the hard work of democracy—how to understand different points of view and forge a consensus behind a course of action toward a solution in a complex, busy, and diverse society.

After all, the success of any democracy is determined by the participation of its citizens. When we do participate, we deepen our understanding of and appreciation for our communities and our country, and make the ongoing experiment of American democracy stronger.

WHY CONGRESS NEEDS TO ASSERT ITSELF

Fact-based deliberation based on a fair, careful analysis of the best available evidence was a problem during the Bush years. Too often we would find out later that solid evidence, dissenting opinions, and the views of experts were being disregarded, and key administration claims were being presented as factual and clearly established when they were not.

This seemed to be more of a problem during the Bush administration than in other presidencies. The Bush administration is not being viewed positively by historians digging into the processes through which key policy decisions were made. And for its part, Congress was remarkably passive during this time, accepting the poor information it was getting from the executive branch. I was beginning to think about the relatively small number of institutionalists there were in the House—people who recognize their constitutional duties to the institution, not just to their party, and who have a strong sense of obligation to see that Congress does its work.

April 14, 2004: "Why Congress Needs to Assert Itself"
Comments on Congress

The last few weeks have seen an irate response to the news that a high federal official threatened to fire the chief Medicare actuary if he gave Congress his true estimate of how much the administration's new prescription drug benefit would actually cost. Newspaper editorialists, academics, and commentators have all condemned the disregard with which both Congress and the policymaking process were treated in the incident.

One voice has been conspicuous in its absence, however: that of Congress itself. Though there have been a few individual members who have expressed their concern, I have been disappointed that the Congress, as an institution, has failed to assert forcefully its need for trustworthy information from the executive branch. This is worrisome.

All partisan loyalties aside, trust is vital to the policymaking process. As Congress set out to reform Medicare, and in particular the drug benefit, it was rightly concerned about the cost of the various alternatives before it. Assured by the administration that its plan would not cost more than $400 billion over the next decade, many members of the House, previously undecided, decided to support it. So the revelation that the chief actuary had actually estimated the figure to be closer to $534 billion—and that the executive branch had withheld this figure from Congress—was not only embarrassing; it called into question the legitimacy of the whole policymaking process. If one branch of government feels it has to deceive the other, it is hard to see how the country can be led well by its public servants. For this reason alone, members of Congress of both parties should have hit the roof.

Yet there is another, even more fundamental, issue at stake. Congress and the executive branch are colleagues—equals—in determining the course of the country. But in recent years, Congress has grown timid, as its lack of insistence on complete data demonstrates. There is no question these days that the initiative rests largely with the White House and executive agencies. As Washington Post editor Robert Kaiser put it recently, "In fundamental ways that have gone largely unrecognized, Congress has become less vigilant, less proud and protective of its own prerogatives, and less important to the conduct of American government than at any time in decades." Small wonder that, as with Medicare reform, administration officials feel a certain leeway to presume on Capitol Hill's good graces.

There are any number of ways in which the Congress of today exercises just a shadow of the clout it wielded a generation ago, but one of the most important is its reticence about initiating policy. The United States at the moment faces a crucial series of tests, from rebuilding Iraq to fighting terrorism to the ballooning budget and trade deficits, yet Congress often doesn't seem to have much to say on these matters. Even on civil liberties and how we handle the difficult question of fair process for terrorists on American soil, it has left the ball largely in the administration's court. Admittedly, there's an argument to be made that terrorists don't deserve the same legal protections as American citizens, and the White House has made it. But there is also an argument to be made that, faced with this new threat, we need to create a framework for handling people who would do this country harm while preserving the hallmarks of our judicial system and its emphasis on fairness. This is an avenue that should be explored fully in Congress, yet it has made little effort to do so.

Why has Congress let its responsibilities slide? Members of Congress themselves give lots of reasons. They range from the legitimate need to tend to their constituents—which now means spending so much time either in the district or en route that only two or three days each week can be devoted to national affairs—to the reality that members know one another less well than they used to, especially if they belong to different parties, and are therefore less inclined to work together. As Robert Kaiser writes, "Few members put loyalty to the House or Senate ahead of their political loyalty to a Democratic or Republican team."

But that's a political calculation, not necessarily a view of the national interest. Good policy, policy that will stand the test of time, does not evolve when all involved march to the same drummer. Good policy is the result of hard work, searching analysis, solid information, and respectful argument about what it means. It is the result of people with different points of view, values, and experiences sitting down together to reason with one another and search for common ground. This is precisely what Congress was designed to foster, and it is what we lose when Congress decides that supporting the party leader is more important than upholding its rights and duties as the institution that most fully represents the American people.

OVERSIGHT AT LAST

Although congressional oversight—keeping a watchful eye on what executive branch departments and agencies are doing—is one of the most important responsibilities of Congress, the quality of that oversight has varied considerably over the years. It's intended to provide fresh eyes, independent eyes to look at the operations and policies of government, and, properly done, it can provide a significant benefit for an administration. Yet Congress did a particularly poor job of oversight during the Bush years.

Republican committee chairs during the Bush years tended to avoid probing into administration actions. One of the few exceptions was when Republican senator John Warner of Virginia held hearings on administration policy on the mistreatment of Iraqi prisoners in Abu Ghraib. The senator's action was such a rare and commendable occurrence that I wrote a commentary on it.

A few years later, the November 2008 elections would mean that the incoming Obama administration would face a Congress that would be under the control of the Democrats. I made a similar point then—that oversight is politically difficult to conduct when you are looking at a president who is of your same party, but it is still crucially important for the nation.

June 16, 2004: "Oversight at Last"
Comments on Congress

As difficult as it has been in recent weeks to watch the testimony coming out of the Senate Armed Services Committee's hearings into the treatment of Iraqi prisoners at Abu Ghraib, one thing about these sessions should give us all heart: the fact that they're taking place at all. Chairman John Warner of Virginia, despite the outspoken distaste of his counterparts on the House side and the less vocal hesitation of some of his own colleagues, has signaled his determination to pursue his inquiry. "When this situation broke, I felt it was the responsibility of the Congress, a coequal branch of government, to start hearings," he commented recently.

It seems counterintuitive in the midst of a war to argue that the nation benefits when Congress is looking over the executive branch's shoulder, especially when it comes to the military. After all, we've been trained by a generation of action movies to believe that the meddling, publicity-seeking congressman only gets in the hero's way. In real life, however, the nation needs both: it needs people willing to serve in dangerous circumstances, but it also needs people willing to ask hard and sometimes discomforting questions about whether our interests are really being reflected.

There is a world of meaning to be read into Senator Warner's passing reference to Congress as "a coequal branch of government." It was a small but pointed reminder that the White House, Pentagon, and executive agencies are not the only shapers of official US policies and activities. Congress—the people's branch of government—has not just the right, but the duty, to be at the table as well. It especially has both the right and the duty to be the body asking those hard questions.

Good congressional oversight is fundamental to our democracy. At its best, it helps Congress—and, through it, the American people—evaluate how well our government and its representatives, whether they're soldiers or bureaucrats, are performing. It can ferret out malfeasance, compel executive-branch policymakers to explain their policies and substantiate the reasoning that underlies them, and ensure that our federal government is truly acting in the best interests of the nation. Done well, oversight protects the country from bureaucratic arrogance, prevents misconduct, and gives voters the information they need to judge the activities of an administration.

Unfortunately, it has been quite a while since Congress really lived up to its responsibilities in this regard. During the 1990s, it fell into the habit of pursuing personal investigations of high-profile public figures at the expense of the more constructive—but less glamorous—work of ongoing policy oversight. More recently, Congress has done so little real oversight—as opposed to hearings designed to score political points—that it's fair to say its reflexes have gone rusty.

So while it is heartening to see the Senate Armed Services Committee stepping into the breach, I'd like to suggest that all it has done is make a good start. Its challenge will be to follow through on its hearings, demand accountability and transparency from the officials who come before it, and determine whether there are aspects of military policy that need fixing. And while all this is going on, let's hope that the rest of Congress is paying attention.

For the current hearings are a hopeful sign only if the habit catches on. Congress needs to develop a continuous, systematic oversight process, one that impels congressional committees to look into the vast range of federal activities that never get into the newspaper headlines. In this regard, it might pay attention to some of the people who invent those headlines—newspaper and television news editors. With the war in Iraq and the upcoming presidential elections demanding space and coverage, some news executives are starting to worry about what is not getting covered. "The war is an overriding issue, but that comes with consequences," Tom Rosenstiel, who directs the Project for Excellence in Journalism, was quoted recently as saying. "I'm sure we'll find out in two years that things went unnoticed—things that will come back to haunt us."

There is a lesson to be learned from Abu Ghraib, and it is this: even in a democracy, appalling things can happen in the shadows. For the press, it is a professional shortcoming when it fails to bring them to our attention. For Congress, it is a dereliction of its constitutional duties. It is Congress's responsibility to shine light on the workings of government, and to ensure that its actions really do reflect the generous and honorable nature of our country. Far from sniping at the senators who are investigating our country's activities in Iraq, we should be praising them—and demanding more from them and their colleagues.

WE URGENTLY NEED REDISTRICTING REFORM

One of the major trends in recent years contributing to the polarization in Congress has been the redistricting by state legislatures that produces politically safe House seats. Skillful redistricting, or "gerrymandering," not only distorts election results—as it did, for example, in 2014 when Democratic candidates in North Carolina got 44 percent of all the House votes statewide but won only 23 percent of the House seats—but also means giving more power to the extremes in Congress and reducing the moderate center, as explained in this newsletter.

> **March 25, 2005: "We Urgently Need Redistricting Reform"**
> **Comments on Congress**
> We can thank the computer for adding much to the convenience of modern life. One of its less noticed contributions, though, should draw our apprehension, not our thanks: the ability of legislative incumbents to escape competitive elections. In this regard, at least, computers are helping to undermine our democracy.
>
> I'm talking, of course, about redistricting. These days, your basic laptop can so finely parse a neighborhood, a street, even a particular house, that the people responsible for drawing new legislative districts can achieve pretty much any political complexion they wish for the districts they produce. Politicians, in other words, now get to choose their voters, rather than the other way around.
>
> Usually, this yields one of two results: a set of districts that gives the party in power a lock on as many seats as possible, or a legislative map that protects incumbents of both parties. The result in either case is the same. Competitive elections for the US House of Representatives and many state legislatures are becoming a relic of the past, and our representative democracy is seriously undermined as a result.
>
> Perhaps the most striking example of this is California, where in 2001 Democrats and Republicans agreed that they would draw

new district maps to protect the registration advantage of whichever party held the seat at the time. They did a thorough job. In the
2002 elections, only three legislative seats changed party hands.
In 2004, not a single one—not one of the fifty-three congressional
seats or one hundred legislative districts—fell to the opposite party.
As one political scientist in the state puts it, it was "surely the
most complete and effective bipartisan gerrymander in American
history."

You might wonder what's wrong with this. After all, every regis-
tered voter in a district still gets to cast a vote, and if most of them
happen to prefer the incumbent, so be it.

Let's think about this from two perspectives. As a voter, would
you rather live in a district in which you knew that no matter how
hard you tried, your preferred candidate could never win, or in a
district in which your party had a realistic—though not certain—
chance of prevailing every other November? For that matter, even
if you take some comfort from living in a district where you're part
of a clear majority, it's hard to get very excited at election time,
knowing that the conclusion is foregone. I think it's hardly an accident that as elections have grown less competitive, the interest and
participation of ordinary citizens have waned.

Even more troubling, though, is the impact of current redistricting practices on the makeup of the US House and of state
legislatures. When a district is drawn to favor a particular party, it
means that politicians running in it don't need to appeal to a cross
section of the electorate; instead, their constituency lies within
their party. Not surprisingly, this means that they focus on appealing to the hard-core base of the party, and tend to be more extreme
than the great mass of voters. Looking at the intense partisanship
and ideological rigidity of our legislative leaders these days, ordinary Americans often wonder what happened to the political center.
My response is that we redistricted it out of existence.

There is a simple solution to this, though it's not a particularly
easy one: remove responsibility for redistricting from the hands of
politicians. Drawing congressional and legislative lines is a state
function, and in most states it still falls to state legislators and the
governor to agree on a map. Several states, though, hand the job
to a bipartisan commission, sometimes made up of retired judges
appointed by the legislative leaders of both parties. Following Iowa's

lead, Idaho, Arizona, and Alaska all switched to this method during the 1990s.

This is a heartening development. Not long ago, researchers at Claremont McKenna College in California studied election results in states where legislators do not draw the political lines. They found unambiguously that districts in these states were more politically competitive. "Looking back at the '90s," the senior researcher told the Los Angeles Times, "there are many more districts that change hands over the decade than where the legislature draws the line."

I fervently hope that this cause gains steam quickly. The US House of Representatives has been known since the founding of our nation as "the people's house," but if its members come to represent only the committed activists of both political parties, it is hard to see how they can live up to the Founders' expectations. Elections need to reflect public opinion as it evolves and changes over time. Political competition forces candidates to understand the needs and desires of voters, requires them to justify and explain their positions, offers voters a true opportunity to weigh the qualities they want in a representative, and ensures that voters can make a choice in the marketplace of politics. A competitive election is the central avenue for our self-expression as citizens, and the legitimacy and vitality of Congress depend on it. We ought not let the convenience of incumbent lawmakers stand in its way.

OUR LEADERS MUST FIND A BALANCE ON IRAQ

There were a variety of factors behind Bush's decision to go to war against Iraq, and the president no doubt wanted to spread democracy and freedom to the region. Yet overall I think it was one of the worst decisions ever made in American foreign policy. The evidence behind the decision was flawed, it did not achieve its goals of a democratic and stable country and region, it damaged the reputation of the United States in the world, and it cost America some $2 trillion and thousands of lives.

The bipartisan Iraq Study Group, which I co-chaired in 2006 with former secretary of state Jim Baker, made one key policy suggestion: resolve the conflict within Iraq through negotiations among the warring factions, backed by an aggressive US diplomatic offensive in the region. The president rejected this suggestion as surrender and authorized a military surge. But even after the initial gains of the surge, the deep sectarian divide remained and later erupted disastrously.

By the time of this commentary, Democrats had regained control of both the House and the Senate in the November 2006 congressional elections, and Congress was starting to assert itself more on the war—much to the irritation of the Bush administration.

April 17, 2007: "Our Leaders Must Find a Balance on Iraq" Comments on Congress

As Congress asserts itself on the war in Iraq, the White House has responded with irritation. The stalemate between these two branches of government is good neither for the Congress nor for the White House, and it is certainly no good for the country.

The Bush administration's verdict on the recently passed House and Senate Iraq supplemental spending bills was swift and stern. One White House spokesman said, "You've got to ask yourself, why go through this long, drawn-out exercise of going and wheeling and cajoling and trying to buy votes within your own party when, in fact, you know it's not going to go anywhere?" Another said, "I think the founders of our nation had great foresight in realizing that it would be better to have one commander in chief managing a war, rather than 535 generals on Capitol Hill trying to do the same."

Yet the founders of our nation never envisioned an unfettered president making unilateral decisions about American lives and military power. They did indeed make the president the commander in chief, but they gave to Congress the responsibility for declaring war, for making rules governing our land and naval forces, and for overseeing policy, and—of course—the ability to fund war or to cease funding it. In other words, they set up a constitutional balance of powers that requires cooperation between both branches of government.

It is hard to find any recognition of this constitutionally mandated cooperation in the White House's recent comments. The president and the leaders of Congress seem unwilling to seek the genuine consultation and pragmatic accommodation necessary to avoid stalemate and produce a more sustainable policy. Instead, each branch views the other as an obstacle to be overcome.

This is a shame. If treated with the respect required by the Constitution, Congress could play a constructive role in forging a responsible way forward in Iraq. Those 535 members of Congress, Democrats and Republicans alike, are the politicians in Washington who have to reckon in an immediate way with the toll this war is taking on our nation. They listen to their constituents' anger and heartfelt doubts; they go to the funerals of men and women killed in Iraq and Afghanistan; they field calls from anguished parents with sons and daughters in harm's way; they visit the veterans' facilities where wounded troops confront the fact that their lives will never be the same.

Congress shouldn't call all the shots just because it has its ear to the ground. The president is, and should be, the chief actor in the conduct of American foreign policy. But Congress can and should serve as an essential resource and participant in policymaking.

Congress represents beliefs found in every American community. And the American people have the war in Iraq figured out— they want Iraqis to take responsibility for their future; they want US forces to leave Iraq, but they want them to leave responsibly; they want to protect US interests in the Middle East. In many ways, ordinary Americans have been ahead of their political leadership in coming to grips with the situation in Iraq.

The war is an American dilemma, not a partisan one or solely a presidential one. We are not going to succeed in charting a responsible transition out of Iraq if the president and Congress are constantly at odds. The president must respect the constitutional role of Congress and its understanding of public opinion. Congress needs to find a balance between responsible criticism and responsible cooperation, supporting the president when it can and opposing him when it feels it must.

The differences between the president and the Congress are real. But consultation, not confrontation, is the best way to work them out. In the absence of consultation, relations between the president and the Congress become poisonous. Charges and countercharges dominate the political discourse. Both sides divert their energies toward political battles, rather than policymaking. Americans lose confidence in their government. Meanwhile, Americans continue to serve and die in Iraq.

The plain fact is that for nearly two years President Bush will have to deal with a Democratic-controlled Congress, while Congress will have to deal with President Bush. Our political leaders have failed the American people on Iraq. If they cannot build bridges between their positions and respect one another's constitutional role, neither side will succeed, our policy will suffer, and another sorrowful chapter will be added to the history of the Iraq War.

WHAT POLITICS SHOULD BE ABOUT

Often when we hear the word "politics," we might think of political campaigns or political contributions or political calculations, and it often has negative connotations: "That's just politics." But in its most basic sense, politics is the way of governing a society, and it lies at the heart of what Congress does.

What can we say about politics? What is politics all about? What are the core components of the basic work of Congress—politics? This commentary discusses some of the main components of politics, starting with a helpful suggestion from noted historian Arthur Schlesinger Jr.

May 14, 2007: "What Politics Should Be About"
Comments on Congress

Over the years, I've met with a lot of high school and college students, and there's one question they come up with time after time: what, they want to know, is politics really about?

Having spent a good part of my life in the trenches, I long ago arrived at an answer that I thought reflected reality and was sufficiently cynical to make me believable. Politics, I would tell them, is about power: getting it, keeping it, and using it to advance one's agenda.

At least, that's what I said until I ran across a comment by the eminent historian Arthur Schlesinger Jr., who died recently. He had a different, and far more useful, answer. Politics is about "the search for remedy," he said.

We live at a time when such a belief seems outdated and hopelessly earnest. Americans have watched their politicians over the years with increasing skepticism, and have come to the belief that politics is about anything but an honest effort to resolve the issues that confront us. It's about personal egos. It's about enriching oneself. It's about winning elections or wielding power for its own sake.

What's disheartening is that politicians themselves have contributed to this abandonment of sincerity. Often they—and especially their consultants—talk about politics as a highly technical and fascinating game whose largest purpose is to experience the thrill of victory. In one of this year's gubernatorial primaries, there's a leading candidate whose advertising ends in the tagline, "The only Republican who can win in November." Don't get me wrong; electability is hardly irrelevant to a primary voter. But should it be the chief thing we look for in a political leader?

What Schlesinger invited us to do was to search beneath the definitions we've given politics over the years, and to find an underlying purpose. All those "abouts" you hear now—it's about ego, it's about money, it's about power—are partly true, or at least true in certain cases. But they're inadequate when it comes to describing what politics in a democracy is truly about: it's how we wrestle with and try to resolve the challenges that confront us.

To see why this is so important, think for a moment about some of the tremendously difficult issues we face. There is a constant barrage in Washington right now of finger pointing and ex post facto analysis of what went wrong in Iraq. These have their place, if only because we should learn from our mistakes, but seen through the lens of Schlesinger's formulation they are political sideshows. The real challenge is to devise a remedy to the situation at hand that can be embraced and implemented by a divided government. That is what true politicians are spending their time on.

So, too, with our health care system. There hasn't been an all-out effort to tackle the many issues that assail it since the failure of the Clinton plan more than a decade ago. The result is that the system has grown more expensive, more wasteful, and less helpful to growing numbers of Americans. It is a situation that calls for politics at its best, an honest and concerted effort to find a remedy that not only is fair and lasting, but also can win the support of a diverse nation.

You'll notice that in both these examples I've added something to Schlesinger's phrase: that solutions have to be pragmatic and broadly acceptable. If politics at heart is a means to an end—the end being an actual fix to a problem—then it is not just about the search for an answer, but about making that answer work.

This means that the best politicians don't just dream up policy solutions regardless of context. They also think about how those solutions would work in the real world; they think about the forces that can help them and those that can block them; and perhaps above all, they think about how to build the broadest consensus possible behind their solutions, so that those solutions have a realistic chance of taking root and flourishing.

Our next national election is a year and a half away. But as politicians start competing for your attention, I'd ask you to keep Schlesinger in mind. Are the people in front of you interested in constructive problem solving? Can they engage wholeheartedly in "the search for remedy"? If so, they deserve our praise. If not, perhaps they—and we—would be better off if they spent some time out of office, contemplating what politics should really be about.

THE TEN COMMANDMENTS OF CITIZENSHIP

During the fall 2008 presidential campaign there was a lot of talk about change in our nation's politics. But as this commentary notes, change begins with us as citizens. This is a commentary that newspapers particularly liked, and it was also widely used in classrooms.

September 24, 2008: "The Ten Commandments of Citizenship"
Comments on Congress

This presidential election, if you believe the polls and the rhetoric, is about change in Washington. Both candidates promise it, while voters clamor for it. It is the cause of the moment.

Yet I have news for you: change in Washington won't happen, and certainly can't be sustained, without change in the country at large. For the point is not to overthrow the system, but to make it function properly. Government does not fix itself. Only a citizenry that is engaged in our democracy to an extent far greater than in recent decades can help to heal our system. To get change in Washington, in other words, it has to begin with you.

Since being a responsible citizen takes commitment, here are some precepts to follow if you want to be effective—what I call the "Ten Commandments of Citizenship":

1. Vote. This is the most basic step democracy asks of us. Don't buy the argument that it doesn't matter. Every election offers real choices about the direction we want our towns, states, and country to take. By voting, you not only select the officials who will run the government; you suggest the direction government policy should take and you reaffirm your support for a representative democracy.

2. Be informed. To be a knowledgeable voter, you need to know what candidates actually stand for, not just what their ads or their opponents' ads say. Read about the issues that confront your community and our nation as a whole. Our government simply does not work well if its citizens are ill informed.

3. Communicate with your representatives. Representative democracy is a dialogue between elected officials and citizens—that dialogue lies at the heart of our system. Legislators and executives can't do their jobs well if they don't understand their constituents' concerns, and we can't understand them if we don't know their views and why they hold them.

4. Participate in groups that share your views and can advance your interests. This one's simple: in a democracy, people tend to be more effective when they work together rather than acting as individuals. You can be sure that almost every issue you care about has one or more organizations devoted to it. By joining and working with the ones you think best reflect your views, you amplify your beliefs and strengthen the dialogue of democracy.

5. Get involved locally to improve your community. You know more about your community's strengths and weaknesses than anyone living outside it. Identify its problems and work to correct them.

6. Educate your family, and make sure that local schools are educating students, about their responsibilities as citizens. As a society, we're not as good as we should be at encouraging young people to get involved in political life. Too many young people—and even many adults—do not understand how our

government and political system work and why it is important for them to be contributing citizens.

7. Understand that we must work to build consensus in a huge,
diverse country. In pretty much every way you can think of,
ours is an astoundingly mixed nation of people, with wildly
divergent views on most issues and a constantly growing
population. This means we have to work through our differences not by hammering on the other side, but by bringing
people together through the arts of dialogue, accommodation,
compromise, and consensus building.

8. Understand that our representative democracy works slowly.
There's a reason for this: it is so that all sides can be heard,
and so that we avoid the costly mistakes produced by haste.
Our Founders understood this 220 years ago, and it's even
more vital now, when issues are vastly more complex and the
entire world is closely connected.

9. Understand that our system is not perfect, but has served the
nation well. Democracy is a process designed to give people a
voice in how they are governed. It's not perfect—far too many
people feel voiceless, and polls in recent years suggest that
unsettling numbers believe the system is broken. And our
system offers no guarantee that you'll get what you want. Yet
it is also true that it provides every individual an opportunity
to be heard and to work to achieve his or her objectives, and it
has served our nation well for over two centuries.

10. Understand that our system is not self-perpetuating; it
demands our involvement to survive. Just because it has
worked in the past does not mean we will have a free and
successful country in the future. Lincoln's challenge is still
urgent: whether this nation so conceived can long endure. Being a good citizen isn't something one does just for the heck of
it; it's critical to the success of our nation.

The Bush years were a time of some significant national successes, but
also some significant failures. When Bush came into office our economy
was strong, the budget was in surplus, and the nation was at peace. In January 2009 when he left office, American soldiers were fighting in Iraq and
in Afghanistan, bin Laden was still on the loose, the federal budget had

turned from large surpluses to large deficits, and the American economy was in the midst of the Great Recession. His administration will forever be associated with intelligence failures and misleading the public on weapons of mass destruction, and with the chaos that followed the intervention in Iraq. He came into office with a Republican-controlled House and Senate, but by the time he left the voters had shifted the presidency, the House, and the Senate all back to the Democrats.

Congress during this time also deserves blame for not doing its oversight job and being too subservient to the president. And the American people fell short too. How many of us contacted policymakers when they were making poor decisions? All of us need to step up our efforts to make the system work better.

Perhaps more than any other presidency in modern times, the Bush years demonstrate the important role that Congress needs to play in our system of government. The Founding Fathers had it right. Power needs to be dispersed, with a lot of checks and balances. Our system simply doesn't work well when Congress is timid and allows the president—any president—to accumulate too much unchecked power. We certainly need a strong presidency. But better policy emerges and our nation is better off if we also have a strong and independent Congress.

NINE

THE OBAMA YEARS
(2009–14)
Continuing Struggles

WHEN BARACK OBAMA FIRST RAN FOR PRESIDENT IN 2008, I SUP-
ported him in the Democratic primary in Indiana—I was one of the few
current or former public officials in the state to do so—and it was his strong
showing that day that made the media predict he would win the nomination over Hillary Clinton. So he was appreciative of my support. I liked
his pragmatic, nonideological approach to the issues, and thought there
would be a change—a new direction—with his administration. He had an
idealism about him that inspired people, and I thought he would be able
to energize young people, minorities, and others who had been outside
the process to become more civically involved, something our country has
needed for years.

During his first campaign I was on a panel to advise him on foreign-
policy issues. Obama had been in the Senate for just a few years, and in the
Illinois state legislature before that, so his foreign-policy credentials were
thin. But in the meetings I found him to be a quick learner. He asked a lot
of good questions and seemed to enjoy digging into the range of issues.

After the disappointments of the Bush years, I thought Obama had
several strengths that were important for an incoming president. He was
cautious, deliberative, and rational in his policy analysis, perhaps a reflection of his many years as a law school professor at the University of Chi-
cago. He seemed to be a conciliator with a willingness to compromise, and
pragmatic rather than ideological. All of this, combined with the benefit of
taking office with both the Senate and the House controlled by his party,
led me to think that these would be productive years.

But his presidency floundered a bit. Certainly he inherited an economy that was in much worse shape than expected; that took a lot of his attention and was a formidable challenge to turn around. In addition, the Republicans from the beginning seemed unwilling to give him many victories that he could use in his bid for reelection, so he faced tougher-than-normal opposition and an unprecedented number of threatened filibusters. Many members viewed him as aloof and not reaching out as much as he should, staying above the fray. He certainly didn't have the enthusiasm for the backslapping and networking of the political process that Johnson or Clinton had. While I thought that his speeches on the major issues were carefully thought out—at times superb—he was not nearly as effective on follow-through with Congress.

Overall, the Democratic-led Congress—with Nancy Pelosi as House Speaker—was active in passing legislation during the 111th Congress, one of the more productive sessions in recent years. Yet most of the major bills were passed by shoring up the support of Democratic members rather than by reaching out to the Republicans to develop broad consensus, which energized the Republicans. And the expensive and poorly targeted economic recovery measures plus the less-than-robust recovery may have also been factors in the big Democratic losses in the November 2010 elections, when Republicans picked up more than sixty seats and regained control of the House.

As Speaker in the 112th and 113th Congresses, John Boehner faced some tough challenges. When he first came to Congress in 1990 he was part of the House Republican "Gang of Seven" led by Newt Gingrich, which attacked the Democratic leadership over the House banking scandal and pushed for a much more limited role for government. A few years later he and other Republican leaders tried to oust Gingrich as Speaker after a series of missteps. I found Boehner to be an able, pragmatic member of Congress, someone you could deal with. But he has had the dubious distinction of being Speaker during a time when Congress was considered to be at its most dysfunctional. At one point during the 113th Congress fewer than one in ten Americans were saying that Congress was doing an excellent or even a good job. Speaker Boehner generally retained the Hastert Rule of not bringing a measure to the floor unless it was supported by a majority of House Republicans. In other words, he did not allow the House to work its will by a majority vote of the entire membership of the House. But Boehner had a difficult time passing legislation under the Hastert Rule because of the ideological split within his caucus.

Both John Boehner and Nancy Pelosi as Speakers during these years had to deal with some deep-seated, polarizing forces that made it a major challenge to get even routine legislation through Congress. As someone who respects the institution of the Congress, it was frustrating for me to see Congress struggle as much as it did during these years. I have never been pleased to see Congress function poorly—no matter whether the Democrats or the Republicans had control—and I always wanted it to be perceived simply as trying to meet the concerns of the American people as it was set up to do.

111th Congress: Key Facts

- January 2, 2009, through December 22, 2010, during the first two years of the first Obama administration
- House of Representatives controlled by the Democrats, 255 to 179 (1 other)
- Senate controlled by the Democrats, 57 to 41 (2 other)
- 383 bills enacted
- Major accomplishments included passing the State Children's Health Insurance Program, the American Recovery and Reinvestment Act, the Omnibus Public Land Management Act, the Edward M. Kennedy Service to America Act, the Helping Families Save Their Homes Act, the Weapons Systems Acquisition Reform Act, the Worker, Homeownership, and Business Assistance Act, the Statutory Pay-as-You-Go Act, the Hiring Incentives to Restore Employment Act, the Patient Protection and Affordable Care Act, the Comprehensive Iran Sanctions, Accountability, and Divestment Act, the Dodd-Frank Wall Street Reform and Consumer Protection Act, the Small Business Jobs and Credit Act, and the Tax Relief, Unemployment Insurance Reauthorization, and Job Creation Act

- Support for President Obama's position in the House: Democrats 90 percent, Republicans 29 percent; in the Senate: Democrats 97 percent, Republicans 47 percent

112th Congress: Key Facts
- January 3, 2011, through January 3, 2013, during the last two years of the first Obama administration
- House of Representatives controlled by the Republicans, 242 to 193
- Senate controlled by the Democrats, 51 to 47 (2 other)
- 284 bills enacted
- Major accomplishments included passing the Budget Control Act of 2011, the Leahy-Smith America Invents Act, the US-Korea, US-Colombia, and US-Panama Free Trade Agreements, the Middle Class Tax Relief and Job Creation Act, the Jumpstart Our Business Startups Act, the Whistleblower Protection Enhancement Act, and the American Taxpayer Relief Act
- Support for President Obama's position in the House: Republicans 20 percent, Democrats 79 percent; in the Senate: Democrats 93 percent, Republicans 50 percent

113th Congress: Key Facts
- January 3, 2013, through January 3, 2015, during the first two years of the second Obama administration
- House of Representatives controlled by the Republicans, 232 to 200 (3 other)
- Senate controlled by the Democrats, 53 to 45 (2 other)
- 297 bills enacted
- Major accomplishments included passing the Pandemic and All-Hazards Preparedness Reauthorization Act, the Reverse Mortgage Stabilization Act, the Agricultural Act of 2014, the Support for the Sovereignty, Integrity, Democracy, and Economic Stability of Ukraine Act, and the Workforce Innovation and Opportunity Act
- Support for President Obama's position in the House: Republicans 12 percent, Democrats 82 percent; in the Senate: Democrats 96 percent, Republicans 48 percent

IS CONGRESS UP TO THE TASK BEFORE IT?

President Obama started out his administration with a different approach to Congress than some of his predecessors. Whereas George W. Bush, for example, would take the lead in crafting specific legislative proposals, Obama deferred more to Congress. He still set the broad agenda, but left it up to congressional committees—which were under Democratic control at this time—to draft the specific legislative language for his proposals. And that raised the question of whether Congress was up to the task.

Although there is risk to such an approach, it is my strong preference to see Congress proactively addressing the needs of the country, and it's what the Founding Fathers expected of Congress. President Obama's signature achievement, which passed the following year—the Affordable Care Act, or "Obamacare"—would come out of this process of letting Congress take the lead in crafting the specifics of legislation.

March 20, 2009: "Is Congress Up to the Task before It?" Comments on Congress

I arrived in Congress in 1965, just as President Lyndon Johnson's transformation of the US government was getting underway. It was an extraordinary time, as LBJ sent up to Capitol Hill his proposals for Medicare, Medicaid, aid to elementary and secondary education, the Voting Rights Act, and a host of other bills that reshaped Washington and its place in the nation's life. The United States was a different country by the time Congress finished.

We are at a juncture that may be as far-reaching and no less dramatic. With the economic crisis as a backdrop, President Obama has sent to Capitol Hill a budget that places the government more thoroughly in American life than at any time in the past three decades, and eschews the antitax, antiregulatory approach to public policy that has generally predominated in recent decades. The White House has put Congress on notice that it intends to reform the health care system, make fundamental improvements to public education, and remake national energy policy. These changes are necessary, it contends, to keep the US economy strong and prosperous.

There is an important difference in the approaches taken by the two presidents, Johnson and Obama. Enjoying the momentum built by his landslide victory in the 1964 elections, Johnson gave Congress specific proposals, like the Medicaid bill and the Elementary and Secondary Education Act. He told Congress precisely what he wanted and then helped shape its response.

President Obama, on the other hand, has given Congress the goals he wants to pursue and the concepts he intends to support, and has left it up to lawmakers to craft the fine print. As the New York Times put it recently, he is "taking a gamble in outsourcing the drafting of his agenda's details" to Congress.

This is not just a leap of faith on the president's part, however. Given the recent past, it also presents Congress with an exacting test of its ability to function effectively and produce policies that serve the American people well.

Congress has a history of not dealing well with the big issues. Now it's presented with a budget and a presidential agenda that offer no letup in big issues. Its challenge is twofold: to act at a time of crisis and in an economy that's being reshaped by the day; and, despite the pressure to act quickly, to act in a manner that allows for the deliberation and consensus building that uphold the democratic process.

How it will respond remains an open question. No sooner had the president's plans landed on Capitol Hill than legislators of both parties and powerful interest groups declared this or that provision badly flawed, seeming to reject the president's proposals without open-minded consideration and debate. Meanwhile, there is a strong likelihood that the leadership, as it has done far too often in recent years, will choose to deal with the issues before it by bundling them into omnibus legislation that permits very little deliberation and requires an up-or-down vote on a bill of gigantic size and complexity. This may be efficient, but it is hardly democratic.

Congress has been given an extraordinary opportunity to live up to its constitutional responsibilities and to function effectively in the national interest. While its public standing has been improving of late, it remains damaged by the perception that its members care more about catering to donors, playing partisan games, and putting in a three- or four-day workweek than they do about tackling the nation's toughest challenges in a reasoned, comprehensive, and fair way.

Now, at a time when Americans are closely tuned in to events in Washington, Congress is being asked by the president to address a far-reaching agenda. It can do so by reviving the tradition of open debate that enlightens the American people and allows its members to weigh the questions before them as they develop consensus, or it can give in to its recent habits of procedural expediency and partisan tactics. The test for Congress is clear. Let's hope it chooses wisely.

POLARIZATION WILL NOT DISAPPEAR QUICKLY

President Obama in the early years made efforts to reach out to Republicans, with limited success. There was still polarization and unwillingness to compromise, and as bad as things were in 2010 in the 111th Congress, they would only get worse in the 112th and 113th.

Every president comes into office saying that we need to work together and move past polarization. But what really counts is follow-through. Presidents need to stay at it, every day. They are the chief actors in the American system of government and they need to reach out and lead in order to move the needle. And, for its part, Congress needs to be more receptive. When President Obama hosted a reception at the White House for the large new class of members after the Democrats took a beating in the November 2010 election, two-thirds of the new Republican members stayed away. Too often the approach of the minority party is what Senate Minority Leader Mitch McConnell expressed in 2010 when he said that his main task was to defeat the president in the next election—an astounding statement given the many challenges facing the country.

With all the dissatisfaction with Congress in recent years, one factor often overlooked that helps Congress function better is the presence of seasoned legislators—institutionalists—who are not in the top leadership positions but have served in Congress for many years and feel a responsibility to make the system work. People like Bill Natcher, who kept meticulous notebooks about every program under his subcommittee's jurisdiction and grilled department secretaries about performance; George Mahon, who took a careful look at every request for federal spending; Wilbur Mills and his Republican counterpart John Byrnes, whose ability to bring to the floor major bills that would pass with bipartisan support was unequaled; Richard Bolling, a master of House procedure; Bill McCulloch, who was able to bring his Republican colleagues along with him on civil rights legislation; Wright Patman, who was constantly looking over the shoulder of the Federal Reserve; Lindy Boggs, who improved the civility of every meeting she attended; Barber Conable, a highly respected member of Congress with considerable expertise in tax policy; and many others. Some became well known, but most did not. They did not seek the limelight, but instead were insiders who put in long, tedious hours on the minutiae of developing legislation, exploring policy options, and constantly networking with their colleagues so they could find consensus and move legislation forward. They had a fundamental belief that the institution had to work, and they made it happen. Often we look for procedural fixes or rules changes to improve the operations of Congress. But just as important, if not more so, is the mindset of members and their decision simply to make Congress work.

February 16, 2010: "Polarization Will Not Disappear Quickly"
Comments on Congress

In recent appearances, President Obama has suggested that it's time for Washington to confront the intense polarization and incivility that mark our politics these days.

His first sally was his back-and-forth with the House Republican caucus at its retreat in Baltimore. He followed that a few days later with a speech to the National Prayer Breakfast decrying the "erosion of civility" in Washington and the inability of politicians in an increasingly partisan culture to listen to one another. "Those of us in Washington are not serving the people as well as we should," he said.

Lots of ordinary Americans would agree with those lofty sentiments. But what's notable is the growing concern in Washington that, when it comes to the actual business of governing, the nation's political leaders appear so riven with conflict that they're unable to move forward on anything. Both Democrats and Republicans welcomed the president's visit with the House Republicans as a first, tentative step in trying to reduce partisanship.

Moves like these are important gestures. But intense partisanship is deeply rooted in the body politic now. Even if the entire leadership at both ends of Pennsylvania Avenue were suddenly to embrace one another in honest fellowship, there would still be a long way to go in reducing polarization. That is because much of our political culture now works to drive people apart, not bring them together.

To begin with, we face a somewhat confusing paradox: In terms of electoral politics, the country is closely divided between left and right, with one side or the other gaining a majority depending on where independents choose to alight on Election Day. Yet in terms of political values, the nation is above all pragmatic and moderate, caring less about ideology than about what works.

The problem is that too much in politics—the extent to which congressional districts lock in a single party's dominance, the increasing importance of primaries dominated by the ideologically driven voters in both parties, and hence the growing ideological homogeneity of both parties' leadership—works to favor division, not pragmatism.

The result is that politics now drives policy on Capitol Hill. Every vote is looked upon as a political vote, with members of Congress asking themselves not, "What's best for the country?" but, "How do we put the other guys on the spot and advance our own partisan interests?"

This trend toward the extremes has also been driven by political developments in the country at large. Demographic trends—the migration of African Americans out of the South, the tendency of people of similar class and ethnic backgrounds to cluster together—have created communities and even regions that are dominated by one party or the other. This has been echoed by an explosion of advocacy organizations, so that groups that used to create consensus out of wildly disparate views no longer do so.

The political parties, which once forged consensus platforms at conventions that were notable for their diversity, now cater to their ideological activists. Advocacy associations—whether focused on the environment, agriculture, health, or whatever—that once needed to build an agenda acceptable to a diverse membership now are so narrowly aimed that they feel free to pursue their parochial points of view.

The media, too, has fragmented. Americans get their information from a bewildering array of sources, and these days need never be troubled by reporting or analysis that doesn't agree with their own preconceived views of the world. Punditry and commentary are what rule the media-sphere now, not hard reporting, and much of it is ideologically driven. There are very few prominent media voices pushing political Washington toward the center.

All of this has made it hard for fair, open-minded, and centrist politicians to gain any footing, and it has pushed their counterparts in the population at large to withdraw from a politics they see as increasingly nasty, closed-minded, and unattractive.

If there's a solution, it lies with ordinary Americans willing to stand up and say "Enough's enough!" The president and other political leaders can certainly try to change the tone in Washington, but they have an uphill battle to fight unless enough Americans make it clear that they are so tired of polarization that they'll set their own ideological prejudices aside and place a premium on politicians who demonstrate that they know how to work with people who don't agree with them.

HERE'S AN IDEA FOR CONGRESS: TRY DEMOCRACY

When I was in the House, a common complaint of my colleagues was that we were doing our work on the House side but that legislation would get bogged down in the Senate. Senators, of course, had exactly the same view about the House. Not much has changed since then.

There are major differences in the way the House and Senate do business. Both of them have their own problems and challenges and both of them can easily become unfair and undemocratic. But, at the risk of showing my institutional bias, there really is a particular problem with the Senate filibuster and the rule that requires sixty votes to close debate—and its dramatically increasing use. In my first Congress, from 1965 to 1966, seven cloture motions—a procedure to end debate through a three-fifths vote—were filed in the Senate. In the 111th Congress, when this commentary was written, there were 139. In the 113th Congress there were 253.

Senate procedures can get technical, but the basic point is that what was once a rarely used way to halt Senate action has now become routine, and sixty votes out of one hundred, rather than a majority, is the hurdle most legislation now faces.

Democratic institutions in this country overwhelmingly operate by majority rule, except the US Senate, where a small minority can completely gum up the works. The majority certainly needs to assure fair procedures that take minority views fully into account. But at the end of the day, Congress needs to be able to do its work, and not be hamstrung by loyalty to a Senate rule that has far outlived its purpose.

April 19, 2010: "Here's an Idea for Congress: Try Democracy" Comments on Congress

Strategists for the Democratic and Republican parties are pondering how best to use Congress's vote on health care reform in the fall elections. Both sides will undoubtedly go overboard in trying to spin the issue in their favor, but it's fair game. Members of Congress went on record with their votes, and now the American public has a chance to weigh the pros and cons of their actions.

But wait. We may get to hold our representatives to account for health care overhaul writ large, but on any number of crucial issues, we don't actually know how Congress might have acted. A public option for people seeking an alternative to the private health insurance market? Not even voted on in the Senate, because a couple of Democratic senators objected to the idea. Malpractice reform as a way of reining in runaway costs? Never made it to the floor for an up-or-down vote. A single-payer system, supported in the polls by a majority of Americans? Not even a floor debate.

These are key issues, and if you step back a moment, it's actually quite incredible that Congress would try to reform the health care system without voting on them.

But then, there are a lot of things Congress doesn't vote on these days. Scores of high-ranking positions in various federal departments have gone unfilled for many months because some senator put a "hold" on the nomination—often for reasons unrelated to the nomination itself. Crucial votes affecting Americans' lives get wrapped up in tit-for-tat political maneuvering that either postpones their consideration or finishes it off altogether. As New York magazine put it recently about an unseemly delay last fall in extending unemployment benefits to laid-off Americans, the bill "spent a month in limbo . . . before the Senate passed it by a vote of 98–0, suggesting lawmakers spent a full month dickering over a measure that pretty much everyone agreed to from the start."

It is especially notable these days that a simple majority of senators cannot work their will in the Senate. That body's rules make it possible to threaten a filibuster—in essence, to threaten endless debate—unless sixty votes can be mustered. This makes it exceedingly difficult to accomplish anything. A single senator placing a hold on legislation—as one senator from Kentucky famously did in March on legislation extending unemployment benefits—can gum up not only Capitol Hill, but Americans' lives.

For much of its regular business, the Senate no longer operates by majority rule. How did that come about in a world-renowned democratic body?

I want to be careful here. The Senate was designed, in part, to temper runaway popular sentiment and to make sure that issues of great import were considered carefully. Its rules evolved differently from those of the House for just that reason, and there's much to be said for legislating deliberately and thoughtfully—even slowly.

What we've been seeing of late, however, is not deliberation but frustration—in both senses of that word. With the rise in extreme partisanship on Capitol Hill, the Senate has become a far less functional body. As New York magazine put it, "The same Senate rules that were designed to check populist passions can, when adopted by passionate populists, turn the place into a governing body of 100 autocrats." This cannot be good for the country.

The issues in the House are different—but quite revealing as a result. There, majority rule isn't the question; it's runaway majority rule. House procedures call to mind Madison's worries about a possible "tyranny of the majority." The House majority routinely and skillfully shapes the rules for procedures on the House floor in order to exclude votes on major policy options and deny members, usually the minority, from offering key amendments that could affect the final shape of legislation. How did that happen in the House—where, supposedly, the people govern?

On one side of Capitol Hill, then, the give and take that ought to be part of the legislative process is now far too easily shut down by the minority. On the other side, it's all too often shut down by the majority. Rules that allowed for a balance between deliberation and effectiveness when followed judiciously are producing the opposite when pushed too far.

The answer, I think, is to reassert democracy as a goal. At both ends of the Capitol, legislators should have the chance to argue over and then vote on the key issues that Americans care about. There are several instances in which our Constitution calls for more than a simple majority, including overriding a presidential veto or ratifying a constitutional amendment. On everything else, let's allow a measure onto the floor through a fair process, then vote it up or down by simple majority rule. Why should the world's greatest democracy not practice democracy?

IN CONGRESS, GOING BIG ISN'T ALWAYS THE ANSWER

An incremental, one-step-at-a-time approach to legislation in Congress makes a lot of sense to me, especially in recent years, with such a deeply polarized Congress and deeply polarized country. As Congress has become more polarized, its legislative output has dropped sharply. During the seventeen Congresses I served in, the average number of bills passed each session was six hundred. In the last two Congresses, the number dropped to less than three hundred. In the current political situation the chances of successfully making sweeping changes on the big issues are, frankly, not good.

Some of the toughest issues may simply need to be set aside, to be revisited another day when the circumstances in the country and in Congress have shifted. But for others, significant progress might still be made, as I suggest here, by lowering our sights.

August 25, 2010: "In Congress, Going Big Isn't Always the Answer"
Comments on Congress

The contrast could not have been more striking. Not long after the passage of comprehensive financial reform in July, Majority Leader Harry Reid announced that the Senate would not be taking up a climate change bill, pretty much dooming hopes of meaningful action this year on reducing carbon emissions.

In some political circles, the Senate's failure to address the issue is getting lambasted as a symbol of its overall legislative impotence. But before we write off the Senate as a has-been, there's another way to look at it—as the latest instance of the never-ending calculation on Capitol Hill of whether conditions warrant going big or going small.

As a legislator interested in shaping national policy on any given issue, perhaps the first decision you have to make is whether to approach it in a comprehensive or incremental fashion. In the end, the decision often comes down to a realistic appraisal of what you can actually accomplish.

In recent years members of Congress have often preferred the grand, omnibus approach—as with this year's health care and financial reform bills. Big problems require big solutions, the thinking runs, and for a politician it's hard to resist the temptation of getting credit for solving those problems. Especially since big bills command far more media attention and public interest.

Sweeping legislation may be politically more complex, but it is often legislatively simpler. It tends to centralize decision making in the hands of key legislators. It gives the leadership greater influence, as bills often take final shape in the leader's office. It makes life easier for the president and executive branch, since they only negotiate with the handful of legislators who are most involved in the bill. And a large, complex bill can give members of Congress the political cover to pass necessary but unpopular measures that are outweighed in the public's mind by the overall accomplishment.

The risk, of course, is that sometimes political circumstances simply won't permit an all-encompassing approach—as appears to be the case with the climate bill. That is why some legislators prefer making progress by increments.

I think most people would agree, for instance, that the tax code is shot through with all kinds of inequities. But Congress very rarely gets around to addressing it, because the code is so far-reaching and complex—and any new legislation would open up so many knotty problems—that it's extremely difficult to take a comprehensive approach to reform. It seems more politically realistic and more satisfying to address one problem at a time.

Moreover, I've always thought that Americans instinctively lean toward incremental change and are suspicious of sweeping attempts to shift public policy—as we continue to see with health care reform. Because taking things step by step is more politically palatable, it makes it far easier to show results. Smaller-scale bills also tend to be dealt with more openly in Congress, going through the regular process of committee and floor procedures that guarantee transparency and wide-ranging input, rather than Congress's cobbling together massive bills largely behind closed doors and then rushing them to a vote. And some big issues may not be solvable, but simply have to be managed; making progress in smaller steps, with time to experiment and gauge results, may be the only feasible approach.

Of course, incrementalism carries its own risks. Sometimes a complex issue—like immigration reform—has so many interlocking pieces that trying to make progress on one or two at a time simply creates more problems than it solves.

Politicians of both parties, for instance, believe in the need to enhance border security, so that is a logical place for legislative efforts to start. But Congress only has so much energy for a given subject at any one moment, and a full-on push to secure the borders runs the risk that lawmakers will then turn their attention away from immigration for a time—leaving businesses scrambling for workers and local law-enforcement agencies puzzling over what to do about illegal immigrants already in the country.

The question of whether to take a comprehensive or an incremental approach, then, is not an easy one. Legislators have to decide based on a pragmatic assessment of what they can accomplish. I'm reminded of the comment once made by the late Senator Paul Douglas of Illinois that when he was elected to the Senate he came with the idea of saving the world, but after a few years he decided he'd be content with saving the United States. After ten years in office he hoped he could save Illinois, and when he was leaving office, he said he'd settle for saving the exquisite stretch of the Lake Michigan shoreline known as the Indiana Dunes.

Not everything can be tackled in a grand manner, in other words. A good bit of the art of legislating lies in discerning when it's feasible to go big, and when it's more realistic to settle for smaller—but more attainable—goals.

IT'S NOT JUST CONGRESS: CITIZENS ALSO HAVE ROOM TO IMPROVE

Ordinary citizens—not just members of Congress—play a central role in turning things around in Congress. But according to the experts, they have not been doing particularly well in their civic involvement in recent years.

I don't think citizens recognize the extent to which members of Congress want to hear from them and the importance they place on their dialogue with constituents. I remember talking to Wilbur Mills early on in my career in Congress as we were walking away from the Capitol one night after a vote. At that point he was one of the most powerful people in the country, as chairman of the House Ways and Means Committee—sought out by the president, leaders of major interest groups, and heads of Fortune 500 companies—and he had just had his picture featured on the cover of *TIME*. I asked him what he was doing over the weekend. He said he was going back to Arkansas for a public meeting in a small rural town, and he expected maybe fifteen to twenty people. He said he never forgot the people back home, that nothing he did came before them.

February 29, 2012: "It's Not Just Congress:
Citizens Also Have Room to Improve"
Comments on Congress
As a member of Congress, you get used to being graded. Interest groups send you questionnaires, check your voting record, and then issue their "report cards." Editorial writers opine freely on your performance. Pollsters issue monthly updates on how Congress is faring with the public.

Members of Congress learn to expect this judgment and criticism. It's part of being an elected official in this country—and should be.

But they also learn that Congress is part of a larger political system that also involves We the People. Our democracy doesn't just require its institutions and political leaders to function well; it works best when we, as citizens, all do our part. So at this moment when Congress's public standing is at an all-time low, it's natural to wonder: how are the American people doing at holding up their end of the bargain?

Every year, the Center on Congress at Indiana University surveys political scientists around the country to get their sense of how Congress is functioning. But it recognizes that Congress is just one part of the picture, and so it also asks these forty experts how Americans as a whole are doing at playing the constructive role our system demands of them.

The questions are instructive, because they give you a sense of a citizen's responsibilities. How well do people actually keep in touch with their members of Congress, for instance? Communication between elected officials and the people they represent—ordinary people with ordinary concerns—is the lifeblood of a representative democracy. It can happen through letters, e-mails, phone calls, and visits; through the interest groups many people join; and through voting. On all of these fronts, a majority of the experts surveyed give Americans about a C average for their participation.

If we're to pass judgment on Congress, then it's also worth asking how much we actually understand it. If we want it to improve, how much do we know about what it does and how it operates? The experts surveyed take a pretty dim view of Americans' performance.

How regularly do Americans follow what's actually going on in Congress? Most of those surveyed gave the country at best a D.

How well do Americans understand the main features of Congress and how it works? Almost two-thirds of the respondents handed out a D, while most of the rest gave us an F.

Do Americans have a reasonable understanding of what Congress can and should do? In other words, do they understand the powers given to Congress by the Constitution, and its role in executing those constitutional powers? Ds and Fs again.

Especially noteworthy is their low opinion of Americans' grasp of the importance of compromise. In a politically and socially diverse country, with two houses of Congress and a president all able to weigh in, most legislation simply cannot be crafted without some measure of compromise. Most of the experts surveyed believe that many Americans don't understand this. They hold a similarly low opinion of the media's ability to explain how Congress works to readers and viewers.

Now, these are the opinions of a handful of political experts. The point is not to berate our fellow citizens for their ignorance, but to understand that if we want Congress to improve, it is not just up to its members to make it happen. Congress will change when we insist that it change.

We can take a lesson from Will Rogers. His statue in the US Capitol is the only one directly facing the House chamber, honoring his shrewd comment, "I always keep my eye on Congress to see what they're up to." All of us need to do this: communicate more fully and openly with our representatives; learn Congress's responsibilities and how it fulfills them—and, even more importantly, how it should fulfill them; and recognize that if we don't like intense partisanship and political games-playing, then we need to give our representatives room to craft legislation with broad appeal.

Without the informed understanding of the American people, in other words, Congress will continue to flounder. And if it does, it won't just be its members' fault.

THE INVISIBLE LAWMAKERS

Many people think that when Congress passes a law setting up a new program or project, that's the end of the matter. It's just the beginning. After the contentious, drawn-out battles in Congress when a bill is being enacted, there can be equally tough battles in the federal agencies tasked with implementing the new law.

Most citizens pay only modest attention to what's happening in Congress, and almost no attention to how those laws are being interpreted and implemented through agency decisions and detailed regulations. But some people, especially the special interests, do.

May 15, 2013: "The Invisible Lawmakers"
Comments on Congress

Want to know what's causing a lot of people in Washington to work long hours right now? Here's a hint: it's not immigration reform or gun control or, for that matter, any other legislation coming down the pike. Instead, it's a pair of three-year-old laws.

The Affordable Care Act (known to most Americans as Obamacare) and the Wall Street reform act known as "Dodd-Frank" both became law in 2010. Most people consider these major pieces of legislation old news, but that's because their civics teachers misled them back in junior high school. In the "How a Bill Becomes a Law" version of Congress that many of us were taught, the story ends when the bill is signed by the president. It doesn't. In fact, the president's signature is more like a starter's pistol.

Because after a bill becomes law is when legislative language—which is often deliberately vague and imprecise, in order to wrangle as many votes as possible—gets interpreted and turned into regulatory language. In other words, Congress drafts a rough blueprint; only then does the federal government decide how the machinery will actually work.

And that's where money—lots of money—stands to be won or lost. A few years ago, a group of academics studying tax disclosures related to a single 2004 piece of financial legislation found that firms lobbying for a particular provision made $220 for every $1 they spent on lobbying. Which may help explain why, as the Center for Responsive Government recently reported, the health care industry has spent more than $700 million on lobbying Congress and executive agencies since health care reform passed.

Indeed, the political fight that begins with the drafting of legislation continues long after a bill is enacted into law—not for days or weeks or even months, but sometimes for years. Unlike the legislative process, which for all its faults is generally visible and accessible to the public, these battles tend to be invisible and inscrutable.

The first arena in which they take place is within the agency or agencies charged with drafting and enforcing the rules that give teeth to legislation. This process can be lengthy—according to one corporate law firm that has been tracking the rulemaking process for Dodd-Frank, only 38 percent of the rules required by the legislation had been finalized by the beginning of May this year. Special interests trying to have an impact pursue a broad range of tactics, from directly lobbying regulators to getting friendly members of Congress to weaken the agency's appropriation, cut funding for regulatory enforcers, or even block presidential appointments to an agency they dislike. They might also take the opposite tack, lobbying to bulk up a rule and make it so complicated that very few people can understand it, or to add little-noticed—but highly profitable—exemptions.

If that approach doesn't work, there are always the courts, which have final judgment over how to construe congressional language. Lawsuits of these types are intensely fought and can go on for years, sometime blocking or restricting implementation until they're settled.

And then, of course, there's Congress. Opponents of a law are rarely shy about relegislating it even after it's been enacted. They can try to get it repealed, or to cut its funding, or to enact exemptions, or, as medical-device makers, insurers, and others are doing right now with the health care law, to overturn pieces of it they especially dislike without taking on the entire thing.

Huge amounts of money are at stake in these fights, which can involve an army of sophisticated players: high-powered lobbyists, former regulators and members of Congress, and the federal officials and current members they're focused upon. As tough and sometimes mean-spirited as the reasonably transparent legislative process can get, these shadow battles, far out of the public eye, can be even more so.

Former secretary of state George Shultz once famously said, "Nothing ever gets settled in this town," and he was right. That is why, as you follow the course of health care reform or financial industry reform or any other high-stakes law, it pays to remember that it can take years before it's really possible to gauge the impact of legislation.

THE JUSTICES AND THE SCRAMBLE FOR CASH

When I first ran for Congress, my entire campaign cost $50,000. In the November 2014 election, spending for a Senate seat cost up to $50 million. The Supreme Court decision earlier that year in the *Citizens United* case was certainly a factor, and, as discussed here, it creates a host of problems for our political system.

I've been writing about the outsized influence of money in politics since the 1970s. Yet trying to find ways to curb the money chase is a particularly stubborn problem to deal with because, despite the grumbling of members of Congress about the time they must spend fundraising, the basic fact is that all 535 members got elected under the present system, they know how to make it work for them, and they know that it has built-in advantages for incumbents over challengers. The chances that they will vote for significant changes in this system in order to make it easier for their challengers are low. That, combined with a Supreme Court that favors removing rather than imposing limits on political contributions, makes it doubtful that this runaway problem of money in politics will be addressed effectively anytime soon.

April 30, 2014: "The Justices and the Scramble for Cash" Comments on Congress

Many trends in American politics and government today make me worry about the health of our representative democracy. These include the decline of Congress as a powerful, coequal branch of government, the accumulation of power in the presidency, and the impact of money on the overall political process.

Recently, the Supreme Court's five-member majority declared that it's unconstitutional to limit the aggregate amount an individual can give to candidates, political parties, and political action committees. Campaign contributions amplify free speech, these justices maintain, and campaign finance laws violate the First Amendment: any limit on the ability of individuals to contribute to candidates is a restraint of free speech. The only legitimate cause for the government to step in is to fight blatant, obvious corruption; it should not act to limit access and influence by well-to-do donors. The result of this decision will almost certainly increase the impact of money on the political system.

The problem is, money doesn't have to be handed over in an envelope filled with one-hundred-dollar bills to be harmful. The Supreme Court decision seems to be insensitive to what money is doing to the political system.

Big money is here to stay in politics. Those of us who wish it were otherwise have lost that argument—at least for the near term.

But we weren't mistaken about the impact of free-flowing campaign cash on the system. Politicians need large sums of money to run for office, and they spend a lot of time raising it. They are keenly attuned to generous donors. Inevitably, this gives more political influence to the relative handful of wealthy donors (only a few thousand at best) who choose to "invest" in politics and often, though not invariably, get what they want. The influence of voters without the financial means to command attention is diminished.

Lawmakers, of course, insist that big donors get nothing in response to their contributions except, perhaps, for a little face time. I am skeptical of that claim. Money buys access that people without money don't get, and access is nothing less than an opportunity to affect legislation. It is a rare politician who can remain entirely uninfluenced by large political contributions to his or her campaign. After all, members of Congress seek assignments to committees that are known to be useful for fundraising, and those wealthy individuals and interests spend large sums on wooing and electing politicians for a purpose: to get public policy favorable to their views and interests.

Over many years both inside and outside Congress, I saw very little outright corruption, but on a frequent basis I could see money's disproportionate influence on the decisions of government and its distortion of our representative democracy. With their decision the justices may have expanded personal liberty, but they've done so lopsidedly: boosting the liberty of ordinary individuals who cannot afford to give to political campaigns gains them nothing in the way of political influence.

The court's decision further empowers a few rich people and disempowers many ordinary people. This is not a desirable direction for our representative government. Our system should encourage a government responsive to all citizens, not just a few.

What can we do? I would prefer that the president and Congress step in and design rules of campaign finance that would reverse the growing influence of money on our campaigns, but that does not appear likely to happen. Indeed, even now opponents of campaign finance laws are preparing challenges to the remaining limits on individual contributions and to the easily avoided disclosure laws we already have. I'm certain they'll get a sympathetic hearing in the Supreme Court.

Paradoxically, this may be our best hope—because I also believe that Americans are growing tired of the outsized impact that great wealth enjoys in politics, and that a backlash to the court's decisions is taking shape. My sense is that growing numbers of ordinary voters are recognizing that money is a poison in our system. I fervently hope that support for public financing and for muscular disclosure laws will grow with time, because our politics will be more democratic, more honest, and more free if we reduce the impact of money on elections.

NOW IT'S TIME TO FOCUS ON THE ECONOMY

There were some major improvements in the economy during the Obama years, as modest growth in our economy was restored, the US stock market more than doubled, and corporate profits hit record levels. Our unemployment rate dropped, and 2014 was the best year in job growth in fifteen years. Not all the improvement was due to the actions of the president, but he played a significant role in bringing back an economy that had been on the verge of collapse.

I felt that the generally positive news made this a time to sort out our economic priorities, with a particular focus on long-term economic growth.

December 24, 2014: "Now It's Time to Focus on the Economy"
Comments on Congress

Recent economic news has been broadly reassuring. Retail sales are strong, November saw the best job gains in three years, the federal deficit is shrinking, the stock market is robust, and the Fed is expressing enough faith in the economy that an interest rate bump next year is considered a certainty.

Yet the public remains unconvinced. This is partly because perceptions haven't caught up to reality. For many middle- and lower-class families, economic circumstances have not changed very much. Average wages, adjusted for inflation, have not risen in keeping with the good economic news. The median net worth of households is actually a bit less than it was in 2010, just after the official end of the recession—and the gap between the wealthy and the rest of us is wider than ever.

Strong numbers do, however, offer one unambiguous piece of good news: the pressure on policymakers to focus on near-term or immediate problems has eased, which means they can now focus on the fundamental question of economic growth. That's where their attention should turn.

A strong economy that is growing for everyone, not just the people at the top, offers many benefits. The quality of people's lives improves. Political problems become more manageable. More people have greater economic opportunity. There's more social mobility and more tolerance of diversity.

Because the economy is always at or near the top of voters' concerns, the temptation for the policymaker is to support another tax cut or the next move to stimulate the economy in the short term. Now is the time for policymakers to resist this and try to understand the large forces—technology, automation, globalization—that drive our economy. As Princeton economist Alan Blinder, political strategist Al From, and others have pointed out, the key is to concentrate on creating the environment in the country for sustained, noninflationary economic growth.

To begin with, we have a chance to get our fiscal house in order and pursue long-term deficit reduction. This is a crucial early step for government to take in creating a sound environment for economic growth.

This means modernizing entitlement spending and shaping a tax reform package that focuses on investments to boost productivity and help the economy to grow for everyone, through research and development, job training, upgrading skills as well as technology, and reducing outsourcing.

At the same time, it means eliminating public subsidies to individual enterprises. That money can be spent on boosting the economic skills of ordinary Americans through education and training. Policies aimed at strengthening our education system, from pre-kindergarten to graduate school, and at promoting lifelong learning and a workforce capable of upgrading its skills to meet changing needs, will have a far more salutary effect on our economy than singling out politically connected enterprises for tax and other benefits.

There are other steps government policymakers can take to improve broad economic growth. We need to expand trade through open markets and simplify the regulatory structure so that it protects Americans without burdening companies beyond reason. And we must address our nation's deferred infrastructure needs, which hinder the smooth functioning of every business that relies on transporting its goods.

The same applies to reforming government itself. A government that does not work well—that wastes money, fails its regulatory responsibilities, and cannot make timely decisions—undermines economic growth. You can see this, for instance, in our current inability to pass comprehensive immigration reform: we cannot increase economic growth without the people our labor force needs, from mathematicians and engineers to migrant farm workers.

Finally, policymakers need to remember that economic growth means providing a ladder out of poverty for the truly needy. Providing opportunity for low-income Americans through the earned income tax credit and programs to upgrade their skills is vital. No one who works full time should be poor in this country.

Free, competitive markets are the best way to deliver goods and services to Americans. Government must not get in the way of that system. Nor should it stand idle. The right response by government to our economic challenges is not to focus on the immediate economic problems of the day, but to invest in economic growth for all.

THE SUMMER OF OUR DISCONTENT

In October 2013, the federal government was shut down for sixteen days over Republican efforts to gut Obamacare. That sent public approval of Congress down to just 9 percent, a remarkably low—even alarming—number for a system of government that rests on the consent of the governed.

It's hard not to become discouraged about Congress. But one of the key lessons I take away from my many years of working in Congress—and one of the main points I've emphasized in commentaries—is that despite its up and downs, we have a resilient, fundamentally sound system and we shouldn't give up on it. We're all in this together, and we have to make it work.

September 3, 2014: "The Summer of Our Discontent"
Comments on Congress

Despite these last few months of hot and lazy days, it's been hard not to notice a cold political wind blowing through the country. The magazine Foreign Affairs captured it with its latest cover, a mockup of a travel poster featuring a crumbling US Capitol with the tagline, "See America: Land of Decay and Dysfunction."

Americans are clearly uneasy. I know it anecdotally, because at virtually every public gathering I've addressed over the last few months someone has spoken up with his or her worry that our nation is in decline. And the polls bear it out. In June, a Washington Post article, "Is the American Dream Dead?" noted a string of polls showing majorities of Americans believe their children will be worse off than they were.

By early August, an NBC–Wall Street Journal poll was reporting that a full three-quarters of those surveyed lacked confidence that the next generation would be better off—the most pessimistic results in the history of the poll. Regardless of income, ethnicity, religion, or gender, Americans don't think much of our future.

This is a ground-shaking turnabout. Since well before I began my political career in the early 1960s, the keystone of our politics was an unflagging optimism that as Americans we could face head-on the task of improving our own and others' lives and deliver on our responsibility to future generations. As Chris Cillizza wrote recently in the Washington Post, "So much of every politician's patter—Democrat or Republican—is built on the idea that America has always overcome hard challenges, always made things better for our kids than for us, always had achieving the American dream as a real possibility." Now, he notes, "a large bloc of the electorate no longer believes any of that."

Why not? Partly, it's the economy: growth has been sluggish, we're not generating enough good jobs, and the benefits of the recovery have flowed more to some than to the many. The growing awareness of a lopsided society—one in which a rising tide fails to lift all boats—has put many people in a surly mood. That problem of income inequality is joined to a host of others—from climate change to crumbling infrastructure to a world in which the forces of chaos and turmoil appear to be expanding.

Yet I think <u>Foreign Affairs</u> has nailed the biggest factor: the perceived dysfunction of our political system. As political scientist Francis Fukuyama writes in the lead essay, dealing with our problems "requires a healthy, well-functioning political system, which the United States does not currently have."

Simply put, Americans have no confidence that our system can resolve the challenges before us. They don't expect miracles, but they do expect political leaders to make progress, and they haven't been seeing much.

I can understand why so many people would be pessimistic, yet I don't find myself sharing their fatalism. That's because political moments are just that: moments. Over the long reach of our history, we've learned time and again that when our political leaders do focus on our challenges, speak to one another directly, and are determined to find a solution to our problems, they can overcome their differences and make progress.

Our Constitution has been in effect for 225 years. The system it created, with its checks and balances, and its carefully constructed equilibrium between constraining and enabling government, has seen us through no small share of bruising times. It has protected our freedom, given hundreds of millions of Americans by birth and Americans by choice an opportunity to pursue the lives they want, and allowed us to speak freely, associate with the people we choose, and openly follow the religious and spiritual lives we want.

There is no shortage of challenges facing the system—from the influence of money on elections to the encrusted rules that hamstring capable public officials to the scorched-earth political culture that reigns in Washington these days. But I am convinced that they are no match for an aroused and determined public that recognizes we are all in this together, that we can adapt to changing circumstances, and that we should not give up on the system.

Obama came into office amid high expectations. There almost had to be disappointments—and there were. But he had some solid achievements. He got through Congress several major bills, including health care and education reforms, new restrictions on Wall Street, and several initiatives that helped stop our economic decline and bring the country out of the

Great Recession. In his first year in office he became the fourth American president to win the Nobel Peace Prize—in addition to Theodore Roosevelt, Woodrow Wilson, and Jimmy Carter—for his efforts in international diplomacy and cooperation. He was part visionary, part pragmatist, certainly an incrementalist. His strength was in analysis and articulation of policy rather than in management and implementation.

Obama showed restraint in foreign policy by drawing down our overseas military obligations. He recognized that he had to wind down the wars in Iraq and Afghanistan and deal with terrorism and the turmoil in the Middle East, but he did not want to be consumed by them. He wanted to focus on issues that would define the next decades: China, climate change, nuclear proliferation, and trade. His administration had great difficulty finding the right role for the US in the Middle East and wavered between staged withdrawal and more intervention. The result was an uncertain leadership in the region. As has become clearer with each passing year, foreign policy has begun to define his legacy.

There was a real transition in his presidency—from his early speeches of hope, optimism, and change, to a president hit hard by circumstances and reality, putting forth limited goals and struggling for his legacy. One of the most serious constraints he faced was running up against an entrenched opposition and an often dysfunctional Congress. He faced obdurate Republican opposition. They really did not want to work with him. My view has been that Obama was not instinctively partisan; he was prepared to negotiate with all. But he had difficulty operating in a highly polarized environment, and he turned increasingly to the use of unilateral executive power—on immigration, gay rights, tax policy, and other matters—simply because he could not get much done through the legislative process.

That was without doubt one of the most notable features of this period—the divisiveness in Congress and the particularly difficult time it had in doing its work. The number of bills passed in the 112th and 113th Congresses was the lowest in many decades. The normal budget and appropriations process failed and we instead had omnibus bills and governing by crisis and shutdown. Obvious national problems like the struggling middle class and our crumbling roads and bridges remained unaddressed, while Congress voted on repealing Obamacare some sixty times knowing it had no chance of success.

The arc of Congress during my fifty years of either working in it or closely observing it has been striking. It's difficult to imagine more of a contrast than between the 89th Congress, brimming with enthusiasm and activity, broadly supported, and the 113th, almost paralyzed, unable to act on issues that mattered, widely reviled by the public.

SOME CONCLUDING THOUGHTS

ON NOVEMBER 19, 1863, ABRAHAM LINCOLN DELIVERED THE Gettysburg Address. Historians tell us that he was the last speaker invited to the event, and that he was invited only after several American dignitaries, including Henry Wadsworth Longfellow and John Greenleaf Whittier, had refused. President Lincoln spoke after Edward Everett, the most celebrated orator of the day in the United States. Everett spoke for two hours; President Lincoln sat the entire time and listened attentively. He kept revising his speech right up to the last moment, and he delivered it in less than three minutes. The prayer that opened the ceremony was longer.

He said that we were testing whether this nation, or any nation so conceived and so dedicated, could long endure. That was the operational question at Gettysburg. It remains the operational question in this country today. A deep vein of pessimism has developed in America, with many people believing that our problems are here for the long haul and our political system just isn't up to the challenge. A Gallup poll a few years back found that our nation is more downbeat, dissatisfied with our political leadership, and concerned about the direction of our country than at almost any point in modern times. Public support for Congress, which the Founders viewed as the central branch in our system of government, remains dangerously low.

Our system certainly has its shortcomings, but I believe we also need to recognize its abiding strengths. We shouldn't ask what is wrong with America without also asking what is right with America. While much of the pessimism centers on our political system and its seeming inability to act, I contend that our political system is actually one of our strengths.

It may be hard these days to find many people who think of the political system as a core American strength, but it is. It protects against arbitrary authority, enshrines fundamental power in a body elected by the broad mass of the people, is based solidly on the consent of the governed, and balances power among the three branches of government. For all its deficiencies, it hears society's varied and conflicting opinions before it acts and moderates tensions among competing interests—doing so in a measured fashion that tends, over time, to force policymakers to find consensus and move toward the center. And, perhaps most importantly, it has the capacity to change, correct itself, and move on. As President Wilson said, the country is always aborning, striving to be better. I believe that self-government is one of the great achievements in the history of mankind.

We have a durable Constitution that has given us more than two centuries of political stability—weathering along the way a civil war, multiple wars overseas, economic and political turmoil, and sweeping movements of social change. And we work out our differences within the generous confines of our Constitution. I've conducted hundreds of public meetings, some of them quite heated, and never once do I recall anyone suggesting that we scrap the system of government set up by the Constitution.

I would be the last person to argue that things are perfect in Washington or within the political system as a whole. Our institutions need plenty of reforms that ought to be on the front burner but are not. It would be hard to argue that, faced with a mass of serious challenges, we are today dealing with them efficiently or effectively. Local, partisan, and private interests too often prevail over the national interest. Our system too often favors the rich and ignores the poor, and the solutions to this and many other fundamental problems often seem beyond our reach. For its part, Congress regularly disappoints us with its timidity and willingness to cede power to the president, its habit of governing by crisis, its failure to follow the well-established regular order that was meant to provide openness and fairness, its endless pandering to wealthy contributors and powerful interests, its failure to carry out the responsibility of oversight, its unwillingness to work out compromises for the common good, and its failure to address the increasing problem of money in politics.

But these problems characterize this particular moment in our history, not our basics. They are certainly discouraging, but they are not crippling. Our challenge as a nation is not to reinvent ourselves, but to use the abundant strengths we possess to find our way through our problems and to emerge stronger on the other side. Our representative democracy is the form of government most likely to lead to wise policy, to provide justice, and to give everyone his or her due. It allows a large and diverse nation, alive with competing interests and factions, to move forward.

President Lincoln ended his Gettysburg Address by resolving that "this nation, under God, shall have a new birth of freedom, and that government of the people, by the people, for the people, shall not perish from the earth." Some of us might share the optimism in Lincoln's statement; others might not. In a sense it really doesn't matter. What is more important than what we *think* about the nation's future is what we *do* about its future: that each of us do our part to make our neighborhood, our community, our state, and our country better and stronger. Our democracy makes a little wager on every one of us: in return for freedom there is obligation; for liberty, there is duty. Our best chance that this nation will long endure is to see things as they are and, insofar as we can, to make them better.

During my time in Washington, I would on occasion visit the national monuments and read, carved in granite, the marvelous words of our nation's heroes—Jefferson, Lincoln, Theodore Roosevelt, Franklin Delano Roosevelt, and Martin Luther King Jr. And then it would occur to me, as it has to others, that as magnificent and inspirational as those statues are, they stand mute. It is for us, not them, to carry forward.

Nowhere is it written in the stars that our remarkable system of government will simply continue on. Each of us must do our part to ensure that it is handed on to the next generation. The challenge is to make the system work.

Although my own view is that our nation's fundamentals are strong, as is the basic structure of Congress—though certainly various improvements are needed—I do recognize that others may be less positive, feeling that America is a country in decline with a political system that is simply broken. Given the current grumbling about the dysfunction of Congress, it's natural to ask whether there is any hope at all. Who is right in all of this? Which direction is America headed in? I would argue that for most of us as citizens, those questions are irrelevant.

Here's a quick story often told about civic duty. One day in 1780, the skies over much of New England darkened at midday. Families lunched by candlelight and people found it difficult to read papers held a few inches from their eyes. It was discovered many years later that the cause most likely was wildfires over eastern Ontario. At the time, however, many people thought Judgment Day was at hand. The Connecticut legislature, which was in session that day, considered adjourning. Colonel Abraham Davenport stood up to oppose the motion. "The day of judgment is either approaching, or it is not," he said. "If it is not, there is no cause of an adjournment; if it is, I choose to be found doing my duty."

So it is with us. Whether we believe our country is rising or declining, our obligation is the same—to do our part. There may be cause for discouragement about the current state of affairs in Washington, but whether Capitol Hill and the White House are falling apart or performing splendidly, our responsibility as citizens is the same: to do what we can to improve our own corner of the world, and to insist that our elected representatives do their utmost to improve theirs.

In short, we must choose to be found doing our duty.

Index

arms embargoes, 131, 141, 187
arms sales, 182, 234
Armstrong, Neil, 71
Article II of the Constitution, 231
Asia policy, 63–65
assassinations, 37–39, 39–43
Assistance for the Newly Independent States of
    the Former Soviet Union, 240
Atlantic Alliance, 167
attack ads, 251
Authorization for Use of Military Force against
    Iraq, 293
Authorization for Use of Military Force against
    Perpetrators of the September 11, 2001, At-
    tacks, 293
Aviation and Transportation Security Act, 293
Azerbaijan, 225

B-2 bombers, 225
B-52 bombers, 167
baby boomers, 272
Backfire bombers, 167
Baker, Jim, 284, 307–308
balanced budgets: Balanced Budget Act of 1997,
    241; Balanced Budget Amendment, 219–23;
    Balanced Budget and Emergency Deficit
    Control Reaffirmation Act, 152; and budget
    battles, 265; and Carter, 147; and Contract
    with America, 257–59; and Medicare, 15;
    and Reagan, 163; and supply-side economics,
    207–208
balance-of-power, 69, 84, 87, 179, 346. See also
    checks and balances; separation of powers
ballistic-missile defenses, 166
Bankruptcy Abuse Prevention and Consumer
    Protection Act, 294
Bankruptcy Reform Act, 240
Bernstein, Leonard, 75
big government, 108–11, 124–26, 261–62
Bill of Rights, 178, 217–18
bin Laden, Osama, 291
bipartisanship: and ethics reform, 205–206; and
    gerrymandering, 305–307; and implementa-
    tion of legislation, 12; and Johnson, 42; and
    Medicare, 15; and Nixon, 46; and "reinvent-
    ing government" initiative, 247–48; and
    Social Security reform, 156
Blinder, Alan, 339
Boehner, John, 317–18
Boggs, Lindy, 323
Boland, Eddie, 156

Boland Amendment, 151
Bolling, Richard, 26–27, 323
border security, 330
boycotts, 73–74
Brady Handgun Violence Protection Act, 240
Brandt, Willie, 106
Branigin, Roger, 40
Bray, Bill, 10
Brown, H. Rap, 29
Budget and Impoundment Control Act, 46, 130
Budget Control Act, 319
budgets and budget negotiations: and Bush
    (G. W.), 291, 314–15; and Carter, 131–34; con-
    gressional budget process, 133, 163–64; and
    Contract with America, 257, 259; and declin-
    ing role of Congress, 301; and discretionary
    spending, 161; and government shutdowns,
    159–61, 263–66; and misinformation about
    Congress, 244; and national spending
    priorities, 210–13; and record of the 105th
    Congress, 282–83; and supplemental spend-
    ing bills, 162–63; surpluses, 269–73, 314. See
    also balanced budgets
bureaucracy, 123–26, 255–56
Bush, George H. W.: and arms control, 223–26;
    background, 197–98; and balanced budget
    amendment, 219–20; and civility in Con-
    gress, 267; and deficits, 189, 270; and ethics
    reform, 205; and foreign aid, 112; and Great
    Society programs, 213; inauguration, 197–98;
    and national spending priorities, 210–13;
    personality, 197–98; relations with Con-
    gress, 198; and Strategic Defense Initiative,
    200–203; and supply-side economics, 207–10;
    and Supreme Court appointments, 230–33
Bush, George W.: and civic engagement, 297;
    and Clinton era budget surpluses, 270; and
    congressional oversight, 299–300, 302; and
    deficits, 270; and deregulation, 143; and Iraq,
    307–10; legacy of presidency, 314–15; and
    lessons of Watergate, 83; Obama contrasted
    with, 320; and political polarization, 289;
    successes and failures, 314–15
Butlerville, Indiana, 44–45
Byrnes, John, 12, 15, 323

cabinet of the president, 84, 148, 150
Cable Communications Policy Act, 151
California, 305
Cambodia, 61, 96
Campaign Reform Act, 293

Camp David Accords, 146
Cape Canaveral, 70
capital gains taxes, 208, 210
capitalism, 106–108, 142–47
Carlson, Frank, 36
Carmichael, Stokely, 29
carrier-based airpower, 166
Carter, Jimmy: assessment of presidency, 129–
31; and budget legacy of Reagan, 189–90; and
budget negotiations, 131–34; campaigning
skills, 115; and deregulation, 142–47; and
election reform, 284; ex-presidency of, 146;
and gasoline shortage, 137–40; and Great
Society programs, 215; and human rights,
120–23; inauguration, 118–20; and Iran
hostage crisis, 140–43, 146–47; leadership
shortcomings, 146; "malaise" speech, 134;
Nobel Peace Prize, 343; and Panama Canal
Treaty, 112, 126–29; relations with Congress,
115–16, 129–31, 147; reorganization of the
federal bureaucracy, 123–26
Case, Clifford P., 36
censures, 268, 276
Center for Responsive Government, 334
Center on Congress, 290, 332
Central Intelligence Agency (CIA), 23–25,
67, 157
centrism, 306
checks and balances, 60, 315, 342
chemical weapons, 281
Chemical Weapons Convention, 242
Cheney, Dick, 183, 290–91
children's issues, 181, 215
Children's Online Privacy Protection Act, 242
Child Support Enforcement Amendments of
1984, 151
China, 68–70, 75, 96–97
Chou en-lai (Zhou Enlai), 69
Christianity, 168–70
Christmas, 48–51
Chrysler Corporation Loan Guarantee Act, 117
Cillizza, Chris, 341
citizenship, 56–58, 312–15, 330–33. See also
civic engagement
Citizens United case, 335–36
civic engagement: and assessment of US political system, 348; and author's background,
5; and Bush (G. W.), 290, 297–99; and community improvement, 298–99; importance to
democracy, 312–15; and lessons of Watergate,
83, 85–86; and proper functioning of Con-

gress, 331–33; and religion in politics, 168;
and voting, 56–58, 287
civil disorder, 29–30, 38–39
civility in Congress, 266–69
civil liberties, 301
civil rights, 28–29, 51, 268
Civil Rights Act, 11, 28, 214, 215
Civil Rights Restoration Act, 152
civil service, 123–26, 192–93. See also bureaucracy
Civil Service Reform Act, 117
Civil War, 169, 268
Class Action Fairness Act, 294
classified materials, 65–68
Clean Air Act Amendments, 45, 47, 199, 236
climate change, 329
Clinton, Bill: and budget battles, 263–64; and
budget legacy of Reagan, 189; and budget
surpluses, 269–73; and civility in Congress,
267; and Contract with America, 257; legacy
of, 287–89; Obama contrasted with, 317;
personal misconduct, 238, 240, 281; political
skills, 238–39; and public cynicism, 250; and
"reinventing government" initiative, 246–49;
and terrorism, 291
Clinton, Hillary, 250, 316
cloture, 325–26
coalitions, 235
Colby, William, 113
Cold War: and arms control efforts, 224; and
China, 19; end of, 223, 237; and the Middle
East, 236; and military spending, 165
Colorado, 254
commander-in-chief role, 308–309
commentaries on Congress, 1–7
committees, congressional: and Contract with
America, 258; function of, 31–33; and Nixon
impeachment proceedings, 81; and seniority
system, 51–53
Commodity Futures Modernization Act, 242
common good, 299
communications technology, 137, 142, 145
Communist Party, 186–87
Community Action Program, 214, 215
community improvement, 298–99, 313
competition in economy, 110, 144
complexity of issues faced by Congress, 1–2,
192, 314
comprehensive approaches to legislation, 330.
See also omnibus legislation
Comprehensive Crime Control Act, 151

Comprehensive Drug Abuse Prevention and
Control Act, 47
Comprehensive Environmental Compensation
and Liability Act (Superfund), 118
Comprehensive Everglades Restoration
Plan, 242
Comprehensive Iran Sanctions, Accountability,
and Divestment Act, 318
compromise: and appeal of Congress, 176; and
Clinton, 239; and Ford, 88; and government
shutdowns, 159–61, 263; and House/Senate
cooperation, 162; and intelligence analysis,
158; and lessons of Watergate, 85; and
Obama, 316; omnibus legislation, 322; and
proper functioning of Congress, 332–33; and
Social Security reform, 156; and strength of
US political system, 346, 347; and term limits
movement, 255
COMSAT, 110
Conable, Barber, 323
confirmation powers, 79–80, 230–33
confrontational politics, 239. *See also* partisanship; polarization
Congressional Accountability Act, 241
Congressional Black Caucus, 37, 51–53
Congressional Budget and Impoundment Control Act, 48, 132
Congressional Budget Office, 172
congressional hearings: and Clinton impeachment proceedings, 281; and congressional
staff, 243; and Medicare, 14; and Nixon
impeachment proceedings, 80; and omnibus
legislation, 164–65; and oversight role of
Congress, 302–303, 303–304; and role of
congressional committees, 32; and the Starr
Report, 274; and Supreme Court appointments, 230–32; and Vietnam, 16, 55
congressional perks, 226–30, 245
congressional process and procedure, 30–33, 81
Congressional Record, 4
congressional reforms, 51–53, 250
Congressional Research Service, 4, 172, 266
congressional staff, 173, 243, 255–56, 258, 278
consensus building, 12, 314
conservatism: and Ford, 89, 90; impact on legislative output, 236; and Nixon's inauguration,
73–74; and Reagan, 195; and Supreme Court
nominations, 233; and term limits movement, 253–56
Consolidated Omnibus Budget Reconciliation
Act (COBRA), 152
conspiracy theories, 138

constituent services, 301–302
Constitutional Convention, 177–78
constitutional law, 60
consultation role of Congress, 37, 88, 94
consumer confidence, 287
Consumer Product Safety Act, 45, 48
containment policy, 70
Continental Congress, 59
continuing resolutions, 164, 263
Contract with America, 257–60
Contra War, 297
conventional weapons, 166–67
Copyright Term Extension Act, 242
Corporate Fraud Accountability Act, 293
corruption, 78–80, 182, 226
Corwin, Edward, 112
cost of living, 155
Council of Economic Advisors, 210
covert actions, 142, 182–86
credit, 103
criminal law, 103
cruise missiles, 188
cynicism: and appropriate role of government,
262; and assessment of US political system,
345–46; and Bush, 297–99; and congressional perks, 227; consequences of, 252; and
declining trust in government, 249–53; and
democracy and capitalism, 106; and Ford,
89–90; and lessons of Watergate, 83, 85; and
Obama, 321–22; and purpose of politics,
310–11; and "Washington fatigue," 89
Cyprus, 157
Czech Republic, 281

Davenport, Abraham, 348
debt: and budget legacy of Reagan, 189;
debt-limit legislation, 265; and national
spending priorities, 211; and supply-side
economics, 210
decentralization, 110
decision-making process in Congress, 66–67,
170–73, 175
Declaration of Independence, 59–60, 178
declarations of war, 308. *See also* war powers
Deep South, 119
Defense of Marriage Act, 241
defense spending: and budget legacy of Reagan,
191; and Ford, 90; and national spending
priorities, 211; and Strategic Defense Initiative, 201–202
deficits and deficit-reduction: and balanced
budget amendment, 219–22; and budget sur-

198–99, 207–10, 212–13, 215–16, 220, 221; and Bush (G. W.), 298; and Clinton, 246; and Contract with America, 257, 258; flat tax proposals, 282; and Medicare, 15; and the middle class, 98, 99–100; and Reagan, 162, 189–90; and record of the 105th Congress, 281; and Social Security reform, 154, 155; tax cuts, 207, 215, 258; tax reform efforts, 282; and voting age reform, 58
Tax Increase Protection and Reconciliation Act, 294
Taxpayer Bill of Rights, 241–42
Taxpayer Relief Act of 1997, 241
Tax Reduction Act of 1975, 91
Tax Reduction and Simplification Act, 117
Tax Reform Act, 152, 209
Tax Reform Act of 1969, 47
Tax Reform Act of 1976, 91
Tax Relief, Unemployment Insurance Reauthorization, and Job Creation Act, 318
technological advance, 145, 180
Telecommunications Act, 241
television, 80–83, 251
term limits movement, 253–56, 258
terrorism, 158, 234, 291, 301
Texas, 27
Thailand, 77
Thanksgiving messages, 18–19, 19–20
Theodore Roosevelt Memorial, 347
think tanks, 278
Thomas, Clarence, 230, 232
Threshold Test Ban Treaty, 199
TIME, 331
"time, place, and manner" of elections, 254
Title IX, 45, 48
tobacco, 281
tolerance, 40–42
Tower, John, 201
Toxic Substances Control Act, 92
trade, 301
Trade Act of 1974, 91
Trade Act of 2002, 293
Trade Agreements Act, 117
Trade and Development Act, 242
trade relations, 69, 126
Trafficking Victims Protection Act, 242
Trans-Alaska Pipeline Authorization, 46, 48
transparency, 84, 330
Transportation Equity Act, 294
travel of members of Congress, 19
travel restrictions, 141

treaties, 126–29
trucking deregulation, 145
Truman, Harry, 295
trust, 300
Truth in Lending Act, 11
tuition tax credits, 133
Turkey, 113, 131
turnout rates, 256, 283–87
Twenty-Sixth Amendment, 45–47, 56–58
tyranny of the majority, 327

Udall, Mo, 10
unemployment: and Clinton, 287; and the middle class, 98; and Obama, 338; and proper role of Congress, 327; and Reagan, 162, 190; and sex discrimination, 103
Unfunded Mandates Reform Act, 241
unilateral arms reductions, 224
UN Security Council, 235
urban riots, 28
USA PATRIOT Act, 293
US Army, 76–77
US-China Relations Act, 242
US Constitution: advice and consent clause, 232; and Agnew's resignation, 78; and balanced budget amendment, 220, 223; and balance of power, 342; and checks and balances, 60, 315, 342; and confirmation powers, 231; and congressional role in foreign affairs, 296; constitutional heritage of Congress, 176–79; and covert actions, 183; and flag protection, 216–19; and Ford's pardon of Nixon, 94; and "high crimes and misdemeanors," 275–76; and Nixon impeachment proceedings, 81–82; and separation of powers, 35, 244, 292; and strength of US political system, 346–47; and structure of government, 59–60; and term limits movement, 254, 256; and voting age reform, 57–58
US Department of Agriculture, 190, 194, 248
US Department of Commerce, 190
US Department of Defense, 194
US Department of Education, 118, 190
US Department of Energy, 117, 139, 190
US Department of Health and Human Services, 194, 248
US Department of Homeland Security, 291
US Department of Housing and Urban Development, 11
US Department of Justice, 78, 190
US Department of Labor, 190

LEE H. HAMILTON is a Distinguished Scholar at Indiana University. He was a member of the US House of Representatives for 34 years and vice chairman of the 9/11 Commission. In 2015, Hamilton was awarded the Presidential Medal of Freedom. He is author of several books, including *How Congress Works and Why You Should Care* (IUP, 2004) and *Strengthening Congress* (IUP, 2009). His current commentaries on Congress and American politics can be found at hamiltoncommentaries.iu.edu.